SURVIVING THE MADNESS

The Story of

PAUL
'ONE PUNCH'
DOYLE

by PAUL DOYLE

in association with

ONTOP
MEDIA LTD

First published in Great Britain as a softback original in 2021

Typeset in Adobe Caslon Pro

Cover Design by *coast-studio.co.uk*

Typesetting and publishing by *UK Book Publishing*
www.ukbookpublishing.com

ISBN: 978-1-914195-75-4

SURVIVING THE MADNESS

The Story of

PAUL 'ONE PUNCH' DOYLE

by PAUL DOYLE

in association with

ONTOP
MEDIA LTD

Chapter 1:

WHERE IT ALL BEGAN

1958 WAS A BAD YEAR FOR MANCHESTER.

Darkness had fallen across the city with the tragic loss of the Busby Babes in the Manchester United air crash disaster.

Tears were being shed by the bucket load, men, women, boys and girls. The place was in shock. My mother was in shock too, but she wasn't crying at the loss of the United team, she was devastated by the news that there would soon be one more mouth to feed.

At the young age of 26 she had already given birth to seven children and little did she know then, but this particular one was going to give the city of Manchester one hell of a headache in the years to come.

Seven kids wasn't that unusual in those days, it was just the way things were. There was no contraceptive pill and only a couple of tv channels and my dad being of Irish descent didn't help matters either.

Our dad was a giant of a bloke, six feet two inches tall with a 60-inch chest. A powerful, hardworking man that wasn't afraid to put in a double shift. He'd regularly be out working on building sites all day long, come home for his tea and then go out again at night, working either on the doors or as a personal bodyguard to one or other of the big-time gamblers in the city. Protection was a natural choice of vocation for him. When it came to fighting, he was in a league of his own. A great street fighter who never gave up, being a super heavyweight worked to his advantage too. He was a good-looking fella with a fantastic physique, fit as a fiddle, largely due to a love of swimming - the opportunity to swim for Great Britain was offered to him, as a school boy but for one reason or another he never accepted it. Maybe his passion for fighting stood in his way. It was a trait that proved to feature heavily in my life also.

In the fifties and sixties street fighters had no real skills, they would go out onto the cobbles and simply throw punch for punch, hence the name 'street fighter'.

To this day people still pop up from time to time telling me heroic stories about my dad, tales of him fighting three or four men at a time, powering his way through the lot of them and coming out with his head held high.

My mother was a Jewish woman (which made me a little Jew boy) and with her looks, I was every bit the Jewish boy, with dark skin and a big nose. Unfortunately, her relatives weren't like the average Jewish family in Manchester, most of whom lived in big houses and had family cars.

Just our luck, mum's family were penniless. We hardly had a pot to piss in.

I was born in Moss Side, which was a decent place back then, apart from it being full of Manchester City supporters. I think it would have been ok growing up there, however before I was a year old, we relocated, not to a smarter house in a nicer area, we downgraded to the biggest shit hole in Europe – Salford.

Salford had its own docks and was very much a working-class city. There was however a class of people lower than the working class and they all seemed to live in Salford too. We had nothing, many families in the area still have very little nowadays, but back then we had it really tough. Don't get me wrong we were far from being the only area in Greater Manchester that was struggling. The city was a dark and gloomy place, smog filled the air and polluted the lungs of its residents, sixty-eight thousand houses were deemed unfit for human habitation. Salford was, for its size, a heavily populated area of nothingness, it had the same dire conditions without the upsides of town. There was no real city centre, it was cobbled street after cobbled street, lined with run down houses and drinking dens on every other corner. For any escape from the boredom of day-to-day life in Salford, central Manchester offered a great outlet, it was only a five-minute walk and Salfordians always refer to it as TOWN, because for them and most districts around Greater Manchester, back then the city centre was the only place that had anything to offer.

Not only was Salford a dump, it was a post-war dump. There was a well-known song written about it called 'Dirty Old Town', originally recorded in 1949, later made famous by the Dubliners and eventually re-released by the Pogues in 1985.

When I was growing up there were a lot of Jewish families living there, as well as an abundance of Irish families. As is the case with most docklands' cities, it was a rough place with tough people. Liverpool used to be the only city in the Northwest of England to have its own docks. For that reason, Manchester businesses were paying over the top prices for international goods. Because of this (and so us proud Mancunians couldn't be held to ransom by the Scousers) twelve thousand Irish Navies were brought over to dig out the Manchester ship canal. This influx of Irishmen obviously had a big influence on the future residents. Many of them settled in Salford and made it their new home.

The Irish Navies were typically fighting men, it was in their blood. After a hard day digging the canal, they would refuel on Guinness, by the bucket-load. After a skin full of booze, often came the brawling. They would spill out of the local pubs trying to knock lumps out of each other. Reputations were made on those cobbled Salford streets and fables were passed down from generation to

3

generation, through proud family members.

My dad made his name in a similar vein and years later I would strive to follow in his footsteps.

Before I had turned four years old my parents had decided to split up. The pressures of having so many kids and such little money finally took its toll on them. It was decided that four kids went to live with mum and the other three with dad.

I stayed with dad along with my brother Michael and our lovely sister Lorraine. We lived in a predominantly Irish part of the city and Lorraine became a mother figure to me and Mike.

My other brother's Wayne, Steven, Mark and Bradley went to live on the other side of Salford in a Jewish area with my mother.

Sadly, it was years before I got to see that half of my family again.

Myself, Mike and Lorraine lived in a 2-up 2-down house that was built pre first world war. It consisted of two bedrooms, a kitchen, a front room and the classic outside toilet (also known as the shit house). Dad had one bedroom and us three kids shared the other. We weren't the only ones living in such conditions, there were thousands of families squeezed into those tiny houses at that time.

From that early age I was already showing signs I wasn't prepared to conform, I wanted to break from the norm, I wanted better. I had my own mind and was determined to be my own man - even though I was still a child.

To say I was a 'little bastard' would be an understatement, stealing from pretty much as soon as I could walk (and before I could talk). When I finally did learn to talk, it hardly qualified as English, only my sister Lorraine could understand my demands.

I was like any other kid in most respects, for example I had a great love of sweets. For families as poor as ours though sweets were hard to come by. The only way I could get my hands on any was to steal them, so that's exactly what I did.

And so it began, the foundations for my life were being laid. What was ahead however, regardless of how much of a little bastard I appeared to be, was still quite pretty inconceivable.

The wheels had been set in motion for a lifelong affiliation with crime, that in turn led to a lifelong affiliation with violence. It was the beginning of a life that would see me residing in many of our fine country's prisons, with the sentence I am currently serving being the longest stretch of the lot.

It was however the beginning of MY life and I was damn sure going to live it MY way.

Manchester was in for one hell of a ride with this little Jew boy in town.

In the early sixties, half of the old houses in Salford were being raised to the ground, which left great opportunities for a few quid to be made. At the end of each school day, I clambered up onto the roofs of derelict houses and tore off all the lead that I could remove with my bare hands, I would then sell it to a tramp at the end of our street for him to weigh in as scrap.

I was making a pound a night which was fantastic money for a young schoolboy.

In addition to lifting lead, I would also boost my income with a bit of shoplifting.

Of an evening we would see my dad for about an hour, he would come home from laboring on building sites, wash up, have his tea, put us three kids to bed and head back out to work on some pub door.

No sooner had the front door shut behind him, me and Michael would be out through the bedroom window and sneak off up the high street to break into some of the local shops. By the time I was 8 years old, Mike 9, breaking and entering had become so routine that we were remarkably relaxed about it.

Mike was a little smarter than me, I was always the first one to go through the window, and as I would head straight for the sweets,

5

he would be emptying the tills and filling his pockets with as much money as he could carry.

One night we broke into an Army and Navy store, just so we could steal the latest fashion accessories for skinheads - Steel toe-capped boots.

The boots I got were three sizes too big for me, but I didn't give a flying fuck I thought I looked great. They didn't work out too well for me though as 5 minutes after falling in love with them, the shopkeeper discovered us still in his store. Mike was able to run a lot faster than I could, mainly because his new boots fit him properly. I was caught after a few yards worth of trips and stumbles. It was like running in clown shoes.

The police came and took me away. I was too young to be sent to court, but I wasn't too young for a good hiding down at the station, I got another from my dad when I got home too - That was the way it was in those days and I soon got used to it.

One night I was coming out of school planning which street to rob lead from, when I was met at the gates by three lads who asked me where Mike Doyle was. Apparently one of them was supposed to be meeting him for a fight. They also said one of the lads wanted to fight his brother Paul too. These guys were clearly oblivious to who I was, so without saying a word I just started unloading punches, finishing one particular lad off in a matter of seconds. He had blood pouring down his face and could take no more.

I couldn't read or write, but at that young age I had already realised, I could steal if I needed to provide for myself, and I could fight if I had to protect myself, in fact when it came to fighting it appeared I was punching well above my weight. That was the first real fight I had in what became a lifetime full of it. From that early age I would fight fearlessly, without panic and I had been blessed with a skull cracking punch that I could use to great advantage.

Little did I know then, but fighting would become more routine to me than thieving, and years later my punch would land me a nickname any fighter would be proud of.

By nine years old I had a ritual of finishing school each day and heading straight to the demolition sites to steal lead, followed by breaking into shops of an evening, then I would roam the streets of Salford and Manchester (which was only a five-minute walk from our house) trying to fight every Tom Dick or Harry that had the balls to stand up to me. I was becoming a thorn in the side of the Greater Manchester police force.

I developed a deep hatred towards the police and got the impression that they weren't too keen on me either. I had already taken a few hidings from their finest boys in blue and it clearly wasn't going to be long before I found myself in some serious trouble.

Eventually the bastards caught me stealing lead. They had already had enough of chasing me around Salford, trying to stop me shoplifting, so that call through to the station that they had caught me red handed, must have been like music to their desk sergeant's ears.

As far as they were concerned something needed to be done to keep me off the streets of Manchester and they had landed that chance. I was still only nine years old though, so I was way too young to go up in front of a magistrate, but because the police were so sick of me and deemed me to be such a menace, they realised that drastic action needed to be taken.

My dad was called to a meeting at Salford police station where he sat with several coppers, who were all sick of the sight of me and between them informed my dad that they believed the best course of action was to send me to a children's home (a reform school).

It must have been one of the hardest decisions that my dad had to make, but in reality he wasn't being given much choice. He was coerced and little did he understand at that time, but once he agreed to me being taken away, I then became property of the authorities and I was only going to be released when they deemed it appropriate.

I wish I could go back in time, not necessarily to right my wrongs, but to apologise to my dad for all the stress and bother I caused him. It must have been soul destroying having to give me up like that after all the years he had tried to do his best by me. It wasn't his fault that I was such a little shit. Lorraine was content to do as she was told and go to bed at 8pm of an evening, but Me and Mike simply couldn't resist sneaking out and causing mischief. It was like a drug to us. There was very little to get excited about as a small kid living in Manchester in the early sixties, so we made our own fun, regardless of the cost. Truth be told though, I was uncontrollable.

I don't know if the police just wanted me off their streets or if they genuinely believed that reform school would change me, if it was the latter however, they were badly mistaken. Uncontrollable is uncontrollable. It doesn't change its face for different environments and nor did I. I already resented authority, so a home for naughty kids wasn't going to improve that, it certainly wasn't going to get me to tow the line.

Nevertheless, off to St George's reform school I went, and it would be a very long time before I was allowed back onto the streets of my beloved Salford.

Chapter 2:

CREATING A MONSTER

I n the sixties, reform schools were run like the military, you had to march everywhere at arm's length from the kid next to you, always in a straight line and when you stopped you stood to attention. You called the teachers 'Boss' or 'Sir' (although there were a million other words, I would have preferred to call them). It was a strict regime which included going to church four times a week.

St George's was a Roman Catholic approved school in Formby, and I was sent there because my dad was catholic. It was an institution for boys up to the age of thirteen, who had severe behavioural problems. Originally the building was simply a catholic school until it became run down and deemed unfit for purpose in 1933, at that time it was converted into an approved school, which was run by Liverpool city council (just my luck). I was only nine, I was the youngest and smallest inmate at the time of my arrival. Being a catholic reform school, St George's wasn't an ideal place to be sent if you were unfortunate enough to have the very distinctive appearance of a little Jewish boy. To say the teachers were little Hitlers would be an understatement, and everybody knows what he thought of the Jews.

If you have ever seen the film 'Scum' well St George's was a similar type of place, a Borstal for young boys. In that film a boy got raped by some of the other inmates, but let me tell you now, nothing like that ever happened in St George's – Thank God I'm not from the South.

That doesn't mean it wasn't a violent place, make no mistakes, it was. It was extremely violent.

Some of the lads in there thought that I was too small to fight. They didn't know me though and they got a shock when I stood up for myself. I had three fights on my first day in the place, losing all of them, but I gave each one a good go. My size in stature bore no correlation to that of my heart, and I didn't take losing well.

We all slept in dormitories in crappy old steel beds. At the end of each bed was a metal bar, that with some gentle persuasion could be prized off. Whoever had gotten the better of me in a fight during the day, would later be rudely awoken from their peaceful night's slumber. I'd remove the bar from the end of my bed and take revenge on all the bigger bullies that thought they could push me around and get away with it.

St Georges didn't have high barbed wire fences around the perimeter, so you could run away if you were crafty enough to get by the guards undetected. Occasionally that is exactly what I would do, just for a break from the bullying and fighting.

One such time I got out of my bed, dished out a beating to this horrible cunt who had punched lumps out of me earlier in the day, then I got on my toes and headed straight to Manchester city centre.

It was 6am by the time I arrived in the city. It was cold and I was hungry, so I stole a pint of milk from a shop doorstep. Before too long the police picked me up. As I was 10 years old by that time, I was given my first charge sheet. I was charged with stealing a pint of milk. A pointless exercise really as I was already in care, but the police like to exert their powers whenever they can. The charge was accompanied by a good kicking in the cells (another exertion of their power). Once they were done with me, I was driven back to St George's where I received another beating for absconding.

Beating up the other inmate, before I absconded actually worked out pretty well for me on that occasion because upon my return I was put in a room on my own. I'm not sure if the teachers wanted to protect me from the bullies or to protect them from me. Either way I ended up with a nice little room to myself which allowed me to sleep a lot more peacefully.

There was one positive thing about reform school, you were made to do an hour's worth of circuit training every day. Nobody had to force me into that, it was the highlight of my day. It was also the start of a lifelong addiction to working out for me. Fitness is to this day an integral part of my daily routine. Some regard me as a fitness fanatic, I've been told I have no 'OFF' switch. I don't know if exercise is simply my momentary release from the pressures of life or if I just enjoy pushing myself beyond my limits. Whatever it is it has kept me mentally as well as physically strong during the darkest times in my life.

Training and my single cell aside however I loathed reform school. The teachers were cunts, the regime was shit, it was a hell hole and I longed to be free. I would often plan escapes with some of the other lads.

One night I broke out with a boy called Curly, he took me on my first car chase. I was eleven years old, and he was twelve or thirteen, we snuck out together in the middle of the night and Curly stole us a car. He was a scouser (a lot of the kids in St George's were) and one good thing about Scouse kids is that they always seem to know how to drive. Stealing cars was their thing, so often when I legged it from St George's I took along a scouse chauffeur.

Curly was my first chauffeur and he drove us to Liverpool. After a couple of hours cruising around the city we were spotted, and followed in what became my first ever car chase. It was exhilarating. The speed, the danger, the ironic sense of freedom.

Curly was pretty good behind a wheel but the skills of a twelve-year-old joyrider were never going to outrun the police for long and we were eventually recaptured.

The customary kicking down the station came shortly afterwards and obviously a further beating back at the reform school. Those beatings couldn't tarnish the thrill I had experienced during that chase though. It had opened my eyes to a whole new level of excitement.

Unfortunately, a few years later Curly died in a similar chase. He was the first of my friends to have his journey through life cut short.

Eventually I was accepted by most at St George's. I was starting to fill out a bit in size, due to my love of training and the lads knew that it wasn't really worth trying their luck with me. I was a stubborn little twat who refused to be beaten and I was growing strong too. After some time, I became settled and learned to get along with the majority of the inmates and even adapted to the routine

Scousers being scousers and having their sick sense of humour decided it was time to make me feel more at home. To do this they insisted I had a tattoo to help me fit in.

They persuaded me to leave it to them to decide on what artistic creation I would be given.

While I was blindfolded, they tattooed the letters A C A B (All Coppers Are Bastards) across my knuckles. Initially I didn't know what it meant, but when I found out I fell in love with it. That tattoo has landed me a few extra beatings over the years, but I still love it and stand by it to this day.

My rebellious status continued to grow, and my desire to be free was getting stronger. One night I ran off on my own. I didn't have the knowledge to hot wire a car, so I found myself wandering the streets alone. I made it back to Manchester where a beautiful young lady called Maggie, who had spotted me sleeping rough, offered to take me in and allowed me to stay on her sofa for as long as I required. Maggie turned out to be a prostitute, she was extremely kind to me and her kindness was a welcome break from the brutality that I had become accustomed to. I tried to repay her kindness by stealing a few essentials for the house, simple things like bread, milk and cereals.

With a roof over my head, I managed to evade the law for a couple of months. I was on the rob day and night. By the time I was eventually picked up I had about £100 in cash stuffed in my pockets and socks which really infuriated the two coppers that pulled me. They were persistently badgering me as to where I had stolen the money, I obviously wouldn't tell them anything and when one of them slapped me, I kicked back in retaliation.

My hands were cuffed behind my back and I was literally thrown into a cell. The two of them followed me in and shut the door behind them, I knew I was in trouble.

I took the hiding of my life (to date) in that cell. They punched and kicked me until they were both heavy breathing and when they were done, they simply turned and left the cell. I was in a heap on the floor, covered in blood and snot and I could feel my head starting to swell.

To my complete amazement as soon as that cell door closed behind them, I got to my feet. Two fully grown men had pounded me into the ground and yet the pain didn't bother me. I was overcome by an adrenaline rush. I felt proud, excited and invincible in equal measures and knew from that day on I would be a force to be reckoned with.

Yet again I was sent back to the reform school, however in my absence they had decided that they could no longer cope with me. It was time to pass the buck and move me on.

I was recategorised and became one of Britain's youngest prisoners.

At twelve and a half years old and had already been denied my freedom for three years when I was put into a special unit called Red Bank. It was a secure unit in Newton Le Willows, which is closed nowadays but in its time, it housed some of this country's worst young criminals. The child killer Mary Bell was being held there when I was first transferred. She was known as the Tyneside strangler. Convicted of the manslaughters of two young boys who aged just 3 & 4, both in Newcastle Upon Tyne, after strangling them both to death. She carried out the 'manslaughters' when she was 10 & 11 years old, respectively. She returned later to her second victim's body to carve the letter 'M' into his chest. That girl was a very strange individual indeed.

In more recent years James Bulgers' murderers Robert Thompson and John Venables were a couple of it's more notorious residents.

Red Bank was certainly no holiday camp but by that point in my life I was used to surviving in unpleasant environments and the penal system had started to become the norm for me.

On my second day I received word one of my brothers, Wayne, was also an inmate. I hadn't seen him for years, and I still didn't see or hear from him for the next month or so, until one day a screw informed me that every other Sunday my mother would visit him. This particular screw being one of the very few more compassionate ones must have pitied me, presumably because I never had any visitors, so one day he took it upon himself to ask my mother if I could join her next visit to see Wayne.

That following Sunday's visit is the earliest memory I have of my mum. It was the first time that I had seen her since she and my dad had gone their separate ways.

Now I'm a great believer in the old saying that 'the apple doesn't fall far from the tree'. It must be true because all of my other brothers were little bastards too. What I couldn't tell you however is who this gene was passed down from but I imagine after that visit my mum would say it certainly didn't derive from her side of the family. She must have travelled back home thanking the Lord that I had gone to live with my dad when they split up.

The visit began with me being seated next to my brother Wayne, across the table from our mum, she had brought us a bag of sweets to share, and she divided them up equally between us. There was very little conversation between me and the two of them, as much as I loved sweets, they were no replacement for the neglect and lack of motherly love I had experienced up to that point in my life. The visit ended and for me it highlighted the gulf between me and her. There was no mother son bond there. I'm sure nowadays a psychologist would have flagged that relationship as problematic. It was the first and last time that she came to visit me.

I thought little of it at the time, as my entire stay at Red Bank was a lonely one, often isolated from the other inmates. As in St Georges I'm not entirely sure if that was for my safety or the safety of others.

Occasionally when I did cause trouble, I was shipped out to other detention centres for a period of time while things cooled down, I was ultimately always returned to Red Bank though.

The types of places I was sent to were designed to give inmates a short sharp shock treatment. They were extremely militarian, you would be beaten for the slightest thing, had to sit in silence at mealtimes, march one metre apart wherever you went and circuit training twice a day was compulsory. The beatings no longer bothered me in the slightest and the training was fantastic as it kept me fit, motivated and resilient, it made me stronger, and strength and power could be used to my advantage.

One time after a particularly troublesome spell at Red Bank I was sent for a prolonged period at such a centre. The place was called Thomas Mores and I was in there for nine months. I trained like a beast for that time and upon my return to Red Bank I was a strong, stocky sixteen-year-old with an air of invincibility. My time in Thomas Mores was intended to break me, but if anything, it made me.

Nothing was working for the authorities in terms of rehabilitating me. I was becoming stronger and more violent as I grew up. My extra strength, fitness and sense of defiance resulted in me being an even more unruly adolescent. The powers that be decided a spell in HMP Risley with some older prisoners might be what I needed to soften me a little and 'put me in my place'. I was told I was being sent to Risley as a last resort, in reality I was simply being moved on again. My first experience in an adult institution merely served to educate me further and expand my criminal mind. Far from rehabilitating me, being in Risley fueled my violent and troublesome nature.

For what was to be the final time, I was returned to Red Bank.

Passing me from pillar to post had simply allowed me to forge friendships with a vast array of criminals throughout the north of England. I had been locked up for the best part of nine years. The whole of my youth had been spent in incarceration of some kind or another. I became a product of the system, institutionalised before adulthood.

Days before my 18th birthday the governor at Red Bank called me into his office. He told me a meeting had taken place and it was decided that I should be released. I wasn't being freed because I had been rehabilitated, it was quite apparent by that time there was no rehabilitation for me, in fact the cheeky bastard actually told me "The future doesn't look great for you Mr. Doyle, the chances of you not returning to prison are slim, that being said, I wish you the best of luck anyway".

I felt like headbutting the ignorant cunt, to this day I wish I had. If my future looked so bleak, maybe some of the responsibility lay at the feet of those who had failed me over the course of the last decade. Almost nine years of my life had been taken away from me and all I got was a 'best of luck and shut the door on your way out'. Now I'm not one for sour grapes nor do I usually feel sorry for myself, I know who I am, and I take responsibility for my actions, but 9 years down the drain and for what? I was essentially nicked for stealing lead from derelict houses that were set to be demolished anyway. I was given a 'care order', a fucking care order. What care was I ever given? They took me off the streets for being a menace at 9 years old. Then at the ripe old age of almost eighteen they sent me on my way with a patronising pat on the back.

To this day I am convinced that they only let me out because it would have been unlawful to keep me any longer. My question to them would be: How lawful is robbing a child of his youth for such minor offences?

Fuck their encouragement, all they did was help to create an aggressive, disturbed animal, before unchaining it to wreak havoc.

Those 9 years were an emotional yet wonderful experience for me. The system had failed me, it had taught me nothing but how to survive on the inside, it had institutionalised me. Nothing was done to prepare me for the outside world in the slightest, a world which I knew nothing of. I couldn't even read or write for fucks sake.

I was going home though, so bollocks to the lot of them.

Chapter 3:

BACK IN SALFORD

By the time I arrived home most of the old houses in Salford had been pulled down and replaced by new builds and high-rise flats, I went to live in one such flat with my dad.

Our Michael was in the Army and had been posted out to Germany, Lorraine was living nearby though, and I felt straight at home (after all the place was full of scruffy cunts) and to my surprise the youth were just as violent as me. Not really knowing anyone I started hanging around with my brothers, Wayne, Bradley and Mark.

We got on quite well and built brotherly bonds. There was one major difference between me and them though, which often proved to be a bone of contention - they were all City fans, and I was United to the core.

One evening me and Mark decided to go to the Chippy for our tea. We were arguing about City and United when some young City fan in the queue fired a smart-arse comment in my direction. The natural thing for me to do was to hit him, (it was after all, all that I knew) so I did. To my surprise he went down with one punch, I wasn't sure whether he was dead or alive, it was the first time I had knocked anybody out, in fact, it was the first time I had seen anybody get knocked out with just one punch. I went home delighted with myself and convinced that I must have inherited my dad's punching power.

As soon as we got through the door Mark told my dad, thinking he may be impressed by me, but it went down like a lead balloon, he started ranting about me ending up back in prison and telling me how I needed to change my ways.

The following day dad came home from work and told me that he had pulled a few strings and sorted me a job in a nearby paper mill. I knew that if I wanted to remain with a roof over my head, I had to give it a go.

As the end to my first long boring day neared, a co-worker invited me to go to the local pub with him and a couple of the guys. Going to the pub was a whole new experience for me, I'd never even had a beer. In fact, there were a whole lot of things that I was still to try. I was still to kiss a girl (or a boy in case any of you southerner fairies were wondering).

In fact, the only girl I ever knew during my time inside was the child killer Mary Bell, in Red Bank.

I was hoping the local girls would be a lot different to her.

As it was my first trip to the pub, naturally I tried my first pint. Bloody hell it tasted terrible. I couldn't stand to force it down, so I went back to the bar and ordered myself an orange juice instead. I sat back down and after a short while a girl named Kath sat down beside me and introduced herself. I came out in a sweat, I was shitting myself, oblivious of what to say or do. Once I had calmed myself down though the conversation started to flow, and we had a bit of a laugh. As the chat progressed, I grew in confidence and was building myself up to asking her for a kiss, when in the corner of my eye I clocked a group of lads on another table staring at us. I paused from my conversation to look over at them. One of them stood up and came over to our table telling me that Kath was going out with his mate and I shouldn't be talking to her. Not wanting to look a coward I gave the lad the perfect answer – "so fucking what" "Get outside you cocky cunt" he replied. As he was with a group of lads,

I told him I'd fight him another time, with that he smirked at me as if to call me a shithouse. That smirk infuriated me, so I decided to wipe it off his smug face. I took him up on his challenge and we made our way outside. He didn't know what hit him though and I found myself walking back into the pub just seconds later. I shove past his friends who were heading out to watch us scrap. One lad said, "are you not going to fight him you chicken?" Smugly I told him and his pals they had missed the fight and that their friend was unconscious in the alleyway.

With that, one of them threw a punch at me, I managed to dodge the full force of it while already throwing my own. That left him sprawled out too, but the rest of his group jumped me. I fought my way free of them and ran home.

No first kiss for me, but it was a memorable first night in the local boozer. I could see why pubs were doing so well, not that I thought much of the beer mind.

The next day at work the guy who had invited me out the previous night told me that the main lad out of the group was spreading the word that he was after revenge.

Thursday night came around and I knew they would be in the pub again, so I decided to go back to do their main lad, before he had a chance to do me. To put the odds in my favour I took a steel bar along, concealed in my jacket.

I walked in through the side door and my target was sat with his back to me. It wasn't exactly sporting but I went up behind him and raised the steel bar high over his head and brought it down with full force. At literally the very last split second, I changed my mind, and instead of busting his head open like a watermelon, I redirected slightly and brought it crashing down onto the top of his shoulder instead. The impact was pretty impressive, and he fell to the ground screaming like a bitch.

In actual fact he should have been thanking his lucky stars that I had shown him such mercy.

It was crazy and a bit cowardly of me to take the steel bar, I suppose it was because of the numbers they had and me being on my own. I knew I could fight though, and I didn't need a bar to beat him. In hindsight I realise I could have killed him if I had landed that bar where I initially intended and much worse than that gotten myself a life sentence. There goes an old saying though; 'No point crying over spilt milk'.

That little incident had made people aware that there was a new kid in town who was ready to take on the world and news certainly spread fast.

Every weekend somebody new wanted to challenge me, it seemed they wanted to remind me of my place. Nobody could though, each and every fight was finished in under a minute. As my opponents came and (swiftly) went, the next one seemed to get bigger.

I was confident I could fight but the size of the guys I was fighting became unnerving. Sometimes the nervous energy and adrenaline (or whatever it was that was rushing through my veins) would give me goosebumps along with a surge of energy that enabled me to fight like a machine. In those early days I didn't come across anyone capable of managing my ferocious onslaught not to mention stand up to my knockout punch.

I developed a well-deserved reputation as a ruthless young street fighter with tremendous power and my name was being talked about.

I found myself thriving on this newfound 'sport' and was thirsty for more. More adrenaline rushes, more violence, more attention, more glory. It was what I was living for, however before long the challengers started drying up. My reputation alone was killing off the competition - locally at least, people didn't want to fight me, if they could avoid me, they did. My only choice was to travel to other areas in search of my buzz.

Me and a group of my more troublesome mates literally went looking for fights. We would go drinking in different pubs, but people saw us coming. They knew as soon as they set eyes on us that we were there for trouble. Half the customers would stop drinking in case it kicked off and the other half simply called it a night and left. To say we weren't exactly good for business would be an understatement.

On the odd occasion we did get a run for our money. More than a few times a whole pub full of blokes set about us and we had to make sharp exits, heavily outnumbered. Still there was the delight of knowing we'd been in a battle, whatever the outcome, we got our adrenaline fix and maybe a few war wounds and battle scars to boot - what more could you ask for on a Friday or Saturday night? Wonderful times and wonderful memories. I was free and I was loving living life with no restraints.

The area of Salford that I'm from, Lower Broughton, is on the doorstep of Manchester city centre, when I wasn't involved in arranged fights or out searching for new challengers, me and the Broughton lads would hit the bars on Deansgate, which to this day is still the hub of the city.

Back then it was the norm for young blokes to have a night out and finish it off with a fight, especially if you were a Salfordian. There were no security cameras to capture any incidents, and no one went running to the police, so people simply fought for fun and the hope of glory. Things went on that you would never get away with nowadays.

The clubs we hung out in were predominantly full of groups from other parts of Salford, which meant half the time Salford gangs would end up fighting against each other. What stood Salford gangs apart from the rest though was that we would stick together if necessary.

If for instance a Salford gang was fighting with another Greater Manchester gang, all the Salford boys, be it from Higher

Broughton, Lower Broughton, Ordsall, Little Hulton or wherever would stand side by side and offer support if needed.

Likewise, if trouble started in a club, the doormen knew they stood little chance against the Salford gangs because they would find themselves heavily outnumbered in seconds.

It wasn't wise to stop us going into a venue. At an early age we had the run of the bars, pubs and clubs throughout the city, including the sought after Deansgate area.

In truth we were a fucking nightmare.

It wasn't just in town (Manchester centre) where we were beginning to totally run a mock.

There were two clubs in Higher Broughton that we effectively had on lock down, they were ours and we called the shots.

Each weekend as many as fifty of us would visit them before heading into town. We'd swagger in, wearing whatever we wanted, regardless of dress code, none of us would pay an entrance fee and if there was a fight inside the doormen often asked us for permission before splitting it up. It was clear for everybody to see, we were more than a force to be reckoned with and frighteningly we were only just getting started.

One night we must have taken things too far and one of the owners of some hot spot in town had had enough. He arranged for a firm from Manchester to ambush us in one of the Broughton clubs. It was common knowledge the days and times we would hit the clubs, so it was just a case of waiting to see which one we showed up in first.

Now as plans go, this was a foolish one. By that time everybody knew that any firm venturing into Salford was effectively going on a suicide mission. It didn't matter how strong their outfit was, they wouldn't leave in one piece. There were simply too many of us and we could have the back-up of the other Salford gangs within a couple of minutes, if necessary.

This particular firm was full of big guys, all bruisers in their own rights, but they didn't have our mentality. They weren't lawless, reckless, feral animals like we were. To them violence was part of their job, but we were doing it for the love of it.

The minute these heavily built guys walked in, the whole club stopped and stared. They swaggered in probably in a very similar manner to how we had swaggered in twenty minutes earlier, and it wasn't long before one of them lashed out at one of the customers. The second he did the entire club steamed in on them, and I mean everyone. There were some serious casualties that night and they became victims of their own stupidity. I mean what did they expect? Talk about a red rag to a bull. Those clowns walked into the place like fucking matadors, completely oblivious as to just how ferocious the bulls inside were prepared to be.

To put it into a context that some of my fellow loyal United fans may appreciate; it was like having a night out in Liverpool on matchday wearing a Man United shirt. There are some things you just don't do, unless you want a night in A&E.

Before too long the police sirens could be heard and forty to fifty of us bowled out onto the streets of Salford and made our way into town to continue our night, on the whole unscathed and already adrenaline fueled, not to mention hungry for more. The Zoo on Deansgate was just starting to take off as the new place to be seen. Although it sounds more like a place you were likely to find me and my crew, it was actually a very classy joint that attracted lots of beautiful women as well as plenty of cash splashers.

Obviously, we liked the sound of The Zoo and that night decided to try the place (not that I was likely to cop for one of those ladies, but still, it was nice to look).

I walked towards the entrance with a stream of lads behind me and a great big smirk on my face aimed directly at the doormen - just to indicate we were ready for action. Before we reached the door, I was stopped by the club owner. He asked if he could have a word with me in private. With a snarl and a glare as if to say, 'what the fuck do you want?' I begrudgingly agreed.

We stepped out of ear shot from the others and politely he said Paul I've spent thousands on this place to make it up-market, the customers are very timid and if they see you and your boys in there, they will shit themselves, leave and probably stop coming back.

Polite or not, initially I didn't know whether or not to take offence to his comments. I had a lovely set of mates, salt of the earth those boys were, and still are today (those that are still with us), but as I glanced back towards them, I could see his point of view. They may have been a brave bunch, but they weren't the prettiest, and I am certainly no oil painting either.

While I was standing there still considering his words and whether or not to knock the smarmy twat out, things got very interesting.

He continued by saying "I am prepared to offer you £250 to keep you and your mates out".

Now £300 is £300, and to a young little Jew boy from Lower Broughton that was a tasty wad of cash in those days (I'm no financial expert, but that would probably be the equivalent to about £1500 today).

"Deal" I said in a heartbeat. "Consider us gone".

I told the boys that we were moving on but that the kind gentleman had agreed to pay for our night elsewhere. And what a night it had started out as.

Everyone knew that I was not shy about having a one-to-one fight. I was happy to test myself against anyone. In fact, I loved it, I saw it as a sport and I wanted to be the best. I was one of Salford's up and coming top boys and eager to prove it. One time however my friends took it upon themselves to arrange a fight for me, without my permission against a lad from Bolton, who was rumored to have an equally impressive record of knocking people out.

When I found out what had been arranged, I became very annoyed. The reason for my annoyance was that they had arranged the fight simply for their own entertainment. I didn't consider myself to be a circus act and so a heated debate (with the odd cuss word) ensued. They knew as well as I did that the fight would happen, but I felt I had to make it clear they had crossed the line.

After a brief pause while they all pretended enough to care about my tantrum, one of them said "We thought you were a student in the art of violence nowadays though Doyley". The other lads started roaring with laughter as I chased him down the street kicking him up his arse. "I'll show you student of violence" I was shouting after him. Two cars pulled up while we were still horsing around, and we all piled in for the trip to Bolton.

On our drive over I ordered that we pulled over at a chippy for me to fuel up.

Literally a couple of minutes after stopping for food though, we arrived at this pub car park, where I could see my opponent warming up.

I put down my half-eaten pie and chips and walked towards him, nothing was said, we both knew why we were there. He could no doubt tell that I meant business by the look I was giving him as I marched over, whereas his giveaway was the shadow boxing he had been doing when we arrived.

A decent sized audience was gathered hoping for an entertaining fight. Unfortunately for them, like many before and many since, it wasn't really what they got - I knocked him out with one hit, then went straight back to the car to finish my pie and chips.

The following morning there was a knock at my door. Fearing the worst after the previous night's escapades, I sheepishly answered but to my surprise a young skinny lad was standing there staring back at me. I looked at him slightly puzzled as to who he was, but before I could say anything he started "Doyley, it's been a while. How are ya? Fancy a day out in town?". He could clearly see I was looking at him puzzled as if to say, 'who the fuck are you?'. "It's me Massey" he continued. "I've just got out of Borstal, after 18 months of hell and could do with a laugh", he said with a devilish grin. "Don't you recognise me?"

The truth be told, at first, I hadn't. Paul Massey was a good couple of years younger than me but before I was robbed of my youth, we had started knocking around together. It must have been ten or eleven years since I had last seen him. Just before I was released, he had been locked up (not for the first time). Like me he had spent an awful lot of his youth in Borstals and reform schools. It was great to see him, and I pretended I had recognised him (as not to offend) but was just surprised he was on my doorstep.

When we were young, we were both quite small, but after years of my fanatical exercise regime we had developed very different builds. I was really beginning to beef up, whereas he was still much more slender. Size wasn't going to hold Massey back though, in the years to come he was to make himself quite the reputation. He became a well-known, highly respected career criminal and a successful one at that.

Although never scared to have a fight, he rarely went searching for them quite like I did, but he was more than prepared to get stuck in and more than capable when he did. His background meant he also had been surrounded by violence most of his life, and there was not an ounce of fear left in him.

I welcomed him into my house with open arms and we had a great catch up. Our friendship rapidly blossomed and before long it was like we had never been wrenched away from each other as kids.

One night in town, during the boom period of bars and nightclubs opening in Manchester, a club called Pip's was standing out as another one of *the* places to be seen. Me, Massey and my close pal Ashy ventured down there to check it out. Most weekends it was full of young up and coming criminals, so naturally we wanted to make our presence felt.

Before long Ashy told me there was a group of lads standing in front of the mirrors that kept staring over like they were also looking for it. We walked over and I asked, "is it going to kick off?" One of the lads looked at me as if I was stupid, which I suppose I would have been if I had hung around and started repeating myself. Before any of them had a chance to throw any punches in our direction, I had thrown and landed five of my own - one at each of them, rendering all five out cold.

Massey and Ashy simply watched on in amazement at my heroics and from that night forth christened me 'ONE PUNCH DOYLEY', a name that stuck throughout my entire life.

I've had some nicknames that I'm glad didn't stick around, for instance 'Banana Ass' because I have a birthmark that appears to come out of my arse, and it happens to be in the shape of a banana - unfortunate I know. Some people think I've shit myself when they see me from behind in the showers, or that I haven't wiped my bum properly. 'One Punch' however I was proud of. Little did I know back then that it would remain with me for so long.

My reputation began spreading even more rapidly once that nickname came about. 'One Punch Doyley' stuck in people's minds a lot more than Paul Doyle from Salford. I had become a real name about town.

As much as Massey buzzed off being by my side and getting stuck in, in the occasional fight, some clear differences were developing between us, mainly regarding our outlooks on life. While I wanted to have a laugh all the time and wouldn't take anything too seriously, Massey already had hard-core desires, he was growing into a determined criminal mastermind, who was set on acquiring an army of loyal friends prepared to fight tooth and nail for each other.

As my study of violence continued to progress nicely, Massey and his friends set about breaking into warehouses, and making serious amounts of cash. He was all about the graft. You could tell where Massey was heading and by that I don't just mean back to prison (although that sometimes goes with the territory), he was going right to the top of Manchester's criminal underworld.

As a young man he was the bravest and most criminally minded person I ever met. Surrounding himself with a set of loyal, equally ambitious friends who were prepared to look out for him 24 hours a day, clearly helped his rise through the ranks though.

Scotty - a happy go lucky lad who was willing to do whatever he was ordered, with a smile on his face.

Matty and Gary McDonald - words wouldn't do those two brothers justice. If they, did you could probably write ten books about that pair. Matty did his first armed robbery, bearing a loaded sawn-off shotgun, aged just 14.

Matt C - the only man I knew who never had to train, would drink 12 pints a night and still have a six-pack.

Navvy - the simple way to describe him (and these words were actually used later in his life by the police) "a very dangerous man that should not be approached."

These lads hated authority and if they ever got nicked, they would do everything within their powers to fight against the system, including fighting with police and screws alike, just as fiercely as the legendary Jimmy Boyle or more recently Charlie Bronson, figures who detested the system and became infamous for spending their lives warring against it.

The way they saw it they fought for themselves and others, to prevent convicts being chewed up and spat out by the system - much like myself and Massey had been in our early years.

Police stations in those days were barbaric. After a good hiding in the cell, you'd be taken to an interview room, you wouldn't get the privilege of a solicitor and your interview wouldn't be on tape. The rotten bastards would have a field day stitching you up with verbal confessions.

They seemed to take particular delight in trying to stitch Massey and his crew up. They had the intelligence to know that those boys would continue backing Paul Massey right the way to the top of the food chain.

Massey had a few tricks of his own to swerve having any false confessions pinned on him.

If he was arrested and didn't wish to be interviewed, he would literally keep the bastards at arm's length. He would cover himself in his own shit so they wouldn't go near him, never mind sit in an interview room with him. He was prepared to do whatever it took, and a dirty protest was just one of his techniques.

Even though I believe both of our firms were full of dangerous young criminals, we were nothing like some of the young gangs of today. The main reason being we rarely carried weapons back then. I wouldn't have survived as a young upstart nowadays. I would have had to be bulletproof to last a week.

Salford certainly isn't the only rough area in and around Manchester though, far from it. We weren't the only youngsters setting out on a life of violent crime.

Broughton neighbours a rundown area called Cheetham Hill. That place has always been full of young (predominantly black) up and coming gangsters, many of whom are notorious for being the first 'professional' armed robbers outside of London.

Cheetham Hill wasn't generally as violent of a place as Salford. The youth there didn't want to know about fighting for fun, but they were more than prepared to use violence and the threat of violence when they were *grafting*. Back in the day a very popular method of graft was 'the snatch' and Cheetham Hill's youth became experts at it.

The best way to explain a snatch: In the good old 1970s small businesses, shops, restaurants etc. used to deposit their daily or weekly takings in the local Bank. These takings would be carried simply in money bags inside perhaps a satchel or briefcase. Lurking around corners and in hiding in alleyways would be thieves ready to snatch the money bags right out of their hands – hence the name 'snatch'.

Normally you would hope to get between £2k and £5k. If you were really lucky it wasn't unheard of for a snatch to bring in up to £25k. It obviously depended on what sort of business you were stealing from and how likely they were to have had a good day or week.

If you got your choice and timing right, you could make some fantastic, easy money, well worth getting out of bed for.

Outside of London and Liverpool the Cheetham Hill firm were the most organised crime gang when it came to such snatches. It was alleged that on one occasion a very well-planned snatch, on a very well-known superstore, earned them £100k. That would be the equivalent to some serious money nowadays. Many of the top lads from the Cheetham Hill firm in the seventies are still legendary figures in today's underworld, and rightly so.

Once the news of the £100k snatch became common knowledge, many other organised gangs decided to follow suit, naturally this included Massey's lot.

Chapter 4:

FIRST TRUE LOVE
– The Red Army

One of the best pals I ever had was Ashy. He was a very unusual character (which is probably why we get on so well).

Ashy had to be one of the most laid-back people I ever met but an extremely switched on individual. He was my look out and my back up from an early age.

If I was in a nightclub without him, I would feel vulnerable. The guy was a star in my eyes, a man whom without his watchful eye I may not be here today. Like myself Ashy was always on the hunt for a good time, he loved his football, he loved stealing and he also loved a good scrap. The average man may think you will struggle to combine all of those things, but me and Ashy found the perfect way to do exactly that.

We started following Manchester United, home and away. Our first ever away game was a trip to St James' park, Newcastle. Me, Ashy and forty other die-hard reds made our way into the Gallowgate end (Newcastle's main home stand). We remained undiscovered for all of about 2 minutes before being attacked by hundreds of meat head Geordies, both fans and police alike. We were eventually dragged around the ground and ceremoniously dumped in the away end, where we were welcomed like heroes.

The buzz from that 10 minutes of mayhem was like something I had never previously experienced. We had found a new love and from that day forward our true passion in life was following United and leaving a path of destruction in our wake, taking liberties with any cunt who tried to get in our way.

In the 1970s being part of United's firm wasn't just about having a fun day out watching a bit of footie and smashing seven bells out of rival hooligans. It was much more complex than that.

A crucial part of the day was going on the graft (stealing). If we were playing, for example Leeds away, we would take about 10,000 fans and to accommodate this the train companies would put on five or six extra trains allocated for the football fans (these were known as specials), each train could take roughly 1500 fans. Now believe me when I say that back in the seventies, out of the 10k travelling fans, about a quarter of them were hooligans.

In the days leading up to the game the local newspaper would hype up such an occasion with articles highlighting the importance of the match, how many Manchester United fans would be invading the city centre, the large police presence to be expected in the area etc. etc.

Such articles would get the local hooligans excited, and no true hooligan would want to miss the entertainment of Man United coming to town.

Come match day thousands of the home fans hooligans would be loitering around the station waiting for us to arrive. If you were on the first train that pulled in, you would be heavily outnumbered, but by the time trains three, four or five had pulled in, there were a few thousand of us and we would rush off the trains in unison and charge into the awaiting fans.

Within seconds it would result in a full-scale riot. Hooligans would be rampaging through the city centre. The police usually couldn't cope – just as the papers predicted, and the city would turn into a place of extreme carnage. A shocking event for the average member of the public to witness or even worse get caught up in, not that we gave a fuck though.

Once the police lost control of the station and the whereabouts of the dispersed hooligans, their main concerns would then be the safety of the public.

A situation like that is every grafter's dream and one they would be looking to take advantage of.

The mayhem at the train station would leave police presence around the rest of the city at a real low, making shops and stores vulnerable. For us, the ultimate prize was jewellery stores. We would lunge over the counters reaching for the cash and if there wasn't much in the tills we would 'enquire' about what stock they had.

What could the poor shopkeepers do? Call the police? Even if they did, they would quickly discover the police at that time were too busy trying to stop a riot at the train station.

The bigger the football rivalry (i.e. Leeds or Liverpool) the bigger the opportunity for us. After a day of grafting before a game like Leeds away, you could go home with hundreds if not thousands of pounds in your back pocket, as we often did.

One of the most famous grafts of all was when United played Ajax away, in Amsterdam.

A jeweler that specialised in watches was done for over a million pounds worth of cash and stock. The hooligans who did the heist obviously didn't want to risk going through customs with their goods, so they sold their stolen watches while still on foreign soil, some for as little as £50 a pop. I opted to buy some of the more expensive watches to ensure a good return when I landed home. My middle pocket was full to its absolute max. I plugged a belter of a watch that I didn't want to risk posting home with the others and obviously couldn't risk wearing (plugging your middle pocket means concealing something up your bum).

The point I'm making is that for me and most of my friends being a football hooligan wasn't just about supporting the team, neither was it just about beating the opposing hooligans black and blue. It was a combination of things and earning good money was well up on that list.

Our greatest rivals were Liverpool, one of my earliest FA cup experiences watching United versus Liverpool came in the semi-final at City's old ground Maine Road. It ended up a 2-2 draw and there was absolute carnage in town on that day. The replay was then held at Goodison Park - Everton's ground.

Goodison is just around the corner from Anfield, in the heart of Liverpool, so I wasn't going to miss it for the world. I knew it would be non-stop violence and I knew United would be taking about 20,000 fans. The hatred and rivalry between the two clubs made it more of a spectacle than any regular semi-final and the fact we had had running riots throughout the duration of the first game at City, simply added to the expectations. Liverpool were one of the best teams in Europe at the time too, which meant their own following was at an all-time high.

I was anticipating that we would give it to the scousers once and for all though. It turned out I couldn't have been more wrong.

I went with a group of friends. When we arrived in Liverpool's town centre, United's firm had fuck all organised and were getting done in left right and centre. It was totally embarrassing. I was furious that we hadn't been more organised. The only positive from the whole night was that we did actually beat Liverpool on the pitch. It was an unbelievable result, given their dominance at that time.

I was buzzing as we left the ground and I had one thing on my mind; getting revenge for the liberties the scousers had taken at Maine Rd.

I was the only one jumping up and down as we left Goodison though, I stood out like a prick. The rest of the United fans didn't want to know. Yet again it was an embarrassment. We had one of the biggest armies in Britain, yet they didn't want to fight. It became everyman for himself as we legged it back to the train station. Heading down Scotty Road the scousers were having a field day, picking us off. The fun was all one sided.

In the early eighties sheepskin coats were all the rage and luckily, I had one. The sheepskin is a heavy jacket with a thick woolen lining and that night my fashion sense may have saved my life.

I was walking a few yards behind my friends, keeping an eye on what was going on. A scouser approached one of my mates, who wasted no time in punching him, before turning and shouting "Doyley leg it". *Fuckin brilliant* I thought. The dopey bastard had just bellowed my name in front of a load of shit house scousers that were prowling like hyenas. I knew I was in big trouble.

I had started to make quite a name for myself in the firm, and on home soil that is a great accolade, however in the middle of Liverpool it was somewhat problematic.

The scouse cunts recognised my name and the chase was on.

The problem I faced was that every which way I turned I was surrounded. The only escape route I could see was back down Scotty Road, so I could disappear in the city centre.

Thousands of scousers were still making their way up the road behind us, but I had no choice.

I felt like a rugby player bursting down the wing as I was running into them, my head and shoulders tucked in as if I was carrying the ball. There was obviously no ball though I tucked in to try to prevent my head from being booted clean off my shoulders.

I was bombarded with kicks and punches, but I refused to go down. I was in the hands of the Gods.

I must have seen the glint of half a dozen blades out of the corner of my eyes as I continued to run. All of a sudden, I felt the tension across my shoulders release. I figured I must have been cut down my back. Was it just my jacket or was I wounded? It was no time to stop and assess the damage. The Scouse fuckers wouldn't stop giving chase, so I had to keep moving. It was a good job that I was fit, not to mention pumped with adrenaline.

I got to the back of Stanley Park where the matchday coaches parked. Just my luck they were all the home fans coaches. The only safe haven I could see was on top of a minibus.

In a nano-second I launched myself on top of one of them. I flew through the air like a pole vaulter, only without the pole.

Scores of scousers surrounded the coach and I soon became their evening entertainment.

At first, they started singing stupid songs at me and then half a ton of bricks began raining down. I managed to catch a few of them and returned fire.

The coach driver being the biggest dick head on the planet shouted, "come down or I'm calling the police". "Call the fucking police" I shouted back as I threw a brick at the dumb fucker. Truth be told it would have been one of the rare occasions that I would have been glad to see them.

When the police finally did arrive (which seemed like hours later) I felt like kissing the useless bastards. My hands were sore from catching bricks, fortunately most of the cowards that were lobbing them at me were pissed up, otherwise I may have taken a few more hits.

I was taken to hospital with a Stanley knife cut to my back, some cuts and bruises and a ruined sheepskin jacket. If it wasn't for that jacket, I could well have become more famous than Joebe (a Manchester United fan that Liverpool fans savagely cut up some years later, leaving him needing over 200 stitches). The next morning, I was discharged and walked back to the train station in one piece, already looking forward to facing Arsenal in the FA cup final.

The night before the final, crowds of cockney hooligans were out hunting for United fans and it wasn't long before they caught up with us. We were enjoying a good old tear up when a panda car pulled up to spoil our fun. The two coppers were heavily outnumbered and must have had a couple of screws loose to confront us, either that or they were incredibly naive. They actually ran at us, throwing punches like superheroes who had left their capes at home.

I'm not sure if it was the buzz of the cup final or being in the capital city that got us going, but me and Ashy hung around like kamikazes and kicked fuck out of those two coppers even after the rest of the United fans had scarpered.

In the distance we could see the blue lights speeding our way. At that point Ashy had to beg me to stop. I was getting that much of a thrill I nearly came in my pants. The rest of that day me and Ashy decided to keep our heads down, in fear of being nicked and missing the final.

The following morning (the day of the match) a group of us met up early. Having fuck all else to do we decided to take a stroll through Soho's red-light district. Some of the lads wanted to go into a strip joint. One of the clubs was lit up like a Christmas tree and it looked the bollocks from outside. We asked how much to get in and the doorman said £20 each. After a debate we got him down to a fiver. Inside it was a dark, seedy shithole, but for a fiver who gave a fuck, it gave us something to do, and we got to see some tits.

We were sitting around a table when this *waitress* came over with big fat knockers that went down to her knees, she took our drinks order, the lads had a beer each and I had an orange juice. There was no sign of any strippers though so after a couple of rounds we decided to leave. We called for the bill and when the same fat-titted bitch brought it over, I thought it must have been a wind up. Nearly £200 for a couple of rounds of beers and orange juices.

I couldn't believe my ears when some of the lads started debating paying the hustling cockney cunts. "They can get to fuck"

I said.

To make my position abundantly clear, when the conning bitch came over for the money, I slapped the stupid look right off her face before heading straight for the two doormen. One hook each and they were both out cold.

For taking such liberties and to restart the day on a more positive note, I instructed the lads to relieve the place of its takings while I watched the door.

As it turned out, that was pretty much the end of our entertainment for the weekend. In the cup final, United, who were 2-0 down after 85 minutes in a drab affair, managed to claw it back to 2-2 just for our hearts to be broken by Alan Sunderland, who scored Arsenal's winner in the depths of injury time. It was a memorable experience in The Big Smoke but for all the wrong reasons.

As I began to acquire a status amongst the United hooligans, mine, Ashy's and Massey's status had also grown back in Salford. Our gang had developed a real reputation and it was one that unbeknown to me was not sitting well amongst some of the other lads. I met Ashy and the others as per normal at a Salford Club before heading into town. Minutes before we were set to leave, I decided to go to the little boy's room. When I finished my pee and returned back to the bar area, I was surprised to find that only Ashy remained there. I asked where the others had gone, and he said they had just taken off. I considered it odd but never gave it much more thought, until the next weekend when the same thing happened again. Then I knew that something was not right.

So, if there's a problem, I thought, let's have it out.

The following day I went to Navvy's house and asked him what the fuck was going on.

Navvy, not being shy, got straight to the point.

He said "it's not worth us going to town with you anymore. We commit robberies through the week, and we don't want to get arrested over a stupid fight on a Friday night. We all know it's routine for you, but we don't need that heat nowadays. If we don't get in a club you'll be fighting with the doormen, inside the place it's odds on you'll be knocking somebody out. You fuck the night up for everybody and no one gets the chance to get laid".

Initially after Navvy's rant, my first thought was *you fucking turncoat shithouse*, however like a professional snide cunt I kept my thoughts to myself.

I simply said "Navvy you're dead right. Just the other day I said to Ashy that I'm getting frustrated with all the trouble we're having, so we were talking about trying some of the nicer clubs where we're less likely to be provoked."

I left Navvy's house feeling he'd breached our friendship, him and the others.

What Navvy said did get me thinking though. If a considered close friend like him, who was a violent man himself, thought my behaviour was too much, what on earth must Joe public think of me? I realised violence had been such a huge part of my existence since I was a young skinhead (with boots that were too big), I had fought most days of my life for one reason or another, either for survival or for fun. Maybe it was time for a change. I decided there and then that the following weekend, instead of looking for trouble I would look into getting myself a girl.

God only knows how but that is exactly what I did. That Saturday night me and Ashy went to a club, outside of our usual stomping ground and avoided fighting at all costs.

To my utter amazement I found myself heading home at the end of the night with a beautiful young lady. Her name was Lynette and she had obviously fallen for my smooth moves and charms. Either that or she may have been a few sandwiches short of a picnic.

Whatever it was that she had fallen for, love was in the air. I went to her house one weekend; she came to mine the next, things were going well.

Throughout my life a pattern appeared to be developing. The pattern was that if ever I had anything going well for me it had a knack of turning to shit before too long.

So, I suppose it should have been no surprise when I found out her brother was a copper. Not only was he a copper, he was the youngest detective in Manchester and keen to get to the top.

Needless to say, this didn't sit well with me.

Lynette soon became pregnant though, with my first child Samantha and my dad and sister Lorraine told me I had to do the right thing and ask her to marry me. It was simply how things were back then.

She was 17 and I was about to turn 20. We had our whole lives ahead of us. This was a positive thing, surely, or so I was made to believe.

When I told her parents about my intentions to marry their daughter, the positivity seemed to spiral somewhat, it was in fact the first time (since my Mother had visited me in Red Bank) that I had seen a grown woman come close to having a breakdown.

I asked Paul Massey to be my best man and he said he would be proud to.

Together we organised the reception for The King's Arms pub on the edge of town.

Across the road from the pub was a doss house for the homeless.

The day before our wedding, Massey's older brother passed away.

I told him not to worry about his best man duties (which he assured me he was prepared to stick to). I said that my brother Mike would step in as best man in his place.

The wedding was the usual sort of thing, but the reception was more like a football match with different supporters congregated at opposite ends of the room.

My family and friends (who were mostly criminals) at one side of the venue. Lynette's family including her brother's friends (who were mostly coppers) gathered at the other.

The atmosphere was tense to say the least. The more people drank, the more electric things got. It was going to take one loose wire to short circuit the whole event and believe me there were a few loose wires in that function room.

Halfway through the night my dad disappeared across the road and invited the tramps over to help themselves to our left-over buffet.

Try to picture the scene; a bunch of criminals stood around the bar, a collection of straight-laced members of the public, with a scattering of coppers, gathered in the seating area and a load of tramps in the middle swarming around the buffet tables like flies over shit.

Massey turned up to the reception (bless his cotton socks). By that time though most of our guests were half pissed. I took him straight to the bar to buy him a drink and thank him for coming. Within minutes some cunt of a copper, who knew him well came over and said something totally inappropriate about his brother's death.

It was the trigger that was needed for the place to erupt like a volcano. It caused an all-out war. Chairs and bottles were being thrown from one side of the room to the other. The tramps found a safe-ish corner of the room and sat back enjoying the spectacle. It was chaos.

One of the tramps actually thanked my dad at the end of the night, saying it was the best food and entertainment he'd had in years.

It wasn't a great shock when the police turned up that it was solely my family and friends that were arrested.

Not only did me and the wife not spend our first night together as man and wife, but I also actually didn't get to spend a night with her for the next 6 weeks. A brilliant start to married life.

Poor Massey got six months. The bastards loved to get one over on him.

It turned out to be the smallest sentence he would ever serve, and he could have managed it standing on his head. As was the way with Paul though he defied the system at every opportunity and spent most of it down the block in isolation.

For me, the six weeks in Strangeways was far easier and less costly than the following six weeks. Most of which I spent trying to win my new wife over. I had to buy us a house. Which I paid a large chunk for in cash.

It was probably the equivalent to about £150k in today's money. You could never get away with buying a house in pound notes today, but in the good old days you could pay for anything with cash – even a divorce as it turned out.

Chapter 5:

QUEENSBERRY RULES

Despite Britain's centuries old history of violence and war, there was a real lack of fighting skills of note. Things were still like they were back in my dad's day when fighters met in the street and the toughest chin and the hardest punch won.

Things began to change though following the arrival of Bruce Lee's martial arts films.

Everybody started to go to the gym to practice their Kung Fu.

Following that came the kick-boxing trend, when anybody who could do a round-house kick considered themselves to be a fighter.

On a fairly standard night out back in Manchester some doorman took a disliking to me. He wouldn't allow me into 'his club' and when I told him I was going in regardless of what he thought, he decided to offer me a straightener. If I won, I would be allowed in, if he won I had to stay away from the place.

He was average height and fuck all to look at and I had no doubt in my mind that I could wipe the floor with him. We went around the corner to a desolate car park with friends from both sides watching on.

I marched in on him and he began to dance around, kicking out at my legs and keeping me at distance. I had to resort to hay makers in the hope of catching him with something and finishing things off. Due to his constant kicking I couldn't get him in range and was missing with everything.

It was a ridiculous fight. I had never fought anyone like him before. It looked more like he wanted to dance with me than hurt me. Some of the old street fighters would have turned in their graves if they had witnessed what was happening.

I tried to rush him, but again he was retreating and firing out his stupid kicks. I couldn't fault his defensive skills, but I began to wonder why he had offered me out if he wasn't going to attempt to land something on me at some point.

In a fight I am prepared to drink my own blood before I'm beaten, so, you're going to have to knock me out to stop me. This particular fight could have gone on forever, as a few bruises to my thighs was never going to bring it to a close.

Five long minutes must have passed before I finally stopped to ask him what the fuck we were bothering for. "We're supposed to be fighting, not dancing" I said. "Try having some fucking guts and fight me like a man".

For whatever the reason, it worked, and he rushed in on me. He put his arms around my neck and attempted to pull my head down. I was too strong for him though and my head was going nowhere. With my arms free I punched upwards straight under his chin. It was a beautifully executed upper-cut, and no sooner had it landed, the shithouse dancing prick jumped back saying that he had had enough.

I looked at him in utter disgust for wasting my time, before giving him a well-deserved bitch slap.

One of his friends had been speaking to a pal of mine during the 'fight' and he told him that the guy fought that way because he was a kick-boxing fanatic. Apparently, he was used to having more success, but my mind boggles as to how that could be true.

Even though I had fought a man with no real heart, it had still been a long fight and one that a lot of street fighters would have struggled with, as their stamina would have failed them. My fitness however was one of my strong points, as I had a lifetime of training behind me.

One positive thing that I took with me from that night was the realisation that I would have to keep my fitness up. If kickboxers and Kung-Fu kids were going to start coming out of the woodwork, then I knew I could have some drawn out battles ahead of me, so for that reason, I joined the YMCA (the best fighting gym in Manchester). Some of the country's best wrestlers trained there in the late seventies and early eighties, and although I had no intention of learning how best to grab another man's bits, I knew I could learn something just from training with those guys.

At the bottom of the gym where they trained there was a punch bag which I spent hours attacking, like a deranged Irish man.

One day when I finished punching the stuffing out of the bag, an old guy approached me and said "why don't you try Boxing. They have classes Monday to Friday".

After a brief chat with the old fella, I decided to go along.

The class had more professionals than amateurs. Two of them were national champions. One was Naz Dayho and the other an unbelievably tough lad called Chris Coady.

Boxing training in those days was all about blood, sweat and tears. No one ever sparred wearing a head guard.

To this day I'm not entirely sure why, but the trainer had me sparring against Chris Coady within 10 minutes of me stepping foot in the place.

I soon realised there is far more to boxing than people give it credit for.

I knew how to punch, but I didn't have a clue how to actually box. I was way out of my depth with Chris, so I opted to storm in on him like a bull in a china shop.

I think Chris punished me even more for fighting like that. He calmly, smoothly moved around me landing punch after punch, teaching me a lesson in the pugilistic art. God knows what he would have done to me if I had caught him with one of my haymakers. Luckily for me that never happened.

After the sparring session I returned to the changing rooms, beaten, bruised and covered in my own blood. I sat down and thought to myself; what a great time I had had. The following night could not come around fast enough.

As I was walking home along King Street (one of Manchester's most famous shopping streets) I decided to treat myself to a new coat. Obviously by 9.30 at night the shops were closed, but I wasn't going to let a little thing like that stand in my way. It was a great coat and the way I saw it I deserved to treat myself after the kicking I had just taken. So, I did a smash and grab.

Brian, the main trainer at the gym, was far more focused on improving the professional boxers than he was the amateurs. It was understandable because he threw his own fight nights. He set up the venues and headlined his own boxers. Naz or Chris were always top of the bill.

Most nights Brian would throw me in the ring to spar with Chris, which at first, I had no problem with, however eventually I felt like I was quite literally being used as a punch bag, simply because I was tough enough to take it.

I had my own aspirations however and they involved learning how to box, being Chris' sparring partner wasn't going to get me there. I wanted to move around the ring, skillfully evading punches while landing my own. So I decided to tell Brian that I wanted to be a fighter, not just a punchbag.

What I had meant was I wanted Brian's help to improve, but I mustn't really have made my point too clearly. Initially I thought my request had fallen on deaf ears, but at the end of another week of sparring against the pros, Brian asked me if I really wanted a fight. In a heartbeat I said "yes, of course". He then asked me "Do you want to fight for money or for some silly cup".

I didn't quite understand what he was asking me, so naively I said I wanted to fight for money.

I filled out the necessary paperwork and turned pro. I presumed Brian would help me hone my boxing skills and give me the kind of attention the other pros were receiving. That wasn't the case though. From then on whenever I sparred with the pros, they showed no mercy and simply outboxed me before trying to take my head off my shoulders.

Following 2 weeks of the same old beatings Brian called me over and told me I was fighting on his next bill. I really thought he was having a laugh, except nobody was laughing, least of all me. I said "Brian I get battered in sparring; I have no skills. When I spar with Naz I never even land a punch. I've not been taught how to box".

Brian exploded into a rage. "I've turned a shithouse into a professional then, have I? What should I do with the pro-license when it comes? Throw it in the bin because you're too scared to fight?"

I couldn't believe my ears. He made me feel so small that stupidly I agreed to the fight.

Brian certainly had a way with words, and a knack of getting you to agree with him.

He wasn't wrong about me being scared, in fact that was an understatement, I was terrified of being a laughing stock.

Going home from the gym that night I decided to do another smash and grab for a jacket. I didn't really even want the jacket; I just didn't give a fuck about getting caught. Being locked up would be an easy way out of the situation I had found myself in. I could do three months standing on my head then come out with a valid reason for missing the fight.

I even dragged my feet during the smash and grab, but just my luck no copper showed up.

Plan A failed.

On to plan B, which was simply not to tell another living soul about the fight. A simple enough plan, or so I presumed.

By the time I had dragged myself out of bed the next day, a few of my mates already knew about the fight. Worst of all Massey knew. He bought a ticket, and then off that one forged 200 more. He was even handing them out for free.

He claimed he was trying to drum up some support for me, but I knew him too well and I knew his sick sense of humour. He wanted a good chuckle at my expense.

I couldn't walk down the street without friend or foe giving me a wink and a thumbs up, no doubt smirking behind my back as I passed.

My brother Mark offered me some encouraging words to build my confidence. He told me that he had placed a bet on me to survive the first round, so asked if I could just dance around avoiding the other guy for the first couple of minutes.

Fight night came around and my nerves were terrible and I struggled to calm myself down.

I was fighting at light heavyweight but at only 5 foot 8 inches tall that probably made me the smallest light heavyweight in the country. I saw the guy I was fighting (JohnJo Green) and thought Oh my God, I'm in trouble. He was 6'4" and had an eight pack. I was hoping my corner had the white towel ready.

The first bell rang and I rushed in on him with my head down, like a ten-year-old fighting in the playground. I think he must have broken the record for hitting a man the most times in one round.

The second round I did a lot better. He landed half as many shots, probably only because he was worn out from his success in the opening round.

It was the same pattern throughout the fight. I took hundreds of punches, but he couldn't put me down. I can honestly say that not one of his punches hurt me.

I lost the fight on points, but it was actually a lot closer than I thought. I had clearly done enough to impress the judges, but he was easily the deserved winner. The most important thing for me was that my head could be held high. I was actually quite proud of myself.

Those who came to see me make a total arse of myself went home bewildered. They were incredulous to how a man could take so much punishment, yet continue to stride forward, throwing punches.

From that night onwards anybody who had doubted my chin, realised not only was it solid, but I also had a no surrender attitude to boot.

A few years later it became even more apparent how well I had done that night when JohnJo Green became a British champion.

A month after my first fight, I was on the bill again. Unfortunately, things went very much the same way. I lacked the boxing skills to get in close enough to land with enough harmful punches, which was hardly surprising as I had never been taught anything. I lost on points again. With a record of 2 fights and 0 wins I became frustrated with myself and annoyed with Brian. I knew I could make it as a boxer, I could take a punch for fun and had my gift from God – my punching power. I needed to learn the art of boxing so that I could get close enough to somebody to land one of my bombs.

It was clear that I had made a mistake in turning pro. I needed to go back to basics, so I joined another amateur boxing gym. As I was technically a pro, I personally couldn't fight as an amateur, so I joined in my brother's name.

I had a long honest chat with my new trainer Bill, and I told him about my two previous fights. I explained that I wanted to learn how to fight properly, how to jab and move and dance around the ring evading punches before counter punching.

He watched me spar and told me straight away that I would never make it as a counter puncher. He told me I was a natural born fighter, but to be effective I would have to fight properly on the front foot, bobbing and weaving, but constantly moving forward. He told me that I needed to get inside and once there, stay there and unleash my fury

Initially I was a little disheartened, but the more I thought about it and the more he taught me, it became obvious to all that he was right.

Bill taught me how to improve myself and use my natural talents. He also taught me how best to land a punch.

When throwing a punch, he told me to kink my wrist slightly to locate my knuckles in the optimum position when making contact with the target. Basically, it makes the punch far more solid. He also drummed into me that I had to punch through my target, not just at it.

Combining those two skills improved my overall punching technique ten-fold. I went from having a naturally great punch, to having a technically great punch too.

Bill was aware of my street fighting tendencies and he warned me not to apply what he was teaching me on the streets, as the risk of seriously hurting somebody would be very high. "To punch in such a manner without gloves on is potentially deadly" he warned.

I spent hour after hour on the punch bag, imagining myself as the hardest man on the planet.

Bruce Lee once said in a film "remember, punch bags can't hit back". Which is obviously very true, but the beauty of the bag is that it can take much more abuse than a man could ever take. I lost days dishing out punishment to it. I dropped from light heavyweight to middleweight, my speed doubled, my footwork improved no end, and I was able to skillfully apply controlled aggression. I had six amateur fights and went from strength to strength.

My amateur record was 6 fights and 6 wins. The time came for me to be back where I belonged, on the professional circuit.

My first night back at The YMCA I sparred with Chris and I actually held my own. The following night I sparred against Naz and I even managed to surprise him by landing a few shots. No one there could believe the change in me, including Brian who I asked to line me up with another fight. He offered me a slot on a bill that was already arranged for the end of the month. With a beaming smile on my face, I agreed.

I had a slow walk home in deep thought about my promising boxing career. There was no smash and grab on my mind that night, just legitimate money making and glory.

I had grown in confidence. I had newfound skills in the ring, a knockout punch in both hands, and even a six pack.

On top of all that if a light heavyweight champion like Johnjo Green couldn't hurt me how could a middleweight come close?

I believed I had all the makings of a champion. What could possibly go wrong?

The week before the fight United were playing Arsenal away. We took a train to Euston station. Unknown to us there were Arsenal hooligans lying in wait. I barely had one foot off the train when they rushed us.

Without really thinking I threw one of my newly mastered punches. It landed perfectly and the bloke was out cold before he hit the floor. I was arrested before I could get out of the train station.

The world was a changing place, and it was just my luck that Euston was one of the first train stations in the country to have CCTV monitoring.

My punch had been caught on camera and I was charged with assault and due in court on the Monday.

I spent the weekend doing press-ups. I aimed to do ten thousand, but I actually did more.

Press ups weren't going to impress the judge though, nor did the footage of me knocking out the Arsenal hooligan.

He scolded me, "I am sick of you hooligans thinking you can come to this city with the intention of rioting. You'll go to prison for 3 months".

I had been expecting a slap on the wrists. I had only pleaded guilty, so I wouldn't need to travel back down to London for a trial.

I leapt up and yelled "I'm changing my plea. The punch was in self-defence. I'm not guilty".

To which the judge replied "Shut up and sit-down Mr. Doyle. It's too late for that, you've already pleaded guilty, and I've passed sentence".

"But I've got a professional boxing fight next weekend in Manchester" I shouted back at him.

That totally incensed him, and he screamed back "If I had known you are a professional fighter, I would have given you six months".

"It's a good job you've already passed sentence then", I cockily replied.

I was sent to Pentonville prison. As I walked up to the reception a gentleman northern prison officer asked me about the fight I had coming up. I told him it was scheduled for the following weekend. He told me that he couldn't get me out for the fight, but he could get me transferred to another prison where I could train. Finally, a stroke of luck, I thought.

Before the end of the first week a screw came to my cell and told me to gather my belongings, I was leaving. I was happy to be getting out of Pentonville. The rumours about the place being the biggest shithole prison in England were true. It's an awful place.

I would have liked to have thanked the officer who got me out of there, but I never saw him again. I was very appreciative of his efforts though. I doubt any of the southern cunts would have lifted a finger to help me.

Handcuffed to a screw I was put in a taxi and taken to Highpoint, a Category C prison in Suffolk.

After booking in at reception it was dinner time, so I went straight for my meal.

I took a tray, collected my meal and went to sit at the nearest table. Another inmate told me that the seat I had chosen was already taken. The same thing happened at the next table and again at the next. I ended up at the back of the dinner hall, sitting with two odd looking fuckers.

One of the oddballs I was sat with asked me how long I was doing. To which I replied, "three months". Some nosey, loud mouthed cockney looked up from his food and said "Fucking hell. What are you a fucking bacon?"

I was puzzled, firstly, by his attitude and secondly at what the fuck 'a bacon' meant.

I clocked the loudmouth and fired him a glare but chose to do no more. I looked back towards the prisoner that I was having the conversation with, but he got up to leave. Before he walked off, he said to me that Bacon meant Nonce.

I was gob smacked.

A sex offender?

What the fuck?

Continuing with my meal, I stewed over why anybody would accuse me of that.

Being a Cat C prison, inmates could walk around the wing and socialise until 8.30pm then everyone had to be back in their cells.

Little did I know, but at that time Highpoint was one of the most violent prisons in the country. It's nickname amongst the inmates was 'Stab-point'.

Everybody in there seemed to have a bad attitude. People were staring right through me.

I decided rather than waste my time with the miserable fuckers I would go to my cell and try to relax.

I laid on my bed like Billy-no-mates trying to figure things out. Why did everyone seem to have such disdain towards me and why on earth would I be called a Bacon. I wondered if it was simply because I was northern, or maybe because I looked Jewish? Or maybe somebody knew I was a United fan? In my view though none of that should result in me being called a nonce.

My chain of thoughts were interrupted when three inmates stormed through my cell door intent on kicking seven bells of shit out of me. Luckily for me they hadn't sent their best men and their plan wasn't too great either. They had underestimated me.

I caught one of them clean on the jaw as I sprung from my bed. The second one I hit in the stomach and he instantly started gasping for breath. The third one had seen enough and began retreating.

Two of them went running out like complete shithouses. The guy that was struggling to breathe on my cell floor was unable to run, so I stood across his throat, making his breathing even more impossible. I demanded to know why they had tried to beat me up. "If you don't tell me right now, I will shut the cell door, barricade us in and stand on your throat until it crushes shut".

I lifted my foot enough for him to speak and he told me that the word amongst the inmates was that I was a nonce or a grass because I'd been seen arriving on my own in a taxi. Also, I was only doing 3 months, when all the other inmates in Highpoint were doing much longer sentences.

I began to understand why they all had a problem with me, even though they had got it all arse over tit. I explained to him what had happened with the Northern screw in Pentonville. That he had done me a good turn because I was a boxer. I told him to pass the word around that I was no nonce nor a grass and that in future if anybody tried to jump, they me would get far worse treatment than I had given him.

I was awake all night psyching myself up for more of the same the next day. However, by the time of unlock the following morning I was in the clear. It had been in the newspaper during the week about the pro-boxer, come football hooligan who had been sentenced to three months after trouble between United and Arsenal fans.

Still, nobody would talk to me, but they seemed less intent on trying to kill me.

Quite ironically Highpoint turned out to be a real low point for me. Nobody took to me and my access to the gym was very limited.

I went there hopeful of being able to use the boxing facilities and continue my progress. Aside from work outs in my cell and the odd occasion on the punchbag all that my time in Highpoint really did was kick the stuffing out of me. My burning desire to be a world champion had all but fizzled out. Upon my release I just couldn't be arsed with it anymore.

The saddest part of my brief spell as a boxer is that two heroes of mine; Naz and Chris never fulfilled their potentials either. Naz Dayho tragically died in a horrific car crash, and Chris Coady was murdered in a street fight, against four other men.

Chris and Naz were two more souls that had their journeys through life tragically cut short. I am proud to say I've sparred with both of them though. It was a tough learning curve sharing a ring with such great men but truly an honour to be beaten up by them both.

My time in the ring wasn't totally in vain. What I had learned during my short boxing career was a set of valuable skills in unarmed combat, that I could use in order to keep myself alive in the violent years that still lay ahead.

Chapter 6:

A RUN IN WITH THE QUALITY STREET GANG

As my boxing career finished before it really got started, so did my first marriage. My life was upside down and inevitably I resorted back to doing what I did best - I returned to stealing to earn a living.

I bought myself a pick-up truck to *collect* old handmade bricks and natural stone flags. There were very few people doing that in those days and the money came rolling in. A hard honest working man probably took home £200 a week, while I was earning about £1500 tax free.

Me and two businessmen I knew set up a reclaim company. We bought a yard, and I did my very best to fill the thing with knock off stone and brick.

One night me and my brother relieved a full street of its stone flags while the residents slept. It was an impressive night's graft.

Two days later the Manchester Evening News seemed to agree with us. Their headline read:

POLICE BAFFLED OVER MISSING STREET

The amusement that article brought to us. We could barely read it through laughing.

On another occasion we stumbled across some flat wasteland that resembled a football pitch in size but was covered in thousands of stone flags. It was very unusual. Thinking no more of it we stripped it bare. Back and forth to the yard we travelled over the course of a couple of days, ensuring we had every flag.

That little escapade also ended up in the Manchester Evening News though. The article told of the theft of flagstones from a mass grave site, of victims of the black death.

I was appalled when I read it. Which disrespectful bastards thought it appropriate to dig a massive hole, put all those poor buggers in it, then just pave over the top of them.

We honestly did not know what it was that we were taking, but by the time we found out, there was no putting them back.

Over the next couple of years, if me and my brothers had saved and combined our money, we could have probably bought a house between ourselves every five or six months. We should have started a small property empire, but like a bunch of idiots, we handed all our money over to the lovely casino owners instead, who were no doubt short of a few quid. We all had bad gambling issues and each of us lost thousands in the casinos on a regular basis.

Why I gambled I do not know. I worked all week and earned that much money that it would have been impressive to spend it over the course of a weekend. For some reason though I felt the desire to risk it all by gambling.

In the sixties, seventies and eighties there was a well-known and very organised firm in Manchester that went by the name of The Quality Street Gang or the QSG. They had their fingers in many pies, but doing security at nightclubs, arcades and casinos was their big thing.

By the early eighties, our gang had developed quite a name for itself. In fact with almost every serious incident that got accredited to a Salford gang, the blame seemed to fall at our feet, whether we were responsible or not. For that reason, the QSG were growing tired of us. They attempted to stop us from entering all the clubs where they ran the door. It became a right headache for me, as I had to beat up their doormen every time, we wanted a night out.

Once inside, our behaviour as a group was rarely what you would call exemplary and the club owners started to moan to the head of the QSG, Jimmy Swords, begging him to do something about us running riot in their venues. It was simply a matter of time until things really kicked off.

In the Summer of 1981 Prince Charles and Princess Diana got married. The government had permitted pubs to be open all day for us common folk to join in the celebrations from afar.

Myself, Massey, Ashy, Matt and Scotty were all sitting around a table in The Salford Club. The lads were enjoying some beers while I was on my orange juice. At some point in the evening, I saw seven or eight tough looking guys stroll in and head straight to the bar. As soon as I spotted them my guard went up. As a warrior of the street and being sober I immediately sensed something was going down.

I remained seated and subtly monitored the situation. Really, I was stupidly waiting for them to make the first move, which I ordinarily wouldn't have done.

I knew the possibility of them just being out celebrating the wedding was slim and after a couple of minutes one of them approached us and headed straight for Matt - probably because he looked the meanest of our bunch. The guy barely said a word before putting a pint pot over Matt's head. It was a big mistake.

I knew the next move would be the guys at the bar storming over to rush us. Without anything more than a glance at each other, me and Ashy jumped up in unison and we met them halfway, with a full Salford onslaught.

Like is often the case in a pub fight, it quickly turned into a bombardment of things being thrown from one side of the pub to the other. Me and Ashy were outnumbered but standing strong. We were buying time for Massey, Matt and Scotty who still had the stupid fucker who had glassed Matt. Somehow, he eventually managed to squirm free and ran out of the pub. His friends hastily followed. Already quite badly injured however the instigator of the whole affair was quickly chased down by our boys, who were in no mood to show him any mercy.

Being professional hooligans, me and Ashy knew when it was time to retreat before the police arrived. The others didn't follow our lead however and on that occasion the retribution went a little overboard.

The police duly arrived, and Massey, Scotty and Matt were all arrested and charged with Section 18 – grievous bodily harm.

GBH is a very serious charge, so they were all remanded in Strangeways. Me and Ashy had more than enough witnesses who could say that we were defending ourselves, so we weren't too worried about getting dragged into it. Also, we knew that never in a million years would our mates drop us in it.

The following weekend I decided it would be wise to keep a low profile, so I offered to take my new girlfriend Donna out for a drink.

As we were walking into town, I spotted a large group of heavily built men standing on a street corner. I could tell straight away that something didn't add up. A shout of "there he is" confirmed it and sweet Donna shouted, "run Paul".

She must have turned around to discover that she was talking to herself however because I was already on my toes.

A loud bang rang out and I stumbled as the pellets hit the back of my legs.

I was in a very sticky spot, but with my heightened emotions, combined with a mix of adrenaline and excitement, there was no way I was slowing down. I knew if I went down at that moment, it may have been my last.

To be excited about being shot does admittedly sound a little strange, but I was living the life that I had chosen and being shot was scary but thrilling. I found myself buzzing from the incident.

The reemergence of the gun on the streets of Manchester and Salford was still fairly new in the early eighties and I was the first of our generation of Salfordians to be shot and live to tell the tale.

Later I found out that while I was being chased and shot at, Ashy was inside a nearby pub, hiding in the women's toilets. He had also been chased by the QSG firm and he too knew they would have killed us that day if they had caught us.

As a child in the reform schools, I had taught myself to show no fear or weakness, so while a serious faction of our firm including Paul Massey was on remand, I decided my best form of defense was attack and so me and Ashy went to one of the QSG stomping grounds to face them up.

Looking back, it was so stupid, we walked into the lion's den, basically leaving ourselves in the hands of the Gods.

We waltzed into the arcade without any problems but once inside all eyes then seemed to be on us. A doorman came over and discreetly advised us to get out as fast as we could, warning that more of the firm were on their way and wanted blood.

We reevaluated our plan and slipped out of the fire escape. Once out the back of the club we could see several cars pulling up at the front, all full of big, tooled up, mean looking men. We had had a very lucky escape and it was all down to the doorman doing us a favour, talking some sense into us. I told him as we were leaving, to pass a message on from us. I said that I would be waiting in the Salford Club the following weekend if anybody wanted to find me.

While I was waiting for their next move, a very good friend of mine, accidentally, drove a stolen Transit van straight through the entrance doors to one of the QSG's illegal drinking and gambling dens, on a street just off Deansgate. He was never known for his driving skills and to be fair to him, having only one eye, you could forgive him for that. I also heard on the grapevine that another similar place had its doors blown off by somebody wielding a shotgun.

Aware of what happened to the last load of heavies that tried their luck in The Salford Club, I doubted that they would be stupid enough to make the same mistake twice, but I wasn't about to make a mistake of my own by underestimating them either. I decided that every time I went to the Salford club, it was essential I was accompanied by at least thirty or forty true Salfordians - just in case.

The owner went completely under the first time he saw us all arrive. The lads were just being boyish, but the 50 plus 'boyish' lads that turned up to stand by my side, were more than a handful for anybody. My mates loved it, we had the run of the place and the pickings of all the loose women in there - of which there were plenty. The ladies soon started flocking in droves too, once they heard so many young men were in the place every weekend. Really the owner should have been thanking me, as his club was packed to the rafters every Friday and Saturday night. On the whole things didn't get too heavy and it was usually harmless fun, but occasionally it did get a little out of hand. One night the lads were beating up some other gang members who had stupidly ventured in. The doormen couldn't stop it (basically because we wouldn't allow them to) therefore the foolish lads took quite a kicking. The owner had obviously seen enough and realised something had to give, if he was to remain open. He approached me and asked if I would run the door for him, he offered me £100 a night on the condition that I stopped the lads taking the piss. I agreed. The previous head doorman, who happened to be Ashy's cousin, refused to work with me because he expected The Quality Street Gang would eventually venture down looking for me. To be fair to him he was in a bit of a predicament because he had known Jimmy Swords, head of the QSG for some years. He suggested that he could meet with Jimmy in an attempt to gauge the situation.

Following a sit-down meeting with Jimmy and the QSG, he came back with a message for me to go to their arcade that Sunday afternoon.

I had a decision to make, and it was a tough one. I knew that it could also have been the last big decision I ever made. The sooner the matter was put to rest however, one way or another, the better all around. If their boss wanted to teach me a lesson for having the cheek to challenge him, then I had to be prepared for that. I had dished out my fair share of good hidings, so I wouldn't be crying myself to sleep at night if I took one myself, as long as I lived to tell the tale though.

I made my decision, I had to go. I asked Ashy to go with me.

"No fuckin way" he said. "I've not got a death wish Doyley, even if you have. Tell them we'll meet at the cafe in Kendals". Kendals is a famous department store on Deansgate and Ashy knew they wouldn't be able to pull off anything underhand in such a public location.

Jimmy Swords was still not to be underestimated though, he was a self-made millionaire, a bloke who started out as a barrow boy, but ended up a very successful businessman and gangster. He had other criminals and the police in his pocket. On the streets he was an unbeaten fighter and off them, in his younger days, a professional boxer too. I knew I needed some back up for the meeting and who better than my wise friend Ashy. Reluctantly he agreed to go with me.

As the lift in Kendal's reached the top floor (where the cafe is situated) I could feel my heart pounding, a million thoughts were running through my head. The pressure was on and I could feel it. I knew I had one chance and if I fucked it up, I could live to regret it.

We strode out of the lift and could see Jimmy sat alone at in the far corner of the room. He was a chiseled looking bloke with a flat nose and a strong jawline. He looked every bit the prize fighter. He stood up to shake my hand. Straight away I noticed he wasn't tall (something I could possibly use to my advantage, if it all kicked off) I looked him straight in the eye for a second or two before offering up my own hand. I did so with a very stoney look on my face, I was prepared to shake his hand, but he needed to know that I was no less prepared to exchange blows with him if need be. He looked at Ashy and with a slight flick of his head he gestured him to leave us alone. Ashy happily obliged.

"Sit down Paul, can I get you a brew or something?" He was taking the lead, but I was unsure of whether or not to let him. "No, let's get down to business" I said. "Very well" continued Jimmy, "this situation needs resolving and I want it to sorting today. I have a proposition for you. I don't make deals lightly, so listen and think carefully before you make your decision". He stopped to take a swig from his cup before carrying on. "You Paul are a loose cannon, far too eager to use your fists and exert violence, but to give you your due, you've beaten some of my best doormen and you do actually remind me of myself at your age, so I can't be too hypocritical. That being said if you continue in this vein, I will need to put an end to you and the chaos you bring. I don't want any of my men doing a life sentence though because we couldn't resolve this issue, between ourselves today". Immediately I liked his style. He was no nonsense and direct, but also seemed smart and calm.

"The attacks on our clubs have to stop, you are jeopardising my businesses and risk me losing money, which I simply can't accept. If you agree to end the violence in our clubs and on our doormen, then I will put word out that you and a small group of friends are to be allowed in our establishments, whenever you so wish. It must only be a small group though, I know how many kids you knock around with and we simply won't allow them all in. Why don't you try taking a nice girl out occasionally and I will ensure you get the VIP treatment" Jimmy's words were making sense, I imagined myself sat wining and dining a fit bird or two, playing the gangster, like in the movies. I nodded my head to show that his words were sinking in, but Jimmy wasn't done there.

"I will also keep my ear to the ground for any bits of work that I may be able to throw your way. It could turn out to be lucrative for the both of us, as long as we can agree to end this war. As an added little bonus, you have my word that if you need any back up anytime, I will support you".

Access to any club that I wanted in town and a potential to make a few quid was way more than I was expecting from the meeting. On top of all that I had the QSG on side if need be, it was sounding like a right result. I was looking at the clothes Jimmy was wearing, and they oozed class, I wanted to follow in his footsteps and make some serious coin. "I can agree to all that", I said "I was getting bored of the agro anyway and wanted to concentrate on boosting my finances. Consider it a deal".

"I don't go back on my word Paul and I don't expect you to go back on yours, once we shake on this, I'll consider it set in stone and immediately inform the rest of the gang that we are no longer on opposite sides." Jimmy again offered me his hand. My heart was now beating at a regular rate and a calmness was flowing through my veins. I was about to take my first backward step in life, reach my first compromise, but far from it being the coward's way out, it felt like the smart thing to do. It felt like a business agreement. It was a compromise that we were both making, which was mutually beneficial. I reached for his hand and firmly shook it, this time with a smile on my face.

Jimmy and I said our goodbyes and agreed we would speak again soon. I turned and left as he sat back down to his brew. I winked at Ashy and gestured for us to leave. The lift doors closed behind us and we both breathed a sigh of relief. "Well?" he asked. "Did a deal" I said. "You Shit house" Ashy replied, and we both roared with laughter. Once I told him what had actually been agreed, Ashy said, "You've made it to the big boys table now Doyley". He was right too, I was on the main stage, I was in the big league and I had a chance to climb the ladder. Making a deal with the Kingpin of Manchester was such a huge step for a young lad of my age but it turned out the transition wasn't going to be quite as easy as I had expected.

Chapter 7:

TOUGH AT THE TOP

I soon realised there were a lot of people out there wanting to knock me off my pedestal. Word had spread that I had reached an understanding with the QSG and it appeared to ruffle some feathers. Grown men that had tried their luck in and around town were clearly disgruntled that a young whipper snapper like me had made headway where they were unable to. Jealous and resentful foes were out for my blood. It was like I had jumped out of the frying pan and into the fire.

In no time at all I couldn't leave the house without having to defend myself. My reputation boomed almost overnight. Every villain, street fighter or general tough guy wanted to put me in my place. The only way that was going to happen though was by them stepping up and beating me and I wasn't about to allow that.

Being only 5'8" and 13 stone, there was no shortage of opponents. I simply didn't look invincible, and the once dried up pool of contenders was back to overflowing again. The new breed of challengers were more ferocious than the previous lot, there were some serious contenders for my mantle. I however was coming into my prime, young, fit, strong and oozing with confidence. Whoever tried their luck simply became another lamb to the slaughter. I was going through them, often still with ease. The common mistake many of those men shared, derived from hearing my nickname. People presumed 'One Punch Doyley' was a one trick pony, how wrong they were. My greatest attribute has always been my punch, but a close second is my ability to take one.

I've been hit on the sly while ordering a drink, while chatting up a girl, while watching football, while taking a piss and on so many other occasions when I wasn't at all expecting it. That many times I honestly couldn't recount. As for the amount of times I've been hit from behind, I doubt it would be believed. The main thing all those shit houses had in common, was that each one of them went home scratching their heads (as well as nursing their wounds) confused as to how the little Jewish boy had turned the tables and destroyed them.

I've always enjoyed being in Salford. I felt that I could relax a little there, as most people knew of my reputation. They knew I was tough and had trained as a professional boxer, so it wasn't advisable to mess with me. It wasn't enough for me to completely sit back and rest on my laurels, but it did help.

One day I was chilling out with some friends in the Salford Club, sat with my back to the wall (as always expecting the unexpected) when Trevor, a pal of mine, approached me with some six foot two, sixteen or seventeen stone, well chiseled tough looking bloke.

"Have you seen Doyley"? Trev asked me "this guy wants to fight him". I looked at the bloke he was with and I definitely didn't know him, nor did I have any reason to fight him. Trev was a long standing, trusted friend of mine who had a fairly impressive street fighting history of his own and he had given me a clear indication not to take the fella too lightly.

I took heed of the warning and stood up, pointing my finger towards a corner of the room and said, "Doyley's over there". As the guy turned, I *sniped* him - A snipe is a sly punch that's thrown when the other person isn't expecting it. Anybody foolish enough to ever be sniped by me found themselves in a whole world of trouble.

He went down like a lump of lead. I leant over him and informed him that I was Doyley, before finishing him off with a punch that rendered him unconscious.

Whoever he was, he had provided me with an unexpected adrenaline rush to kick off my evening. So, when me and a couple of my pals made a swift exit from the Salford Club, we headed into Manchester ready to pounce again should the opportunity present itself.

As it turned out, the big lump who had come looking for me that evening, set the wheels in motion for what would become a very eventful, not to mention very expensive few days of trouble for me (through no fault of my own of course).

At the next bar we attempted to get into, an argument broke out between us and the two doormen, who didn't want us inside. Within no time all hell broke loose, I fought with one of the doormen, who initially put up a good fight, but when I stepped up my ferocity, he simply couldn't deal with what I had to offer.

The other doorman was beaten senseless and ended up being repeatedly stabbed.

Having already made a smart exit from the Salford Club, half an hour later I found myself again making another sharp retreat. I told the lads that we would be pushing our luck if we stayed out together, so we split up and went our separate ways. I decided to go home and surprise Donna.

The next morning, I got wind that the police had been out in town, making it clear of their interest in speaking to me about both incidents. I needed more information and I knew just the man to speak to.

In those days at the bottom end of Deansgate, on the border of Manchester and Salford, Bob's pie van was situated between a taxi rank and a bus station. It was the prime location for a fast-food joint. Loads of the Salford lads would stop at Bob's van before leaving town after a night out. I would often call by there and have a chat with whoever was about, or if it was quiet then Bob himself would keep me entertained and updated with all the gossip.

I always thought Bob had a great job. He got to know everybody. The man did as much chatting as cooking. He got to hear all about the week's excitement and also had a front row seat for the countless incidents that took place right in front of his little van each weekend.

That night me and Donna headed to Bob's van for an update. I was chatting away with a couple of acquaintances who had heard some whisperings from the night before. It seemed the police knew exactly who they were looking for and it would be a matter of time before me, and the lads received knocks on our doors. As we were talking, I spotted two tall, athletic looking lads, both clearly pissed, heading straight for Bob's. They had just joined the queue as Bob shouted, "Doyley here's your coffee". As I walked over to pick up my coffee, I noticed them staring at me. One of them then blurted out "Is that One punch Doyley? Look at the fucking size of him". The pair then had a little giggle, clearly at my expense.

Such words were nothing new to me, I had been hearing bullshit about my size for years, and often I'd let it slide. But laughing at me in front of my girlfriend was unacceptable. I chucked my coffee into the gob shite's face and knocked the prick out before he had time to scream about it.

His friend got all brave and threw down his coat before rushing me. Now rushing somebody when drunk is not always a wise tactic. I side stepped his advance and he steamed straight onto a right hook.

Unfortunately for the obnoxious pair it was one of the rare occasions where I actually lost my cool. I showed them little mercy. Donna finally made me see sense and was able to drag me to the car to make our getaway.

Admittedly, with hindsight, I went too far, but their ignorance that night cost them. It would soon end up costing me too.

In a little over twenty-four hours there had been five people seriously injured in three separate incidents and I was a wanted man.

It was back to Bob's the following day to find out how badly hurt the two piss heads actually were.

I went with a pal of mine called 'Ready'. Out of all my mates he is one of the least harmless, so I figured he would be a good person to go out with. Ready was always comical, but he also has a bit of a lip on him. He can be a cheeky twat when he wants to be, but usually nothing too offensive.

While I was stood by the van chatting to Bob a car pulled up full of smart looking middle-aged guys all suited and booted. They weren't typical of Bob's usual customers.

As they approached the van, Ready popped up at the front of the queue and said, "you'd better wash your cups for these posh cunts Bob".

Not seeing the funny side of Ready's wisecrack, one of them dropped him with a beauty of a right hand. As impressed as I was with the punch, I found myself in a bit of a pickle. I had just watched my mate get poleaxed by this bloke and what made it worse for me, was that there were some girls in the queue that knew us both well. I simply couldn't not do anything and risk looking like a shithouse, I had no choice but to stick up for my mate.

I gave the bloke some run of the mill street chat and asked him to try his luck with me if he thought he was a hard man. Deep down, I was hoping that nothing further would come of it as more trouble was the last thing I needed.

The bloke was clearly feeling confident after his first impressive punch, so he took me up on my offer.

We walked away from Bob's van and had a fair fight, one on one. I put him down with ease but did him very little damage. As I headed back to the van, hoping for that to be the end of it all, the guy, pride damaged, started demanding another shot.

As much as I enjoy a fair fight, I tried my best to talk him out of it. I told him to go home and forget about tonight. "This is a fight you can't win" I said. My words did little to deter him and still he demanded a rematch. I couldn't get out of it without completely walking away, which I was never going to do.

I had to fight him again.

After flooring him for a second time, he was still trying to get up for more. I bent over him and landed a punch that had some serious body weight behind it.

Out of all the fights I had that weekend, he looked the worse off (apart from the bouncer who had been stabbed up, but I wasn't responsible for that one).

It actually crossed my mind that I had hit him too hard, and he might even die.

One of the girls that I knew in the queue was a nurse, so I asked her to look after him. Me and Ready made our retreat, while she was giving him first aid.

Even though it had been a *busy* weekend for me, I was technically defending myself or a friend on each occasion. That however didn't matter in the slightest when the police came calling and I was charged with four section 18s. The big guy in the Salford nightclub, the two doormen in town and one of the rude athletic looking smart arses.

It turned out that the smartly dressed guy that I had been worried about was only knocked unconscious and the only thing that was really hurt was his pride, thankfully.

I offered the two doormen 3 grand each to drop the charges, and the big guy from the Salford Club took 2 grand not to turn up at court (even though I was furious about it, because he had come looking to fight me). He turned out to be a bus driver and a straight member of the public. It seems he wanted a straightener to test himself and wasn't happy that I had sniped him - Boo Fuckin Hoo!!

In those days 8,000 pounds was a hell of a lot of money. It could have been £10k or more, if it wasn't for one of the athletic lads wanting his day in Court, which meant I was still potentially looking at a 6 year stretch for his GBH charge.

When I was initially interviewed, I stated that I was defending myself. The bloke had run at me and I was only being charged because I won the fight not because I was at fault for it.

The CPS thought they had enough to charge me though.

Eventually my trial date came around. I had to appear at Crown Square. Where the plaintiff arrived looking very smart, clearly trying his best to get me sent down.

When he took the stand however his plan began to crumble. He was going on with himself, enjoying his fifteen minutes of fame, when he stated that the last thing, he remembered was throwing his coat to the ground and charging at me.

At that moment, the judge intervened, he dismissed the jury and called me (along with my solicitor) and the prosecution up to the front. He said that he was appalled with the amount of violence in our country and did not condone any fighting, however as the plaintiff had just stated he took off his coat to voluntarily fight, either both men should be charged or neither man.

He basically had agreed with my initial belief, that prosecuting me was unjust, simply because I was the victor. He gave the prosecution a few stern words and told me to be on my way.

He was certainly one of the wiser judges I have presented in front of.

Although I had escaped a prison sentence, that weekend had to go down as one of my most costly ones, and there was little point in me kidding myself that I had everything under control. Things could have easily turned out very differently for me.

A few weeks before my trial Massey and the others had been up in court for the attack on the QSG member outside the Salford Club. They had all pleaded not guilty. Unfortunately, their judge had been less insightful than mine and they were all found guilty and received five-year prison sentences. The judge described them as being "violent young gangsters".

The victim had turned up at court in a wheelchair. His wife also read out a victim statement proclaiming her husband was so seriously injured that she had to help him dress each morning.

Those words proved just as effective as the CPS had hoped and helped seal their fates.

Massey being Massey was determined to fight the system.

He put in an appeal straight away, bearing in mind he had already served 9 months on remand.

Almost three years into his sentence he finally went to the Old Bailey for his appeal.

Massey's QC presented the judges with a video recording that had been filmed a few weeks after the original trial date. It was an amateur martial arts film, the star of which, performing his Kung Fu kicks was no other than the poor victim who had been wheeled into court a few weeks earlier and apparently required assistance getting dressed.

Massey won his appeal and headed back to the streets of Salford hungry for success, and with some new ideas about how he wanted to achieve it.

Chapter 8:

OPERATION TWENTY MEN

I n the 1980s the Europeans saw us English as fairly honest, trustworthy folk. Massey had come home from prison with an idea that would change all of that though. He had come up with a brilliant scam of travelling to Europe with stolen credit cards, buying as much stuff as possible in as short of a time as possible, then getting back home before the crimes were even detected.

Back in the day if you went into a store in England and spent over £50 on a credit card the store had to check to see if the card was stolen. In Europe you could spend £300 or more if you had your passport with you (or 'A' passport with you).

Massey got some bent passports made to match the names on some stolen credit cards and he was in business. Such scams are no big deal nowadays, but in the early eighties it was revolutionary. It took some organising but Massey with all his guile, thrived on the challenge and he put everything into place.

First time around he did the job correctly, he took just three lads with him and they came back with thousands of pounds worth of goods. Not just rubbish either, most of it was the latest in fashion, the type of stuff you couldn't even get in England back then.

The next time he went with six lads. Once again, they came back with cases full of gear, not to mention beaming smiles to boot.

News spread however and no one wanted to miss out on the fun or the chance to be parading around Manchester, donning all the latest fashions. For those reasons by the time Massey's third trip came around more than twenty undesirable Salfordians went along, and I was front of the queue.

We headed to Belgium. No more than an hour after arriving we were on the high streets spending like kids in a sweet shop. We hit all the beautiful towns. Those poor Belgian folks had no idea that they had some of the most violent, opportunistic criminals from the North of England taking advantage of their good nature.

At the end of day one, we were all buzzing with the thousands we had fraudulently spent using the knock off cards. Never before had 20 lads from Salford been so smartly dressed

So, inevitably it was time to party.

The first bar we visited was full of girls flaunting themselves at us. A very beautiful girl came over to me and said if I bought her a glass of champagne, she would sit with me. My first thought was 'is this girl already pissed?' A glass of champagne for a chat? I should be smashing the back out of her for that. Stolen credit card or no stolen credit card, she wasn't mugging me off for a glass of anything, so I told her to jog on.

While the lads were having a ball, I was chilling at the bar, when I noticed a cash box under the counter. I got a friend to keep the barmaid talking while I did a sneak for it. A 'sneak' is basically where somebody keeps the shopkeeper/bartender busy, while another tries to whip some stuff from behind the counter or from out the back without anybody even noticing. You walk away from the crime scene and nobody is any the wiser.

After pinching the money box, naturally me and my pal fucked off and disappeared up the street. It wasn't until we stopped to check the box that we realised what a result we'd had. The cash box was full of hundreds of pounds worth of Belgian Francs. It must have been the full day's takings and possibly more.

My little theft was unbeknown to the rest of the boys who were still drinking in the bar. So, when the staff discovered that the box was missing and the doormen tried rounding up the remaining lads and accused them of robbery, it didn't exactly go down too well.

In fact, it went down like a rather big, explosive, lead balloon. Me and my pal heard the commotion from a street away, we stashed the stolen money under a hedgerow and got back to witness the bar being torn to shreds.

That was just the tip of the iceberg too, once the fun and games started it carried on all night. We ran riot throughout the town, causing carnage in each and every bar we went in.

It even continued back at the hotel where somebody took the safe from the office. That was a foolish move though, because stealing from where we were staying meant that we had nowhere to retreat to. After the hotel raid, we all knew we had to clear out of Belgium and sharpish.

Naturally, we headed straight to Amsterdam.

Not only did we have bent credit cards on us, we also had a few thousand quids worth of fake £20 notes. We were changing them in hotels, using them in bars, giving them to taxi drivers and even to working girls. Those conning Dutch gits thought they were ripping us off, with shitty exchange rates and extortionate fares. Little did they know it was us having the last laugh. Consider going on holiday with monopoly money and every fool just accepting it. That is exactly how we felt.

After two or three days a few of us had become bored of shopping, so we decided to try our luck at pulling off a 'sneak' or two.

We went into a very smart jewellery store, but the shopkeeper could see we had no class and didn't belong in there, so we were watched like hawks, before finally being asked to leave.

Unfortunately for the shopkeeper that didn't go down very well, he got knocked out and we took what we wanted anyway. It wasn't exactly 'sneak' like, but it was equally effective.

What we hadn't really given enough credit to, was the fact that we weren't in Salford and our behaviour was drawing a lot of unwanted attention. To us it was just another day at the office, but to the Dutch we were a serious problem and they wanted to clamp down on us before we caused any more trouble. Word spread quickly and the atmosphere in the entire city seemed to change. When Gary McDonald got shot at, we knew our time was up and we all split up to get out of Amsterdam.

Once out of the city, we headed for the borders to make our way home. I went home via Germany and sent most of the money and jewellery home by post. I didn't want to take any chances with one particularly expensive watch that I had *'bought'* so I plugged it.

Carrying all my shopping through customs made me sweat a little, I had thousands of pounds worth of clothes in two very expensive, designer suitcases. They were the first cases I had seen that had wheels on the bottom.

I'm not sure if I must have a dishonest face or something, but more often than not I get pulled going through customs, so you can imagine my delight when I walked straight through unscathed.

I was also relieved to be back on home soil. God only knows how many serious offences we had committed on our trip, but our behaviour had been disgraceful and we were all lucky to get home. Out of the twenty of us that travelled, not one got arrested or even pulled at the airport.

Little did we know then, but lady luck was about to turn her back on us.

Our firm stood out in those days, partly because we were taking liberties, partly because with Massey's genius criminal mind, we were years ahead of our time. Some of the scams we were pulling off, thanks to his ingenuity, had to our knowledge never even been tried before.

There was a pattern developing though, the crimes we were committing were pushing boundaries, people were being hurt, damage was being done and huge amounts of money was being unlawfully made. There was often a serious path of destruction left in our wake. The Belgium and Holland trip had highlighted that we were no longer able to remain under the radar, in fact, we were very much on it. Unbeknownst to us the police had already assembled a special police unit to bring us to justice. The little European jolly had simply been the tip of the iceberg. I believe the reason we all got through customs was because the officials had been made aware of the ongoing operation and told to leave us alone.

The special unit monitoring us was called *'operation twenty men'*, it was the biggest single operation of its kind taking place outside of London. None of us know for sure why it was named 'twenty men', whether it was because they considered our firm to be made up of twenty main individuals, or if it was because of the excessive number of forged twenty-pound notes we had put into circulation, either way, we had a serious problem heading our way.

The night I arrived back from Germany I spent at my girlfriend's house.

The first thing I noticed as I drove onto my road the following morning was a police car parked outside my house. Naturally, I spun my car in an instance and drove off. I went to my mum's but discovered her front door had been kicked in and there was no one home. The net was closing in on me.

I soon received information that a heavy-handed team of policemen had gone through more than thirty doors, arresting over 50 individuals, including friends and family members.

The arrestees were being held in different police stations across Salford and Manchester.

Strangely they released my brother Bradley in the hope that he could find me and pass on a message. He tracked me down the next day at a mutual friends' house and informed me that they had nicked our mum, but if I handed myself in, they would let her go. Unfortunately for mum it was a Saturday and at that time I couldn't have imagined anything worse than having to spend a weekend in a police cell of my own free will.

I know I owe my mum an apology for that little stunt, but I did at least ensure my Saturday night was a good one.

When Monday morning arrived, I handed myself in bright and early. Me and Salford's best solicitor, Mr Bastel attended the station together. Back then we thought he was a decent solicitor, it was before he acquired the nickname 'Bastel six months' – which he got labelled because every clown that used him got at least six months.

Bastel did quite the job for me, I was charged with 8 conspiracies and of the 35 co-defendants I was the only one remanded in custody. The prosecution said that I was at the head of the indictment. I'm not usually one for sour grapes, but I felt like whacking Bastel six months right in his useless mouth.

The investigation revealed that more than a million pounds had been spent using the bent credit cards and tens of thousands of pounds in bent twenties had been used both home and abroad.

The plan had been to exchange all the twenties in Europe, however after our swift departure some of the lads had brought a bundle back to England with them, resulting in us all receiving an additional charge of importation of forged notes.

I was extremely unhappy with the situation, I believed the police were clearly trying to stitch me up and what made it worse was that I had only really wanted to go on the trip for a bit of a jolly with the lads, it hadn't been about the money for me, I had the reclaim yard at the time, which was earning me a good crust. I have lost more in a weekend of gambling than I made on that trip.

After spending six months on remand the judge at one of my hearings decided that as I was the only one of 35 defendants on remand, I could be granted bail.

I was delighted and went out that night to celebrate. I met up with the lads in a pub called The Town Hall Tavern. Although I was happy to be out, I was still feeling a little disgruntled at being the only one who had been remanded, especially after the cock up involving the fake twenties being brought back to England was nothing to do with me. Before long, an argument broke out between me and some of the lads. It was heated for a while but it got settled without too much fuss. I felt better having had my say so was happy to try and put it behind us.

Later in the evening we met up with some of the other lads in The Salford Club, I was at the bar ordering a round of drinks when Navvy, who is well known for his violent nature, approached me with his new sidekick. Navvy had a nasty glare in his eye - I had heard that him and his sidekick had robbed a security van to the tune of £80,000 (which was a massive result back then) just a few days earlier, so I expected him to be all smiles, clearly though he wasn't.

No sooner had he reached me, he exploded into a tirade of abuse, saying he had heard I'd been arguing with some of the lads and that I was out of order running my mouth off.

I looked at him and raised my arms as if to say, 'are you putting it on me?' (offering me outside). His position shifted slightly and he said, "I'm not stupid enough to fight you now with a few drinks inside me, but I'm sick of your shit, if you take liberties again I'll come after you and I'll cut you from head to toe".

I was in shock. I couldn't believe the level of his threat, nor could I believe that he expected me to lie down and do nothing. I had no choice but to retaliate, Navvy was not a man to make idle threats, I knew I had to deal with him immediately.

"You've started something now" I snapped at him, "so why wait till tomorrow?" At that moment I hit him with full venom, and he was out for the count before hitting the floor. I bent over his unconscious body and bit one of his ears off, before turning my attention to his sidekick (the getaway driver he had used to rob the security van) "Tell him that if he ever threatens me again, I'll gauge his eyes out".

I left the club feeling very upset about the whole situation, my response had been fairly extreme, but my emotions were running high and in that kind of environment in front of a dangerous man like Navvy, you have to fight fire with fire. I couldn't have shown him any weakness, that was the world we both lived in and for that reason I was especially surprised that he had chosen to go down that path with me.

A couple of weeks after our fight Navvy and his co-defendant getaway driver were arrested for the security van heist. Navvy made a 'no comment' interview but during an ID parade three people picked him out for being the man with the gun. He was remanded to Strangeways.

In the meantime, Massey had broken his bail conditions for stealing thousands of pounds worth of petrol and was also on remand. Massey and Navvy were padded up together and began forging a lifelong friendship.

Strangeways was always split into two main parts, one side was for inmates on remand, the other for those who had been sentenced. Massey and Navvy were housed on a remand wing that was located close to the rear prison walls. In those days, the original walls were half the size of what they are now and you could shout up to inmates from outside the prison grounds and even chat with them. We often went down late in the evening to find out what the lads needed, before returning the next night to deliver their orders.

We would put ladders up against the back wall with a rope tied to the top rung, then we'd climb the ladder and abseil down the other side of the wall. It was then a quick dash over to the cover of the prison wings, once there, bold as brass we started passing whatever they wanted through cell windows. When we were finished, we climbed back over the wall using the rope, shimmied down the ladder and would slip off into the night leaving the guards none the wiser.

It wasn't long before Massey wanted to try the wall for himself though, so he planned an escape. He requested a saw be passed into him, and he and Navvy took turns sawing through the bars. When they were finally ready someone with a ladder and rope went to the back walls of the prison and waited for the shout.

It didn't quite go to plan, however. As they were running for the wall, two screws saw them and released the dogs. When Massey and Navvy realised, they couldn't make it, they decided to head for the roof instead. To cover up a failed escape, they said they were actually protesting. When the Governor asked the reason why, Massey said that he was an innocent man who had spent too long on an overcrowded remand wing that wasn't fit for human beings. Navvy said something about there being no scent in the soap.

The riot was all over the regional news. Massey was protesting about the conditions and becoming a voice for the prisoners, while Navvy was just enjoying himself, throwing roof slates down at screws and police alike.

Massey quickly had the support of all the inmates who could be heard chanting his name from way outside the prison grounds. His reputation in Salford and Manchester was growing all the time, that little stunt saw it grow nationwide too. I went to the walls of the prison to shout up to him, knowing he would love to hear the encouragement and I couldn't believe how many people were gathered there showing their support. A girl in the crowd stood out to me, she was actually throwing Mars bars up to the roof for them. Being a lover of chocolate, I told her not to waste them all and she gave me one. Little did I know then, but that was to be the start of a beautiful relationship and that she (Jeanette) would end up being my second wife.

What a story to tell the kids!

After several days of protesting and enjoying the English summer, the lads came down and were duly thrown into segregation. In those days, in Strangeways, you would get a beating from the guards for talking on the landing, so you can imagine the hell unleashed on Massey and Navvy down in block.

As well as embarrassing the governor and his screws, what they had also done was lay down the foundations for change within the prison system.

A few years later, in Strangeways, the largest English prison riot of modern times took place. That riot lasted for 25 days and was accountable for £52 million worth of damage, one death, 147 injured prison officers and 50 inmates requiring hospitalisation.

Just like Massey and Navvy had done, the inmates took over the roof and threw tiles and slates down at the screws, police, firemen, in fact anybody who got within chucking distance. The 1990 riots actually left Strangeways in need of rebuilding and those little perimeter walls then doubled in size.

Despite the lads denying it, the governor suspected Massey and Navvy of trying to escape and ordered that they be treated like escapee prisoners.

In the 80s when an escapee prisoner went to court, he had to be transported handcuffed to a screw in a taxi. That's what they did with Navvy. It was a very naive mistake to make with one of Manchester's most dangerous men. In the taxi he showed them just how dangerous he could be by beating two screws up (with one hand), stealing their keys, uncuffing himself and going on the run.

Navvy's co-defendant was sentenced as the getaway driver during the robbery, he received 10 years, which was a harsh sentence for those times, and it meant that Navvy was probably looking at a 15-20 stretch if he was recaptured. Such sentences were fairly unheard of back then unless you had murdered someone.

Massey remained in the block while all this was going on. He was down there for months, segregated beside some IRA prisoners.

All high-risk prisoners in Strangeways had a separate visiting room from the rest of the population. Before a visit, the cons were placed in a cage (which happened to be located by the prison wall) until all visitors were seated.

The night before a visit, Massey had a loyal friend get over the wall, saw the top of the cage and tape it back in place. A rope was left on the top of the cage so he could get over the wall once he was out of the cage.

Massey's second escape attempt took place on Christmas Eve.

Everything had gone smoothly, until he was pulling himself through the roof of the cage and a screw spotted him. He had just enough time to raise the alarm before grabbing Massey's feet as he was climbing free.

Another masterplan had narrowly been scuppered. The things he was attempting and the scales of which he was attempting them, are what later left him being recognised and infamously titled in numerous newspapers as 'Manchester's Mr. Big'.

The headlines that time however in the Manchester Evening News read: 'Manchester man spoils IRA escape from Strangeways'.

That escape had fuck all to do with the IRA though, it was all Paul Massey. The Governor knew that and stripped him of everything, he was left in solitary confinement, doing his time the hard way, no contact with anyone, restricted visits, absolutely no perks. My heart bled for him, but he was a true warrior, and I knew they couldn't break him.

None of us saw him again until the 'operation twenty men' trial began.

Out of an army of co-defendants only me, our Mike and Paul Massey himself pleaded 'not guilty'. Mike got the first decision - a well-deserved not guilty. Massey was found guilty on two counts, but muggings here was found guilty on all 8 counts.

Massey received six years in total, with his additional charges.

I got three years and 10 months. Bastel-six months – only a fool would have used that man.

In truth I was looking forward to getting on with my sentence, I'd been on bail almost two years, and I needed to move on with my life. Getting my time done was for the best and the sooner it started, the sooner it would be done. It would have been nice to have spent a bit more of my sentence with Massey but as he was still considered high risk, the only people he was housed with were terrorists and the likes of the Infamous Black Panther.

Chapter 9:

THE BIG HOUSE
– Strangeways

I arrived at the prison from court in a sweat box along with the other 'newbies' that day. To my delight a top-ranking member of the Quality Street Gang, Billy McPhee, had passed on a message to his friend who was working on the reception, that I was to be looked after - My earlier agreement with Jimmy Swords had clearly been a wise one and was finally reaping rewards for me. Billy's friend said he could sort me a cushy job alongside him if I wanted. I gratefully accepted the offer, I wasn't interested in fighting the system like Massey and Navvy, I was all about the easy life and with the right contacts I knew just how to make prison work for me.

I don't really feel bitter against the system, I'm a born criminal and I expect to be locked up from time to time. One thing the reform schools had taught me as a child was to turn the other cheek where authority was concerned. Back then If a screw called me a Jewish cunt I would just smile back and nod. I'd have been in big trouble if they could have read my mind, but I learnt not to give them the satisfaction.

When working on reception the day would start at 06:30 and finish at 20:30. It was a long day but all that most cons would do in their cell is sleep, so in my eyes, it's much better to be busy.

We cooked our own food. The screws had a Chinese guy cook them the best food from the kitchens, steak, eggs, bacon, homemade chips, fresh bread and proper butter and we were allowed to cook up anything that would be unused. Obviously, we made sure that there was plenty of surplus stock so we could feast like the screws, meanwhile the poor sods on the wings were served food a dog wouldn't eat.

The hatred between most screws and inmates was intense, there was no conversation between one another. The screws on reception would see more of us than their own wives though, so they did us the odd favour, as long we didn't take the piss. We got to phone home occasionally. On the wings inmates got one phone call a week and a thirty-minute visit a month. We were allowed one visit a week that could last all afternoon if we behaved. The most entertaining perk from working on reception though was watching new inmates coming in from sentencing. There were some funny sights. If anyone was spotted crying the other inmates would taunt them, saying they were going to be sexually abused and warning them not to drop the soap in the showers. I've seen some tough looking men go under within the first twenty-four hours. It was cruel really, but it broke up our days.

Strangeways' induction wing used to be a long wing, a new inmate would firstly be put in a holding room to have some checks on health etc, before being stood in front of a screw and told to undress and bend over so the officer could see right up their third eye (in case it was loaded with any goodies, or naughties). They would then have to shower and get into their new desirable prison clobber, following that came the daunting wait before being thrown into the jungle.

Newbies have their belongings; tobacco, soap, shampoo, toothpaste and similar items taken from them. The screws would hand them over to us reception workers, I think, looking back that maybe we were supposed to store it for the prisoners, but we called it perks of the job.

If any of my friends came in (as quite often they did) I would make them bacon, eggs and chips with a mug of coffee, so everybody knew they were with me and weren't to be fucked about with. Sometimes I would give them some of the belongings that had been taken off other newbies too.

If a new guy came in that didn't know anybody then they had to pave their own way. Some would do it by keeping their heads down, others by trying to make a name for themselves (which can be a tough road to take).

One night a nonce came into the reception. Usually, such criminals are put straight onto protection and kept away from the rest of the population, on a vulnerable prisoner's wing.

This particular smug prick had gotten off with a fine, for some kind of indecency with children, which he then didn't even bother to pay, resulting in him receiving a custodial. He was so arrogant that he thought no one would know what his unpaid fine had been for but unfortunately for him, a screw working reception that day read his court papers out and asked me if I would like to welcome him to Strangeways on behalf of us all.

A free chance to do a nonce doesn't come around very often, so happily I agreed.

While the despicable scumbag was taking his shower, I told the other cons in the holding cells who he was and what he was in for, when he came through to collect his food I gave him a left hook, putting him flat out. I then left the cell and shut the door behind me.

Later that day when the screw went into the cell to take the other inmates over to the wings, we all got a fright. Red faced he came running out like he was going to have a heart attack. He asked me what I had done to the nonce. "Nothing, I only hit him once, why?" "ONCE" He screamed, "the guy's half dead in there, he's black and blue. I've got to get him to the hospital wing immediately".

After I had left the holding cell the other inmates must have felt it was necessary to punish him further and if I'm honest and I didn't exactly have a sleepless night worrying about it.

A couple of years into my sentence I was milling around on reception one day with not a lot to do, when I noticed that a cell door down the wing was taking a serious kicking.

I walked over to see what was going on, I peered through the door's hatch and to my surprise looking back at me was Navvy.

"How you doing Doyley? You Jewish bastard" he said.

I was pleased to see him. It was the first time we'd spoken since I had bitten his ear off. It cheered him up no end when I took him bacon egg and chips, with a cup of coffee to swill it down. He was used to being fed pig swill in segregation.

We had a good chat about old times and put our differences behind us. The following morning, he was due up in court after finally being rearrested following his escape. I went to his cell before he left and wished him all the luck in the world, I didn't let on but deep down I was feeling for him because I knew he was up against it, especially after his getaway driver had received a ten stretch.

Later that afternoon I could barely believe my eyes when I saw him strolling down the wing towards me with a great big smile on his face. "Doyle you Jewish bastard, come here and give me a cuddle" he said. I told him to fuck off with the cuddle but asked what he had to be so happy about. Navvy told me the judge had thrown the case out because the Identity parade - which was the only evidence against him, could not be seen as conclusive. When Navvy committed the crime, he had two ears, but (because of me) by the time of the identity parade he only had one. The other members of the parade all had two ears, which made it unfair and therefore deemed the identification as insufficient evidence We both fell about laughing. Life has a funny way of surprising you.

The following day Navvy was transferred to another prison, it was the last time I ever saw him. It was also the last time I bit a friend's ear off.

With the outstanding food on reception, I ballooned from 13 stone to over 16. Put simply, I had become a fat bastard. I usually use my prison time as a health kick, but I had been sitting around, stuffing my face and lounging about. I needed to lose weight and get fit before my release.

Lindholme was a Cat C prison in Doncaster that was rumoured to have the best gym in the system. I decided to get myself relocated there.

Within days of me asking a screw if he could sort it for me, I found myself on a prison bus out. I had had it cushy in Strangeways, but I wasn't sad to be leaving and I suspected I would see the inside of the Big House again sometime in the future. In my eyes I was going to a health farm and I was going to work my bollocks off to get back in shape.

On day one me and the other newcomers were shown around the prison. I got excited when I saw the gym, it was state of the art. After being given the tour, we had to do a test down in the education block. That threw a spanner in the works right away. I had barely done a day's education in my life; I couldn't read or write. Anyone that was poorly educated, or illiterate had to do half a day in the 'Noddy Shop' the other half down the education block. The Noddy shop was aptly named because everybody who spent any serious time in there ended up like a nodding dog. It was a sweatshop for making mail bags. Some inmates would sit and sew Monday to Friday for their whole sentence.

I was mortified and found myself actually missing Strangeways.

My first day in the Noddy shop I sat in front of a sewing machine doing the square root of Jack Shit. The boss asked me if someone had shown me how to work the machine, but I told him it didn't matter as I would be sewing fuck all. He then informed me that if I didn't work, I would be put on report. I duly found myself on report.

I got two weeks' loss of pay and no canteen for a month.

The next day the same thing happened, I refused to do anything and was sent in front of the governor. He asked me what my problem was and I told him I'd been working the reception at Strangeways with impeccable behaviour and that a reputable screw had helped me to get a transfer because I had put on far too much weight and as Lindholme had the best gym facilities in the system, it would be the perfect place for me to get trimmed up and healthy in time for my wedding when I got out.

The governor smiled at me, seemingly appreciating I was giving him my best sob story, before, the gentleman that he was, asked "How would you like the gym orderly job then Mr. Doyle". I couldn't believe my ears. I had gone into his office on report and was expecting a dressing down and left with the best job in the prison.

Within no time I was resembling my old self again. I would have backed myself against any other inmate in a fitness test, however there was a gym screw named Pete Bell that no matter how many times I went up against him I just couldn't beat him. Sometimes he would only beat me by a second or so, but he always won.

He had speed and stamina. His reactions were so fast, he could catch a fly, let it go and then catch it again. Pete was the fittest man I'd ever met.

Training alongside him did me a world of good, he pushed me on and inspired me to keep testing my limits.

I was nearing my parole hearing and as I was fit again, which meant there was only one thing left to do before I got out, I needed to earn some cash.

I had gone into prison penniless. By rights I should have been a millionaire, but because of all the gambling and my extravagant lifestyle it had all gone.

I had to find a way to generate some much needed money.

In the 1980s cannabis use in prison really boomed. It helped the cons sleep at night.

Having a reputation like I did it was relatively easy to get inmates working under me. I had someone selling cannabis on each house unit (wing). Every week I would get a nine bar of black smuggled into me, from which I could earn £1200. It was fantastic money.

I went for my parole hearing, but like most of the Salford lads in those days, I was refused it. I did get a six-month review though. If you got a parole review your case would be re-assessed without you needing to be present. If you cleared for parole off the back of your review, a screw would simply approach you one day and tell you that you would be going home.

After failing my hearing, I just cracked on with getting fit and making money.

One morning as I was going for breakfast a screw came over and said "Every dog has its day Doyley, pack your shit up you're going home".

My first thought was 'Brilliant', but I could have done with staying another six months as the money I was earning was great and the added bonus was I couldn't spunk it all in the casino while I was behind bars.

However, as the screw had so delightfully put it, it was this dog's day.

I spent my first day out as a free man with Jeannette. We had a lovely day together and I felt very lucky. I felt that lucky that I couldn't get the casino out of my head. Unbelievably I had earned enough money during my eighteen months in Lindholme to buy me and Jeanette a house, so after some serious begging and agreeing to start house hunting, she finally said that as long as I treated her to a slap-up dinner beforehand, I could finish the night uninterrupted in the casino.

I took a grand of my Lindholme earnings out with me and after our dinner I went to the best Casino in Manchester, The Midland Hotel.

I have a very aggressive attitude to anything I do (believe it or not) and that includes gambling. I started out betting like I had a hundred grand in my pocket and within 2 or 3 hours I was up by over £90,000. What a rollercoaster my life had become. That morning I had been ready for just another mundane day in prison and by the end of the night I had relieved the Midland hotel's casino of seventy four thousand of its finest pounds. I could barely get to sleep when I got home, I was on such a high.

It had been a great day and I was determined to use the money more wisely than I had previously done so in my life. I spent 20 grand setting up a reclaim business. I knew the business inside out as I had dabbled at it on and off all my adult life. I knew if I did it right, I could double my money buying and selling reclaim materials, and so I set about doing it 'right'.

I had my brother Michael running the business while I did what I do best, I stole our stock.

One day I was at the yard when a lad who had been selling cannabis for me in Lindholme came by to see me. He said he wanted to sell for me on the out and he wanted to sell it in the area I'm from – Lower Broughton. A man with a plan I thought, how could I refuse.

Little did I know but my life was about to change forever.

I knew fuck all about buying and selling cannabis outside of the prison system. It is all very sheltered inside. Someone gets it into you, and you simply dish out the goods, before paying your bill and counting your profits. There are no fussy customers, not grumbling and no running off without paying (there was nowhere to run after all).

Outside of the prison walls it seemed a lot more daunting. You need to set up meets to view and buy the merchandise. You might get shit stuff that nobody wants, so then you need to sort out the supply end. You might get people trying to do a runner without paying, so then you need to sort out that end.

I had to establish a few good sources and get it moving though, because my man with the plan could sell half a kilo of green a week and I was getting excited about our prospects.

My first move was what any respectable gentleman drug dealer would do, I got my girlfriend to buy some cannabis for me. She had some family friends who could get us started.

I knew I had to learn the ropes though and fast. I needed to keep up the supply to meet the demand. In no time at all I had five people selling cannabis for me around Salford. It turned out it wasn't exactly rocket science. In fact, the hardest part was keeping my customers in stock.

That year cannabis seemed to really explode up and down the country. Joe Public wanted to relax at the end of a hard day, and I tried my best to do Joe Public a service.

Drug dealing around Salford was hardly organised crime back then, there wasn't too much of it about. Once the demand had increased, I began to be supplied by an old criminal acquaintance of mine from Cheetham Hill. Before long though, he simply couldn't keep up with my demand.

I knew that the only people in the North West with any serious experience were the gangs from Moss Side or the Scousers, which meant Moss Side or Liverpool were my only two realistic options to get the quantity of weed that I required. Both are very seedy places, but fuck going into the heart of Moss Side I thought to myself. I wasn't brave or stupid enough for that.

I got in touch with a scouser called Granty who had spent the majority of his youth with me in special units. We arranged to meet at a boozer in Liverpool. I hadn't seen him in years, but he greeted me with the most welcoming of words "fucking hell Doyley you Manc twat, it's good to see ya".

After a lovely chat I told him I had a 'blooming' cannabis round, but I was struggling to keep up with my customer's demands. Immediately I knew I had gone to the right man. He became very business like and quizzed me on what I needed, how regular, where and when. Then he began to tell me how to do the job correctly. He had been a lifelong friend, so he was happy to help me, but I think secretly he enjoyed professing his knowledge to me too.

The very next day he sent his driver down to Salford with five kilos. It was a massive step up for me. I even started supplying my old dealer from the Cheetham Hill firm.

Chapter 10:

START OF THE DOOR WARS

Most of my customers were from Broughton, the town I call home. It's a very cliquey place and it goes without saying over there that if one of your own was in trouble all the lads would turn out to assist. Other areas around Salford have taken a dislike to Broughton lads over the years. I think mainly because having a large firm with that sort of location (right on the edge of town) it gave us the advantage of having the run of the city centre.

At the same time that my new business was really taking off, a friend of mine, Jimmy became the landlord at a pub in Broughton. He wasn't having it so smoothly though; he had a problem that would worry any landlord. Every Sunday night a large group of lads from Salford were going into his pub and causing trouble. The troublesome young lads were actually a very strong outfit, especially so as they were from two different Salford areas but were combining forces.

If anyone in the pub stood up to them, they were quite seriously dealt with. I was disgruntled to hear that people from my own area were being beaten up, so I told Jimmy I would try my best to sort the problem for him.

Jimmy was a straight member of the public and was considering going to the police, but we wouldn't allow him to do that because he would be breaking the most important rule in Salford: YOU

DON'T GRASS.

If he had done that, we couldn't have helped him and no doubt his business would have been burned to the ground. I told Jimmy the only way to deal with young violent thugs was, ironically, to fight fire with fire.

I had to ask myself whether or not this firm was pushing its weight around so they could get a foothold in Broughton and start selling drugs on my patch. It was a possibility and it gave me more of an incentive to deal with them. Maybe they thought I was already over the hill, pushing 30 years old. They were in for a shock if they did, I still hadn't neared the pinnacle of my criminal career, so I had no intention of being mugged off or edged out.

Without meaning to brag I believe I have experienced more violence than anyone I know. I was raised in violent institutions, I was a street fighter, I had been a boxer and I was a professional football hooligan who had fought up and down the country. At that time there was a special police squad assigned to follow me and the United lads because they knew that wherever we went, violence followed.

I knew the young gangsters that I would be going up against would be brutal, I knew they would show no mercy and I knew they had a point to prove. I still had all that in me though, as well as my vast experience and knowledge to fall back on, and I would use that to my advantage.

I told Ashy to get the lads together and make sure we had at least 40 members, because I was expecting them to bring 20. It's always nice to have the odds in your favour and within an hour or two Ashy phoned back informing me that everyone was not only ready but looking forward to it. Throughout Britain the most popular weapon on occasions like these is a beer bottle. Readily available, easily disposed of and very effective. Each firm would have a front man who would go into a fight first to kick things off. Immediately followed by the hyenas, mostly armed with such bottles. It's usually a blood curdling display.

Somehow word got back to this other firm that we were expecting them. For that reason, they came down with 30 plus lads.

Extremely foolishly they came through the front doors in one big group and received a warm welcome from our lot. We waited for them all to be inside before bombarding them with beer bottles.

How no one got killed I just don't know because the onslaught was brutal. I've seen plenty of savage affairs, but nothing quite like that one. For the lucky ones who did make it outside they didn't have time to get in their cars, they were chased clear out of Broughton. The small number that did make it away unharmed must have been mentality wounded by what they had witnessed.

That night really marked the start of the door wars in Salford and Manchester.

It also left Broughton with a bit of a legacy and did no harm to my reputation either.

The following weeks a number of club owners contacted me asking if I could stop gangs causing trouble in their venues. Me of all people, who had caused as much trouble as anyone and given Manchester and Salford a splitting headache for the last decade, was being asked to stop the trouble.

Courage wasn't a problem and I still felt riddled with excitement walking into men throwing punches at me, so I figured I might as well get paid for it.

A friend of mine, Paul Quinn was doing the security at a famous Salford pub, The Inn of Good Hope. Each weekend it was wall to wall with customers. However, the same predicament was developing, gangs of youths from in and around the area were causing trouble, behaving menacingly and no doubt putting the fear of God into the other customers.

Quinny was a natural fighter, 6'4" and Salford born and bred, he was willing to have a go at any man. Paul called me one day to ask if I could help him and his other doormen tackle a gang that had been going into the pub and causing unrest. Naturally as the request came from a friend I agreed to help. It was to become one of the biggest mistakes that I would ever make, and it led to war with one of the most violent firms Manchester would ever likely see.

The leader of that firm was my old mate, Paul Massey.

Naively I thought that as it was my old friend and ally, all I had to do was tell him I was doing the door there and as we had been like brothers for years, he would simply stop his firm from going in or at least from causing trouble.

After Massey's most recent release from prison he had relocated and the firm he was running was from his new hometown of Ordsall.

To say that me and many members of his firm didn't see eye-to-eye would be a huge understatement. I disliked an awful lot of his new friends and vice-versa.

Not just for me, but for my whole family growing up, we experienced so many conflicts with the Ordsall gang that I had lost count of the incidents. From the time that Massey took over at the top of their hierarchy, rather than things becoming easier, I believe they got worse. The fact that me and Massey were such good old friends really seemed to rile the rest of his crew. They hated that we had history and a mutual respect for one another, but deep down that was never really going to change. We had been through too much together in our younger years for our relationship to just dissolve without serious cause. Clearly, we were not close like we used to be, but we actually had a tighter bond at that time than I believe he had with a lot of his so-called friends. For that reason, when he invited me and the family to a birthday party he was having at The Salford Club, it was hard for me not to go.

Rather unwisely me and Jeanette went along, even more unwisely we went with my brother Bradley.

Walking into that party was like walking into the wolf's lair with a leg of lamb strapped to your back. There were hundreds of Ordsall heads, and they would all have happily feasted on me and my brother. Of all the people to go with as well, Bradley was renowned for being a loose cannon. In fact, he was probably one of the loosest you could ever expect to meet.

We'd hardly had time to take our coats off and get a drink before Bradley had punched one of their crew for staring at us. This did nothing to ease the tension and when the guy disappeared shortly afterwards, I seriously started to question what we were doing there.

It wasn't long before he returned with a handgun and he had only one intention - to shoot my brother.

I heard the gun go off and spun around to see Bradley on the floor bleeding. I rushed across and stood over him, protecting him from the Ordsall members that were hovering over him, while Jeanette helped get him to his feet. He had only been shot in the leg and was able to hobble to safety with Jeanette's help.

Their attention then turned to me and the shooter pointed the gun straight at me to prevent me attacking him. Only a fool would have attacked him in that club though, if he hadn't fired a bullet into my skull, half the club would have happily killed me for him.

I had to front the situation and stand strong. If I had turned my back, he would no doubt have at the very least put one into my leg too.

People were screaming at him saying "this is your chance" and "shoot him, shoot him". With a cool head I pointed my finger at him, whilst he was still levelling the gun at me, and I told him that I would be coming for him.

In hindsight it was stupid of me to say anything, I should have said fuck all and got out of there, then dealt with him at a later date. It was unprofessional but the moment had gotten to me. The adrenaline rush was near lifting me off my feet. I was heavily outnumbered and alone and my brother had just been shot, I couldn't totally control my emotions.

I tried to remain calm and casually backed up a few paces before walking towards the exit like it was just another day at the office. That steely exterior I was showing was not exactly mirrored on the inside. The confidence that I was displaying was merely for show. I was still expecting the gunshot to ring out at any moment. I could feel my heartbeat pulsing in my head and with every step closer to the door that I got, the more ferociously it beat.

I took my first step outside and as the fresh air hit me, I could barely believe I'd made it in one piece. The danger had far from passed but whilst inside I was at their mercy, outside my odds of surviving were improving with every second that passed and each step I took.

They had missed another massive opportunity to get rid of me, either by a mob handed beating or simply by shooting me and covering it up.

Once outside the club I began to walk backwards again as I was being followed by six members of their firm, not to mention the mass of onlookers congregating by the doors. One of the following hyenas was a stocky black guy from Moss Side called Tony Mac, who was obviously wanting to make a name for himself in our area. He was closing in on me with a knife in his hand. I was egging him on, daring him to attack me. Whenever somebody pulls a weapon on me, my preferred method is always the counterattack. I've done it successfully several times. Wait for the attacker to make the first move, then respond with venom. Tony having a knife didn't scare me, it just made me angrier.

I continued slowly backing up, beckoning him forward. There was a bit of distance developing between him and his mates and I knew I could take him out if it grew much bigger. The shit house glanced over his shoulder for moral support and upon realising his mates were 20 yards behind him, he stopped walking forward and backed up to rejoin them.

With the few remaining Ordsall boys not displaying enough bravery to actually attack me, I slowly turned and continued walking. My ears were pricked like a dog's. I wasn't stupid enough to believe they wouldn't have a go with my back turned. After 50 or so yards I glanced back to see them all ambling off back into the party.

I caught up with Jeanette and Bradley and we walked to a nearby telephone box, where we arranged for the two of them to be taken to hospital. I stayed and made several phone calls for the lads to come down and back me up. There were no mobile phones in those days, so it was a little slow getting the word out. I knew I would have a bit of a wait before my backup arrived.

As I was waiting for the boys, whilst stalking the venue, one of the Ordsall lads came out with a doorman who I knew well. I was in no mood for a pointless chat however, so I hit the doorman before either of them got a word out. He went down and the other guy ran straight back into the club. Before my boys could get to me, a squad van pulled up and I was dragged into the back and taken to the local police station where I duly was thrown into a cell without questioning.

While I was stuck in a cell the police were trying to close down Massey's party. The Ordsall Firm were having none of it though. Massey started a protest because the police had spoilt his birthday. They barricaded themselves in the club, while the police remained outside, probably too scared to try to enter.

Morning finally arrived and the police simply let me go. They knew what had gone on in the club, so they pulled me in to stop me from taking revenge - and they as good as told me so. In hindsight I'm glad they did really. Prisons are full of cons doing time for things they did in the heat of the moment. Unprofessional and stupid mistakes often either costs or ruins lives. Being in the cells gave me time to not only cool off, but also to plan my revenge.

Later me and Massey arranged to meet and discuss things. He told me that if he had known the lad was planning on shooting

Bradley, he would have told us to get out of the place. He filled me in about the standoff with the police and said he had had a debate with a senior copper to bring the incident to a close. The copper had told him that the police didn't want a tit-for-tat war between the Broughton and the Ordsall firm taking up all of their time and efforts. Both Massey and the police knew the strength and stubbornness of our Bradley. He would keep going back and back and back until you killed him and naturally, we would all be standing right beside him each and every time.

Massey admitted that he didn't want to lose one of his friends or gang members to a life sentence over a loose cannon like Bradley and subsequently have an all-out war with me and my family. So, he offered Bradley £10,000 as compensation for being shot and me £5,000 as a gesture of good will.

Although I wanted to see the Ordsall firm suffer I had no desire for Massey to get hurt. I agreed to his offer and we shook on it and he personally arranged the money.

Bradley however wasn't happy with the deal. He was even more unhappy that I was getting £5,000 as I hadn't even been shot. In fact, I honestly believe that if he had had a gun at that time he would have shot me himself to justify me getting paid. He soon cheered up when he saw the colour of his money though.

The following Thursday night I went to the Inn of Good Hope to start my new job. In the car park I was approached by a bloke for whom I simply don't have the words to describe. He was a once in a lifetime kind of individual. The mold was really broken when they made him.

He put his hand out for me to shake and said in a brilliantly well-spoken and wonderfully posh form of the Queen's English; "Paul welcome. Let me introduce myself, I'm Graeme and this is Alan". He continued before I could get a word in, "Alan is a salt of the earth individual and a very brave man, not to mention an excellent doorman. I must say on behalf of both of us, we have been looking forward to your arrival". I was about to say 'hi' when Graeme continued further: "It's a great honour to be working with you, there's no doubt your reputation precedes you. Some of the stories I've heard about you are legendary, brilliant, simply brilliant stories. By the way Paul did you know we have a free bar policy for doormen, would you like me to get you a drink?"

I must have stood there with my mouth open in amazement for a good few seconds, before I even replied, "no thanks, Graeme I'll go up and get my own, but thanks".

I had to go and get my own drink, as I needed time to process who the hell I had just met.

Graeme was the most unique character I had ever come across. His vocabulary and his mannerisms certainly did not fit in in Salford, not to mention his posh voice.

Immediately Graeme made an impact on me though. He looked a powerful man and had a fantastic physique. He was 5 foot 11' and 16 stone of solid muscle.

He was a good looker to boot. He looked like Roger Moore and would no doubt have made an excellent James Bond.

For the next hour or so I was taken aback by him. Watching him was pure entertainment. When a customer arrived Graeme would open the door then say sir or madam "welcome to the Inn of Good Hope, I do hope you enjoy your evening". Most of the customers were left in shock because they had never been spoken to like that before, however it put a smile on the faces of a lot of them and I had to chuckle to myself.

Graeme should have been working at a posh establishment, like the Millionaires Club in town, not a pub in the middle of Salford.

Before I had arrived at the Inn that night, a group of lads had already been let in. While I was at the bar getting my orange squash, I noticed them sat around a couple of tables. These lads fancied themselves as a bit of a tough firm and I'd had some problems with them in the past. These fellas went by a very unusual name (it was very apt but unusual) they were known as The Ugly Firm.

The Inn of Good Hope was on their turf so I shouldn't have been surprised to see them there. Due to our history and bad blood nor should I have been surprised that they were not too pleased to see me working there.

Amazingly the Ugly firm caused me no trouble all night and most of them left fine too. There is always one gobshite in any group that can't help but stir things up though, and it was no different that night. This particular gobshite walked passed me and snidely hissed "Doyle why the fuck are you working here? This isn't your area".

At the ripe age of thirty I had survived long enough on the streets to know when it's time to have a discussion and when it's time to throw a punch. This was the latter. So, I launched one in the general direction of his loud mouth.

Unfortunately, I didn't catch him as sweet as I would have liked. He fought back and we ended up going at it in the car park. The ugly bastard did actually put up a good fight, but there was no way I was going to lose, especially on my first night not to mention in front of Graeme.

Eventually I delivered the knockout blow and left him sprawled out in the car park. After finishing him off I made my way over to the front doors wondering how badly Graeme and Alan had been beaten up by the others. To my surprise there was no sign of them, but there was a scattering of ugly firm members lying unconscious across the entrance hallway.

I looked around and saw Graeme and Alan arriving back from chasing the remaining members of the Ugly firm down the street.

"Paul" said Graeme, in his finest queen's English "did that bloody scumbag hurt you?" I told him I was fine and with that Graeme disappeared inside the pub.

After thirty seconds or so he reappeared shouting "Damn it, damn it, damn it". He was devastated to find that there were no

Ugly firm members left for him to beat up. I told him not to worry as we had more than taken care of them, which I hoped would console him a little. I was convinced it had when him and Alan started giving each other high fives and bear hugs. It also helped confirm to me that something wasn't quite right in Graeme's head.

After my shift I went home quite bewildered. Meeting Graeme was like discovering a new species. I'd never before or since known anything like him. To say I was impressed would be an understatement. The guy was fascinating. I couldn't wait to see him again the next night.

Word spread quickly around Salford that I was working at the Inn of Good Hope. It annoyed some people (mainly villains) in the community and the word was out that I had taken liberties with the handling of the ugly firm. Trouble was brewing.

On the Sunday afternoon, before work, knowing there could be reprisals at any time, I had discussions with Graeme and Alan to make sure they had their wits about them. I made them aware that Salford was just about the most violent city in our country and that some of its best men may well be turning up to test us.

I told them that the situation we found ourselves in was not going to be about chucking drunks out or stopping the odd tough nut overstepping the line. It was about stature, respect and dominance. I told them to expect the unexpected, knowing that trouble could start at any moment.

I always have and always will protect myself at any cost. Firms often came for me tooled up and serious gangsters don't make a habit of giving second chances. For that reason, I usually have a hammer or a bat close by. I suggested to Alan and Graeme that they got themselves a weapon. Graeme asked "would a hammer head do Paul? Because I could fit that in my hand". I agreed that would be fine but warned him only to use it if necessary and only against gang members, not on Joe public. I told him that we didn't want any needless injuries to innocent victims, and I certainly didn't need any police charges looming over us.

Halfway through the night, what I had been expecting finally began. Firstly, one car pulled up, then another, then another. Eventually about 15 cars lined up outside the pub. I knew who it was, and I was more than impressed with Massey's turn out.

I walked out and met him with a beaming smile on my face, knowing that it would annoy some of his entourage. He was a very clever man and I figured he would have something planned to either diffuse the situation or work it in his favour.

Car doors began opening and hooded figures started emerging from inside them. Massey walked forward with four more of Salford's finest gangsters, all of whom you would not want to get on the wrong side of. There stood about 40 lads behind them, filling the car park, all staring at us, looking mean and ready. It was no time for a hammer or a bat. I had to use my second-best weapon, my chat.

Massey started first, he had clearly planned his initial spiel. "Doyley we've heard you're planning on barring the lads. You do realise we won't be much of a pushover as the ugly firm, don't you?"

I said "no Paul, I'm not barring your lads, it's the landlord that is barring them because they scare the customers. I'm simply earning a living as a doorman and he's paying the wages".

Massey argued back and said that I could earn my money anywhere else in Salford without there being a problem, but that I was doing it as a favour for Quinny who wasn't the landlord, just the head of security, and he, according to them, was overstepping the mark.

I argued back that there were plenty of other pubs in Salford for him and his boys to drink in without it being a problem, and reiterated that I was simply earning a living, and it was the landlord who was giving the orders to protect his business.

By Massey's side stood a very tough Irish lad who was head of a hard Salford family. Me and him also went back years and I had done a big favour for him back in the day.

Graeme could see that my plan to smooth things over wasn't going so well and he walked up and stood fearlessly by my side.

Massey looked him up and down, then continued to talk as if Graeme wasn't even there. He could be quite dismissive like that. It was an arrogance combined with a lack of fear, an impressive quality which he had developed.

"Under normal circumstances I would set the lads off their leashes and chase Quinny right out of town" Massey said "but I believe he fancies himself as a fighter – so I've brought my pal Mark along to fight him. Winner takes home twenty grand", he said patting the Irish lad on the back.

I told Massey that Quinny was neither there nor were we expecting him that night, but I would pass on the offer.

I don't know if it was Massey's sick sense of humour or if he was just itching to see a fight, but he then suggested that I fought for the twenty grand instead.

You sneaky cunt I thought to myself.

Firstly, I would have been right up against it fighting Mark, and secondly Massey knew that I would fight anyone on the planet whether I thought I could win or not, but he also knew me well enough to know that if I did lose and he and his boys went partying that night with my twenty grand, I would have been suicidal. Forget the money, my pride would have been taken from me.

I suggested to Massey that he knew exactly that, but to prove I wasn't afraid I raged "Fuck the money, but I'll have the fight, right now around the back".

Mark wasn't there to fight me though – thankfully - and he said as much. He told me he was still grateful for the favour that I had done for him a few years earlier and he was only there for one reason, to fight Quinny for the twenty grand. He finished by asking me to pass on the message.

My expression of anger returned to a smile and I nodded my head in agreement. They all then left as quickly as they had arrived.

It was one hell of a tricky situation and when Quinny came to see me to find out what had been said, I informed him of their offer. Quinny's heart was ruling his head and he was considering taking up the challenge.

I told him he was either very brave or very stupid for even considering it. It would have been like entering into the lion's den and there would be a house full of lions home.

It was a 'one-on-one' fight that he could not have won, mainly because it wouldn't have been a one-on-one fight. He would have been going up against the whole firm, and he knew how violent and ruthless they could be. They had already visited once with 40 lads hoping it would kick off. It could have easily been 60 or 70 turning up on the promise of an arranged fight.

Then there was his opponent to consider. A well-oiled street fighter, who knew the ropes and played by his own rules – which were there were no rules. He would no doubt exchange punches for a minute or so, but if he suspected Quinny to be capable of taking his punches he would soon switch tactics and start biting the face or body and gauging the eyes.

I commended Quinny's courage but reminded him of a one-million-pound security contract he had recently sealed outside of Salford. I advised him to avoid the fight and focus his efforts on his new enterprise. There was no need for him to go down that road. It was a trap, and he could have ended up dead.

I don't know who would have won in a fair fight between the two, but it would no doubt have been one hell of a fight, and under different circumstances I would have enjoyed watching it.

Fortunately, Quinny put his emotions to one side and let common sense prevail. He relocated and concentrated on his new business. He passed over the security contract at the Inn of Good Hope to me and Graeme (rather than selling it on). He was obviously trying to repay us for our loyalty. To be honest I have been given better presents in my time, but we accepted, and I became partners with Graeme.

What can of worms had I just lifted the lid off?

Becoming a partner with Graeme Boardman was the start of an interesting period in my life to say the least. The fact that it was coinciding with the seeming demise of mine and Massey's relationship would make it all the more so.

After Massey and his boys turned up, looking to assert themselves on me, I knew things would no longer be quite the same between us. I considered it a serious breach of our trust and friendship and there was clearly a battle for power on the cards.

The years that followed were destined to be explosive and many events that occurred went down in Manchester folklore.

Chapter 11:

A NEW PARTNER IN CRIME

I spent a bit of time trying to understand Graeme. I wanted to know what made him tick. How (if at all possible) to control him and what was it that made him such a fearless fighting machine.

Graeme was certainly one of a kind. He was born to deliver punishment. Whenever there was a disturbance inside the pub Graeme would be first there. By the time I got there I would usually have to put some unlucky sod in the recovery position.

One night me and my pal Tet watched on in amazement as Graeme destroyed three guys in a matter of seconds.

During my violent journey through life, I have seen fighters of the highest level. Stand up fighters like Paul Quinn, street fighters like Damian Noonan, champion boxers like Naz and Chris Coady, kick boxers, wrestlers, martial art experts. I've seen them all but not one of them, I believe could match what Graeme had. He was a staggeringly efficient fighter, but it was hard initially to comprehend what made him so good.

His initial onslaught was frightening to watch, it would be so fast and ferocious that usually the fight was over before it began. However, if an opponent could get through that, Graeme had other tools to fall back on. He was super fit and although not the tallest his outstanding physique had him easily weighing in at heavyweight. He trained daily after eating half a dozen eggs for breakfast. His waist was only 32", but he had to wear 38" pants because his legs were so muscular, he couldn't fit in anything smaller.

It didn't matter to Graeme if you were 6'6" or 5'2", whether you were pissed up, drugged up or you were called Susan and had three legs. If you were asking for trouble, he would have no problem in rendering you unconscious.

He had a serious competitive streak. As a teenager he played football for Coventry until one of his teammates upset him and he beat up half the squad in a rage.

One time I introduced him to some friends who were playing for a local football team. Graeme made one appearance for them, but after bitch slapping himself for playing a bad pass, he then beat up two of my mates for laughing at him.

I eventually concluded that the reason Graeme was such an expert in combat was probably quite simple. He wasn't right in the head. He was an unhinged psychopath, and it was his super intense, frenzied, psychopathic onslaught that made him unstoppable.

There was something inside him that I'm simply not educated enough to explain. He would have made a great study for some professor at some university.

The one thing I grew certain of was that I had landed the most fearsome man I would ever meet as my new business partner. My plan, therefore, was simple. I had to take advantage of Graeme being a psychopath and work it to my favour. I was streetwise enough for the both of us and had the knowledge to take our partnership to the highest level. It was the perfect combination for a security business, and so I decided to expand it.

When applying for contracts and meeting club owners Graeme would do the talking. His posh accent and queen's English made a great first impression. I would stand behind him looking aggressive and mean. My host of scars and the broken knuckles obviously added to the effect.

Whenever we met with other gangsters however it was the opposite way around. I'd do the talking because I knew more about dealing with those kinds of characters and Graeme would be stood close by, ready to strike.

In no time at all our security business was booming. We had bars, pubs and clubs all over Greater Manchester. Each weekend we would go from venue to venue. I would take care of paying the doormen their wages while Graeme would busy himself with hurting somebody or other.

Graeme's tendencies to explode on people at any given opportunity kept our staff on their toes. They already knew who and what I was about, but they quickly learned that Graeme was an equally formidable force.

His reputation grew and grew. Not only as a ferocious fighter but also as a terrible womaniser. He could charm the knickers off most women in a matter of minutes though. It's just the fact that the poor beggars he took home were often left in shock due to his perverse obsessions. Some of the stories that I heard actually shocked me.

He did things to them that must have bordered on abuse. It certainly would have broadened their horizons.

I'm more of an old-fashioned Casanova. I still make love between the sheets with the lights off. I wouldn't have trusted Graeme with my wife, sister, mother or even with our Mark, now I come to think of it. He was ruthless.

On one occasion at the Inn of Good Hope we were standing in the hallway between the doors to the lounge and the toilets. A couple came out from the lounge, the guy went straight into the gents and Graeme immediately hit on his girlfriend.

He started his patter with "You are truly beautiful. What the bloody hell are you doing with him? He must take you to some exquisite places."

"Does he fuck" she replied in her best Salford accent. "Well," Graeme continued "I certainly would if you were my girlfriend".

"Are you faithful to him?" he asked, "no, not really" replied the girl. And before her poor fella had finished his piss Graeme had given her his number, lined up a date and snogged her face off. He really was the best charmer.

I used to know an incredibly beautiful girl. We became friends in our early twenties when we both lived in Salford, but later on in life she married a millionaire and moved out of the area. However, every time her millionaire husband went away on a business trip or sunning himself playing golf, she would get in touch with me and I'd take her out for a bit of fun.

During one such occasion we arranged to meet at the Inn of Good Hope. My plan was to take her to a nightclub after work, then to a Casino and finish the night off at her place. There was no need for me to go over the top with fancy restaurants and hotels. We both knew the score and had been friends for long enough anyway.

As she walked up to the doors of the Inn Graeme's jaw hit the floor. He couldn't believe how classy she looked. I knew straight away that he wanted to test his charms on her. I told him to behave himself, and he replied "Good Lord, of course Paul. I wouldn't dream of touching somebody with you". I doubted the honesty in that statement but appreciated him saying it anyway.

Towards the end of that night Graeme received a phone call from a pal in need. Graeme asked me if I would go to a nightclub in Chorlton with him after we had finished at the Inn. He said his friend was having trouble with some local bully boys. Naturally, I agreed to go and support him.

When we arrived, Graeme stayed outside chatting with his friend while me and my lady friend went in for a drink. The club was full of locals. Everybody seemed to know each other.

I was waiting my turn at the bar when some bolshy prick came up shoving customers aside and barking his drinks order at the barmaid. Obviously, I've seen this sort of behaviour a thousand times before and didn't think too much of it. He looked like a troublemaker though so I had a look over to see where he disappeared off to.

He went and sat back down with five other lads. All of whom looked of a similar ilk. Before we had even been served the same guy came pushing his way to the bar again. I was amazed that not one of the other customers said anything to him.

As I was watching him, he clocked me and stopped to say those infamous words "what the fuck are you looking at?"

I never understood why people say that. It simply tells the other person they're looking for trouble, and also offers them the initiative, giving them the chance to strike first. Naturally, I accepted his invitation and put him on his arse with a massive left hook.

I glanced over in the direction of his mates, two of whom were already rushing over. I met the silly twats halfway and knocked them both out. I was left with no other option but to rush the table where his remaining friends were sitting. It was the sensible option to eliminate them before they attacked me.

I flipped the table in the air and while they were gawping at the drinks flying everywhere, I landed two more punches, rendering the final two unconscious.

From start to finish the whole affair had lasted no more than 30 seconds. I must admit I was actually quite impressed with myself.

I wasn't finished though. I wanted to give the rude cunt a boot to his head to knock some manners into him. Just as I was about to volley him, an 18st doorman put me in a bear hug from behind. Instantly I heard Graeme shout "get your hands off him" which the doorman immediately did.

I turned round with an undisputable anger in my eyes and told the doorman "don't ever fucking touch me like that again you cunt, or I'll kill you".

Graeme said, "Paul cool down, this is my friend we've come to see". Graeme introduced us and the doorman apologised for grabbing me, before saying those other famous words I'd become accustomed to: "I've heard all about you, but, and not being rude, I expected someone bigger. Are you a martial art expert Paul?" he continued.

With my childish sense of humour, I said "yes, now count yourself lucky I didn't teach you a move or two for bear hugging me. Now you'll have to excuse us but me and the police don't see eye-to-eye, and I have a funny feeling they may be paying you a visit soon. Do me a favour and make sure nobody remembers anything".

"No problem" he said "one favour deserves another. I only wish I'd called you and Graeme down sooner". I looked at him confused wondering whether or not he was taking the piss, when it dawned on me that the five lads, I'd left spitting out broken teeth inside the club, were the bully boys we had gone down to sort out.

A good job well done I thought and me, Graeme and my lady friend set off for the casino.

While I was gambling at the tables Graeme kept my lady friend company. There was no doubt whatsoever Graeme would be giving her his best chat up lines. Once or twice, she came over asking me to take her home because the night was turning into morning. I was on a winning streak though and every gambler knows that it's not possible to leave a table when you're on a winning streak.

I called Graeme over and asked him to do me a favour and take her home. Graeme very honestly responded with "Paul I don't know if I would be able to trust myself with her". I smiled and said, "feel free to smash her all over but just don't spoil my winning streak".

He laughed a strange sinister laugh and said, "you're impossible to work out Mr. Doyle" and off they went.

Looking back, it was a funny old night. I went home with a smile on my face. I had single handedly thrashed five wannabe gangsters in a matter of seconds and impressed all those who bore witness to it. I had also won big at the casino. However, from that day forward, whenever my lady friend's husband went away it was

Graeme who got the phone call to entertain her, not me.

Such is life, I suppose.

Each Sunday evening at the Inn of Good Hope a local rugby team would come in after their game. Now in case you don't know, rugby players are a total fucking headache when they're pissed. With me being aware of Graeme's mental health issues I had told him that I would be the one to deal with them if there happened to be any trouble. Graeme was to remain an observer and could just back me up.

One Sunday a barmaid came over saying she had a problem getting paid by one of the rugby lads. I approached the six or seven of them who were all already pretty drunk. I really didn't need any drama and I was hoping to smooth out the situation in an amicable way. So, I asked the guy why he didn't pay his bill. He told me he had put £20 on the bar and that someone had eaten it, so he wouldn't be paying again.

I was starting to tell him that he wouldn't be served any more drinks until the last ones were paid for, when one of his mates said, "don't tell him what he can and can't have and If you've got a problem with us then come and try your luck with me". Oh God I thought, here we go, not because I was concerned about the big guy, but because I had spotted Graeme had approached and was standing right behind him.

Graeme being an ex-professional footballer had been taught to headbutt through a target, for optimum power. So, when Graeme spun this guy around and headbutted him, he was knocked out cold before he hit the deck.

Like a lot of pub fights, the first minute was mayhem. It's when everybody wants to join in and is full of adrenaline and confidence. After the first few violent acts however you can usually spot the men from the boys.

I ended up in front of two of the rugby lads with a broken chair leg in my hands. I could see they didn't really want it and I didn't really want to hurt them anyway, so I told them it was in their best interests if they fucked off quickly, which they did.

When I turned round, I could see two unconscious on the floor, one either side of Graeme.

Graeme himself was like a human sandwich, between two further guys - one grappling with him from the front, the other from behind.

Approaching from the rear I had a free shot, which usually I aim straight at the jaw. However, the previous week I had been at home making a cup of coffee and after stirring the boiling hot drink, I jokingly pressed the teaspoon on our Mark's neck. Of course he reacted furiously and as I was trying to run away, he punched me in the centre of my back - leaving me in horrific pain.

So, in an instant I decided to hit the guy with a 90% punch into the centre of his back. To my horror the punch had no effect. He turned around and picked me up by the waist, literally leaving my legs dangling in the air.

He may have been a big cunt, but he obviously wasn't the smartest, as he had left my hands free, so before he squeezed me to death I pulled his head back and pounded his jaw. After, having learned from my first punch, I let him have the extra 10% in the second one.

He fell back onto the bar stunned. He was at my mercy, but I could see the look on his face had changed and he didn't want anymore. My next problem was stopping Graeme from finishing him off. I growled at him to make a quick exit, while I attempted to restrain Graeme.

He was jumping up and down with rage. I realised in that moment that it would take a 30 stone Silverback gorilla to hold Graeme down. His power was immense.

The following Sunday the nearest thing you could get to a Silverback gorilla came down to the Inn. He was one of the biggest men I ever saw and he was screaming that he wanted to fight the man who beat his friends up. Not being a hero I said, "I think he means you Graeme".

The guy was clearly the hard man of the rugby club, so when Graeme disposed of him in under 30 seconds the team received the message loud and clear that no one man could beat Graeme, so either come in and behave or don't come in at all.

The Sunday after 40 or more (basically the entire rugby club and associates) rocked up with only one thing in mind, which was to seriously hurt the us. Chaos quickly ensued, and we had to retreat back through the pub and over the bar defending ourselves with pool cues and chairs before we could lock ourselves in the back room. It was carnage but we lived to fight another day - even if the pub looked a little worse for wear.

That incident confirmed something for me, the whole community officially hated us.

Chapter 12:

ROCKWORLD

On a Friday and Saturday night, after finishing at the Inn, I would usually work at one of our night clubs called Apple Jacks. It was one of the perks of being the boss. It was a pleasure to once in a while work at such a peaceful place.

The rave scene in the UK was booming at that time, and Manchester was becoming a haven for clubbers and gangsters alike.

A nightclub called Rockworld opened its doors once a week for an all-night rave. The place could hold 1200 customers. It was an extremely dangerous place to work. Some of the most notorious gangs from around the North went there to party hard and flex their muscles. It was a venue where they could show off their strength for all to see.

A security firm named Lock19 had the door. The two lads running Lock19 were good friends of mine, Mickey Francis (one of three notorious brothers from Moss Side, who ran Manchester City's firm of hooligans) and Steve Bryant (a dangerous man, not to be messed with), both of whom were notorious figures around Manchester.

One day they asked if me and Graeme would give them a helping hand controlling some of the Salford gangsters that were causing havoc at Rockworld.

I knew firstly this was not something that I wanted to be in the middle of and secondly that you couldn't really control Salford gangs. Once they were in you were in trouble.

I said to Mickey and Steve that the only way to control them is to not allow them in. Then Graeme sensing an opportunity chipped in saying he would gladly stop them at the door if that's what was needed.

I couldn't believe what I was hearing, Graeme clearly didn't get that I was trying to swerve the offer. I once had told Graeme to always expect the unexpected. In Rockworld fuck all would be unexpected. There was guaranteed trouble from the time the doors opened until (and often beyond) the time they closed.

Why would I want to work on the front line and battle the shit storm at Rockworld when I had it nice and easy at Apple Jacks, where the worst thing that would happen was, I may get attacked with a handbag.

I didn't want to look like a coward, but I really didn't need the extra hassle in my life, so as Graeme had stuck his size twelves into the mix, we agreed that he could start on the door at Rockworld, and I would continue at Apple Jacks. Then if things got too heavy, I could be on call to provide some back up.

I told Mickey and Steve that there were a lot of Salford lads that I would simply struggle to refuse entry to because of my close connections to them, and it may actually bring even more trouble if I was a regular on the door. They were happy with the proposal though, fully aware of Graeme's capabilities and he started work there that same weekend.

A few weeks later I bumped into Mickey and I asked him how Graeme was doing. He said, "Paul the guy's a fucking monster". They were averaging 10 serious incidents a night more with Graeme on the door than they had before he worked there. Mickey looked ill when he was talking about Graeme. I could see he was concerned about what he might do next.

I told him not to worry and that I would speak with Graeme.

I knew deep down that speaking with him would be pointless. He was great to have on side, but if you could have had him on a chain and release him solely when some prick needed destroying, that would have been perfect. Unfortunately, that was obviously not a realistic possibility. The truth of the matter was that Graeme was a hard man to contain.

I spoke with him and asked him to reign it in a little because I didn't want to be dragged down to Rockworld as I was happy working at Apple Jacks. He agreed to try, but I knew in truth that it was a pointless conversation. I also knew that Rockworld really needed someone like Graeme who could and would destroy gangsters single handedly without worrying about the consequences. That club was so dangerous that the doormen had to walk around in groups for their own protection. Not Graeme though. He genuinely didn't give a fuck.

There are a few nights each year that doormen tend to dread. The last Friday before Christmas for example - which is nicknamed Black Eye Friday. This is when a large number of businesses will have their staff Christmas do.

Essentially, they all get overly pissed up, fall out, and try to kick fuck out of one another. It becomes a real headache for bouncers, especially because you have to tiptoe around Joe Public a little more than the local hoodlums. You can't rough them up and give them a proper slap on the way out. The risk of one of them crying all the way to the local police station is far too real.

Another bad night to be a doorman is St Patrick's day. Every Irish man worth his salt seems to want to dress in green and drink till they pass out or piss their pants. I've never understood it to be honest. It's often left me wondering; Was St Patrick a total piss head or something?

One St Patrick's day evening, I arrived at Apple Jacks and it was full of pissed up jolly green giants. Which is never a great start to your shift.

One of the pillocks came over to me straight away asking where the toilets were. I said, "do you see the fruit machine over there" at which point he cut me off in mid flow and said, "I didn't ask you where the fucking fruit machine was". Completely bewildered, I shook my head trying to register how rude he had been, then I continued "the toilets are next to the fruit machine". With that he walked off without saying so much as kiss my Irish arse. As it fully sank in just how rude he had been and how humiliated he had left me feeling in front of my friends, I began to fume. I asked another doorman to stop any customers going into the gents for a minute or two while I taught the Paddy prick some much-needed manners.

Seeing the loudmouth tosser sparked on the floor with his dick still out did make me feel somewhat better. Volleying the nasty cretin between his legs completed my satisfaction too.

That same St Patrick's night Graeme had an incident at the entrance of Rockworld with a high-ranking member of the Cheetham Hill Firm. Graeme refused him entry and knocked him all over the street when the guy protested. Later while Graeme was on his break (down the road in his favourite kebab shop) a number of the Cheetham Hill firm rushed the doors of Rockworld for revenge resulting in three doormen being badly stabbed up. Injuries that were intended for Graeme.

I was the next to dodge a bullet (so to speak) because the following weekend at Apple Jacks, while I was down at Rockworld having a meeting to discuss Graeme's general demeanor, a van full of Paddies turned up looking for me and ended up giving the bouncers that were working, a bit of a pasting.

The Cheetham Hill firm were clearly not happy with Graeme and nor was the promoter at Rockworld. The promoter was in fear of further repercussions from the Cheetham Hill mob. Even though Graeme was obviously not bothered, I begrudgingly agreed to swap doors, for a few weekends.

Once again, I found myself back on the front line.

For all his faults Graeme had done a good job at not allowing Salford's finest into Rockworld. They would have had a hundred lads in there regularly if it wasn't for him.

However, I was to take his place on the door and the news spread fast. Massey came down on my very first night, to see how the land lay. He asked me if I would sort it for him and some of his friends to be able to get in.

We had a chat, and it was agreed that as long as his lads didn't arrive mob handed, they could get in. It had to be in small groups, and they needed to behave (as well as you could expect them to).

A couple of hours later I had lost count of the number of Salfordians I'd let in for free. Things weren't quite going as I had hoped, the numbers were growing, however I had promised Massey that I would allow them in, and I was a man of my word.

Another small group arrived alongside a high ranked member of the Ordsall firm, a black guy called Jay. Sticking to my word I politely said go straight in Jay, you don't have to pay. I don't know if he was high on drugs or what, but he completely took the piss. "Don't fucking talk to me Doyley" he said as he swaggered by.

I was livid. I delivered a clean knockout punch and then threw him outside into the road. Seconds later Massey and his firm were back in the entrance hall, arguing the toss with me. I told them that the ignorant cunt showed no respect and so he was treated in exactly the same manner. I said that he should count himself lucky I didn't go overboard with him.

There can be no doubt that me and Massey had an enjoyable youth together, growing into criminality and fighting the police shoulder to shoulder. Things had changed though and over the previous few years our lives had moved in very different directions. Really, we were the same people deep down and we still enjoyed each other's company. Our problems were obvious though, we lived in different areas of Salford and we clashed with each other's friends and that caused friction between us.

Massey told me that he found it very hard stopping his lads coming for me because they all hated me and wanted my blood. I told him I didn't give a flying fuck about his mates and that I had only let them in that night because of mine and his friendship. "So, if that's the way your mates feel then tell them anytime" I said. It didn't go down too well, but it needed to be said.

The following week myself and our Bradley pulled up at some traffic lights when I noticed the car behind us was full of hooded lads. As I was looking through the rear view mirror, I recognised Jay as being one of the passengers. It then became clear to me that it was a car full of Ordsall boys and any thoughts of it being a coincidence faded when I noticed Jay and a passenger in the back pulling down balaclavas.

I am a true believer that in the art of war, the best line of defence is attack. I had to strike first. I told Bradley what was going on. I asked him to set off as normal when the lights changed, but then to pull up quickly so we could jump out and rush them.

My plan worked. We were both smashing their windows through with hammers before they realised, we were on to them. They sped off but I wanted to strike while the iron was still hot, so we gave chase. The van we were in turned out to be no match for their sporty hatchback though and they ditched us with ease.

The troubles between our Broughton firm and their Ordsall firm had become intense and neither side was about to bow down.

That Friday night, literally minutes after Graeme had left me at the Inn of Good Hope, to start his work at Apple Jacks, a car pulled up carrying five members of the Ordsall Firm, two of them relatives of Paul Massey, who were starting to make names for themselves in the criminal world. I was alone aside from our Mark who had had two fights in his whole life (one was a draw, the other one he curled up in a ball after one punch). The odds weren't exactly in our favour. I stood tall however, directly in front of the pub doors waiting for what was to come. I was in the hands of the Gods, but I had a job to do.

I told them they weren't allowed in. One of them asked "who's going to stop us?" To which I replied "you're not the brightest are you. I'm clearly the only doorman here". With that he pulled out a knife. In a boxer's stance, hands up to my face and elbows tucked in, I stepped towards him, gesturing for him to come at me. One of his friends threw a beer bottle which hit the side of my face but bounced off. To my surprise that sparked a violent response from Mark. He ran at them wielding a hammer above his head, shouting all sorts of obscenities. I could barely believe it as they ran for their lives and piled into the car for a speedy getaway.

My brother had possibly saved my skin - for the time being at least.

I knew I had a major problem ahead of me which would present itself later that night.

I had no choice but to turn up for work at Rockworld, or I would have been labelled a coward, and that kind of talk spreads fast.

Upon arrival I could see the party was already starting without me. The doormen were out on the pavement taking a verbal volleying courtesy of Paul Massey.

His attention turned to me as soon as he saw me. "What the fuck are you doing attacking my family with hammers?" he spouted.

"What are you doing mouthing off at me like you're capable of doing anything about it you cunt" I snapped back. I offered him out there and then, but the doormen stepped in between us and kept us apart. At that point he slipped into the club shouting back "I'll show you fucking hammers".

One of the doormen started begging me to leave. Massey had obviously already told him what to expect. I said I wasn't going anywhere as he would tell people that I fucked off rather than fight him.

The entrance to Rockworld had large double glass doors. Beyond the doors was a long hallway which led into the club. There was only ever one door open so the doorman could control the flow of customers entering. I took up position in front of the doors with my hammer in my hand.

If ever I needed it, it was then. I had to hold my nerve as I saw a large group running down the hall towards me.

My mind had been made up, the decision had been made and the adrenaline was coursing through my veins. I was switched on and ready for it and I wasn't going down without a fight.

In that moment I knew that my years as a football hooligan would stand me in good stead. The hundreds of mob fights I had been in had prepared me well. I knew I couldn't let them through the doors in numbers, so I stood there swinging like a madman, daring anybody to feel the wrath of my hammer blows.

My tactics were working perfectly for the first minute or so, until they smashed through the other glass door which gave them the opportunity to surround me. I knew I had overstayed my welcome.

I fought my way through them, still frantically swinging my fists and hammer. Only the foolish got too close to me.

I was gradually making my escape, but I was being followed by a large number of violent thugs who wanted to kill me. I literally started running for my life.

I think I actually overtook several cars while I was speeding down the road. I was still pretty fit at that time and the Ordsall thugs obviously weren't so. The hyenas finally gave up their chase and began returning to the club. Some were dawdling behind the others, swaggering back feeling brave and victorious, stupidly making the mistake of considering me long gone.

Once I was confident, I had outrun them, I doubled back to pick off some of the strays.

I rushed a small group and gave a few of them very severe headaches. They had had their opportunity to finish me off and they had wasted it. Very sloppy on their parts, amateur and very sloppy. I didn't intend on gifting them another opportunity like they'd had that night.

I headed straight to Apple Jacks to discuss my next move with Graeme.

In those days, a form of punishment that was becoming popular was a 'legging' (a bullet to the leg). I never used to carry a gun though and anyway I thought that a legging was a crap punishment. The victim would spend the following day or two pumped full of painkillers, chilling out, reading the paper whilst being fussed over by doctors and nurses. If you were a gunshot victim, you got the full care package.

What we planned to do was dish out a number of serious beatings. We could inflict injuries that I knew wouldn't require all the care and attention of hospital staff but would leave my victim wishing they had been shot. Broken ribs, snapped fingers, burst eyeballs. The sorts of injuries that take days to stop throbbing. Waking up after a beating like me and Graeme could dish out was like waking up in hell.

We paid visits to a few of the Ordsall firm, in the early hours of that morning, and we considered nobody to be untouchable. I didn't want any dust to settle, I wanted my retribution while they still believed I was on the ropes and running scared. Most of what went on was too brutal to elaborate on, but I got a good deal of revenge that night and Graeme got more than his fix of the kind of violence that he craved. We targeted main players in the Ordsall firm and showed no mercy. There were a lot of people that simply believed nobody would have the nerve to do what we did that night.

The situation had become extremely serious for both sides, and a couple of days later Massey called me and asked to meet up.

We agreed to meet at my brother Mike's pub in a neutral part of Salford. We had a long discussion and Massey was clearly shocked that I was prepared to take the fight directly to the houses of his family and friends. I told him that he had crossed a line at Rockworld and if he was prepared to up the ante like that and prepared to target me, then I would have no boundaries as to exactly what I was prepared to do in return.

We came to the conclusion that nothing could be done to stop the fighting if our opposing firms kept coming into contact. We agreed orders needed sending out that our gangs needed to stay away from each other.

The talk was as successful as it could have been. Poor Mike actually got the shittiest end of the stick because the police closed his pub down off the back of that meeting.

Massey had a fall out with some of his lads over the agreement because they wanted me gone.

As for me and Graeme, we agreed it would ease tensions if we stopped working at Rockworld. Which was not a bad result for anybody concerned.

Most of the serious gangsters around Manchester and Salford were setting up security businesses, and door firms. Everybody was chasing the same jobs and drastic measures were being taken to make firms stand out from the crowd. Some would put pressure on club owners as well as the other security firms.

That period in time was the height of the infamously named 'door wars'. To me it didn't feel so much like a competition between all the firms, it felt a lot more like every other fucker against us and as we were already well established, we had a lot more to lose than most.

For me and Massey during the few weeks that followed our 'truce meeting' we both felt mounting police pressure. One night after finishing work at the Inn of Good Hope I found myself surrounded by the old bill. They searched my car and found my work tools, namely two hammers, a machete and a couple of bats. I didn't think the weapons were too heavy. I knew plenty of people carrying worse. In fact, I considered them as fairly standard accessories to carry in Salford. The CPS thought differently however, and I was charged with five counts of possession of an offensive weapon, with each charge carrying a potential of up to four years imprisonment.

In court I informed the judge that I was a doorman and I worked in some very violent places. I had taken the weapons from customers but had not got around to discarding them. Fortunately, I was believed and was only handed community service. Usually, I would have been happy with a result like that, but on this occasion I was far from happy. Such a let off made it clear to me that there must have been an ongoing operation on me. I was already under surveillance.

The signs had been there but with all the chaos I simply hadn't picked up on them. The closure of Mike's pub should really have started the alarm bells ringing.

I had two pretty big problems to negotiate, and I had to be fully switched on if I wanted to survive with my life and my freedom both intact. I felt naked without my tools at a time when I had Manchester's most notorious firm breathing down my neck, as well other security firms eyeing up our doors. As I already had a community service order for carrying offensive weapons, the last thing I needed was to be stopped with more, but on the other hand if I was caught out by any enemies, I knew that my weapons could have been the difference between life and death. The thought of an operation on me was like the cherry on the cake. It really was the last thing I needed.

Chapter 13:

ESCALATING TROUBLES

Me and Graeme had the doors of a nightclub in Bolton, called Kiss. It was away from the competition of the Manchester gangs, or so we thought. One night I received a phone call from one of our doormen there informing me that three well known Bolton gangsters were inside Kiss and wanted to see me. I knew one of the blokes well, he was a hardened villain named Baz. I was 'doubled up' with him in Strangeways when we were younger. He was a good, confident fighter who had become notorious in Bolton.

Immediately I was suspicious of what Baz wanted. Although I had never had any trouble with him historically, I knew I had to be prepared for any eventuality, so on our way to the meeting I made some calls, trying to get an insight into what Baz might want. I received some information that indicated he may have been sent by the Ordsall Firm.

So much for our 'truce agreement' and staying out of each other's way. Their new tactics were to hide behind other people. The Ordsall firm clearly wanted me gone, not to mention the door job at Kiss.

Over the years one thing that I've developed quite a skill for is the face-to-face 'sit down' meeting with other gangsters. It's important to be relaxed and to seem confident, especially in tricky situations. I would often try utilising my Jewish charms for a more friendly approach. Although there have been many a fool that have mistaken my kindness for weakness. Not so many have made that mistake twice though.

Usually, it is pretty apparent the path a meeting will go down straight from the get go. Some people arrive with the intention not to budge from their initial stance, so may need a 'push' in the right direction. Others will be more realistic and are prepared to negotiate.

Upon arrival at Kiss, we invited Baz and his two friends up to the office to talk. Straight away I had a gut feeling about the direction that meeting was going to go in.

It resembled something out of a gangster movie. Baz was sitting there on one side of the desk with his friends standing either side of him, doing their best to look menacing. I was sat behind the desk with Graeme beside me ready to pounce.

Right away I said "let's get straight to the point Baz. Why have you come here with two lads that look like they're wanting to take on the world?"

Baz replied with "we go back a long way Paul and we've always got on, but you're running a door at a nightclub in Bolton. This is our city, and we don't like the idea of Salford gangsters thinking they can run it."

I told him that I thought of him as a friend. I told him that I didn't consider myself a gangster, more just a 'grafter' and also that I had been living in Prestwich (an area in Bury) not Salford for the last six months. I also pointed out to him (even though he was well aware) that the doormen which I employed to work at Kiss were all from Bolton.

I left him with no real comeback. He had to put up or shut up. He wasn't about to let me know that the Ordsall boys had asked him to visit me, that would have made him look like a liar and a coward. Baz told me he would give some consideration to what I had said, and with that him and his moody looking sidekicks left. There were no pleasantries on his way out, he was clearly no happier than when he had arrived, but I had played my hand well and effectively left his hands tied.

Massey had warned me he would struggle to keep his boys from coming after me. Now I knew they definitely were. It would have made no difference if I had given up the door at Kiss. They would have sent someone to the next place, then the next, then the next. There was no way I was showing any weakness nor was I giving up any doors unless I genuinely wanted to.

A couple of days after the meeting with Baz he sent a messenger to tell us; that if we continued to work in Bolton, we should "expect the place to be targeted and whoever gets hurt gets hurt". He also sent me a personal message that there would be a bullet with my name on it.

There goes an old saying 'don't shoot the messenger', and we didn't, he got one hell of a hiding though. I had to send back a message of my own, and the time for talk had long since passed, much like my friendship with Baz.

Where I was living at that time was a nice peaceful Jewish area four or five miles from the Inn of Good Hope. Like a naive fool, I would always take the same route to work, from the house to the pub. Back then the car of choice for young gangsters was the Golf GTI or the Sierra Cosworth. I still had a trusty Mitsubishi Shogun, which was a very different type of vehicle and the kids weren't exactly queueing up to buy them.

I was taking my predictable journey to work one weekend, accompanied by Jeanette, who was sitting in the passenger seat. When I noticed three Golf GTIs coming up behind us, travelling at quite a pace. They moved out to overtake us and the first two flew past at speeds my Shogun could only dream of. The third one slowed slightly and when it pulled out alongside us, we heard an almighty crash of glass as my back window shattered into a million pieces.

I said to Jeanette "those little bastards have stoned our car". I gave chase, but it was like a donkey chasing after Red Rum. Angrily I conceded defeat and continued on my way to the pub.

When we arrived, Jeanette got out of the car and headed straight inside, not even looking at the damage. She passed by Graeme like she didn't have a care in the world. In fact, she told him that I had damaged the car.

I walked after her shouting "don't worry love, I'll clean up the glass", when Graeme's roars of laughter distracted me.

"What's so fucking funny?" I asked. "Something amusing you, is it?"

Once he had stopped laughing long enough to speak, he said "I don't think your missus has the faintest idea you've just been shot at", he pointed to the bullet holes in the rear door of my car. I had to laugh myself as I genuinely thought we had just been stoned. Times had changed and it wasn't the first or the last time I was shot at, but back then it simply wasn't my immediate reaction to think that it was a bullet that had exploded my car windows.

Graeme couldn't wait to tell Jeanette that she'd been shot at, and when he did, she simply replied "No Graeme, that prick got shot at, not me".

Shootings in Salford were becoming all too common. They were happening all over the city of Manchester too. Moss side was divided in two and the Gooch and Doddingtons were in the midst of an all-out war with gunfire being almost a daily occurrence. There was a member of the Cheetham Hill gang called White Tony Johnson who was also making a name for himself as a gunman. He had been arrested, but not convicted for a murder in Manchester and another in Leeds and was allegedly behind a further handful of shootings.

The gun game is a very dangerous game to be involved in, as White Tony found out, when he and an associate were both gunned down in Cheetham Hill. Tony died from his injuries. The well-respected Noonan brothers Dessie, Damian and Dominic were all arrested and charged with his murder. Twice they were tried and both times the trials collapsed. White Tony Johnson's murder remains unsolved to this day.

Manchester was a changing place. More and more gangsters were acquiring guns and there was no shortage of members prepared to use them.

As our truce with the Ordsall firm had clearly fallen apart, me and Graeme decided to make the most of an unplanned, fortuitous opportunity that presented itself to us, by taking bloody revenge on the shooter that I believed had blasted out my car windows.

Understanding the lay of the land, we awaited their retaliation.

Presuming the simplest thing for them to do would be to target me at home. Me, Mark and Wayne decided to do a stake out. I had recently moved, and we were living directly opposite Heaton Park in Middleton. Me and my brothers hid ourselves in the park with a perfect view of the house. I had a gun that Hitler's grandad must have fought Napoleon with. It was the oldest, most hideous looking gun on the planet. We spent three consecutive nights out there, sat around whispering at one another and making hand gestures like you see in SAS movies.

When the sun came up after the third night we walked back to my house, wondering when they were going to make their move. I opened the front door as Jeanette was hanging up the phone 'You bloody idiots' she snarled in our direction.

It turned out my prediction was wrong. The Ordsall firm had actually gone to my best mate Ashy's house and shot that up instead.

I headed straight out to the telephone box and started making the necessary calls. It didn't take too long to discover who was responsible. The tit for tat nature of our little war meant that our next move was obviously to plan our own revenge attack.

We discovered where the Ordsall member responsible lived and paid him a visit at home. His house turned out to be like a fortress. A lot of gang members had steel gates fitted over their windows and doors, as did this guy. An attack on the house looked tricky, but we wanted to fight fire with fire, so we had to come up with a solution.

It turned out to be a fairly simple solution too. One night somebody kindly drove a stolen thirty-ton wagon right into the front of the house.

In the days that followed Ashy was arrested and questioned. Luckily for him he had been in the casino all night and knew nothing about it.

Yet again me and Massey had arranged a sit down. We were both grafters and the more time the police spent sniffing around, the less money was being made, not to mention the increased risk to everybody concerned. He had spoken to his boys and they had agreed that they were ready to focus on business matters and would put our dispute on the back burner.

Upon hearing his new stance, I agreed that it was time to call a halt to our gang wars and refocus my efforts elsewhere. I was under no illusion that that would be the end of it, but I realised that if Massey's profits were down, then he had a new way of approaching the truce talks with his men. And at the end of the day, he was the head of their firm and if he felt strongly enough about something, then it would be so.

Over the next few weeks, it was a big relief going to work, knowing the only people likely to be attempting to take my head off would be rowdy drunks.

The majority of my fights have been over after the first few punches. For that reason, I never felt that I really got the credit I deserve for being able to take a punch. Like any true fighter, I have a do or die attitude - you've got to knock me out or kill me to stop me getting back up. I'm no fool though, I realised there were plenty of blokes out there stronger, faster or more skillful than me and they would no doubt stand a good chance of either beating me into the ground or knocking me out. Graeme had a similar mindset to me; his initial onslaught was breathtaking. An ability to take a punch or not I would have been lucky to get through his explosive start to a fight and I never met another man that could handle him either. Thankfully, we were soldiers on the same side, I had his back and he had mine and he was one person I didn't have to worry about.

On the odd occasion, where I knew I was up against it, I had the know how to either throw the first punch, or at least avoid theirs. The key to victory is not to allow your opponent to get a foothold in the fight. On one occasion, however, I failed to stick to my own game plan.

It was a rare but beautiful, warm Manchester summer's evening as I pulled up for work at the Inn. Graeme and a few others were already there enjoying the late afternoon sun when my hopes for a peaceful night were shattered before work had even begun.

Two cars pulled up moments after my arrival. I recognised all the occupants of both cars and I knew to expect trouble.

These guys were all at the top of their respective food chains. Serious hardened criminals.

I felt my stomach flip over. These blokes don't just rock up somewhere to chat, men like that only head out on serious business. Massey was in the front passenger seat of the first car.

I gave Graeme the nod and he shot over to be by my side as I walked towards the cars, heading straight for Massey's door. "I thought we had an understanding", I said. "I thought we were avoiding each other from now on?" "Calm down Doyley" said Massey, almost chuckling. I could see in his eyes that he was up to something. He had a devious, smug look on his face as he spoke. "We're not here to cause trouble, we're only here because I know how much of a betting man you are, and I thought that you would appreciate the chance to win £20k".

"Cut the bullshit" I snapped "What the fuck are you talking about?" I already knew by that point that whatever it was I wasn't going to like it. He was playing mind games again and it was pissing me off.

"I've come down here with these friends of mine to offer you the chance to win twenty grand in a one-on-one fight". As he was speaking, the one man in Manchester that nobody at that time (except perhaps Graeme) would have wanted to fight stepped forward. Standing at six foot two in height and almost as broad as he was tall, he was a street fighters worst nightmare. Damian Noonan was the head of the notorious Noonan family. He was more like a bear than a human. He was an intimidating bloke and certainly not somebody to be taken lightly. I could almost hear Massey's thoughts. He knew very well that I would be up against one of the few men that realistically could beat me and that was precisely what he wanted. It was what they all wanted.

My mind was racing. I knew Damian and his brothers were running some doors in Manchester and he was making quite a name for himself. What I didn't know was if this was all a ploy to get me to fight him in the hope that I would lose and they could attempt to chase me out of town and take my doors, or if Massey just wanted me out of the way for once and for all and if he had to pick someone who could that, then Damian would be his man.

I told them they could fuck off with their bet. A few sniggers could be heard coming from around the cars. I was wearing a denim jacket and I began to take it off. "I said you can fuck off with your bet, I didn't say I wouldn't fight him". What else could I do; I couldn't exactly say that I wasn't in the mood.

Damian strode towards me, looking as mean as I try to look. He had everything you could wish for to be a top fighter, size, strength, aggression, arrogance. I could see he was oozing with confidence too. He threw the first punch, and it was a beauty, it split my nose right down the middle, to be honest it almost took my fucking head clean off my shoulders. I was temporarily blinded. For the first time in my life, I was fighting a man that I couldn't even see.

It took me a full minute or so to get my eyesight back, but it felt more like a lifetime. In that first minute he gave me the worst beating I had ever received; blood was pouring from my nose and he wasn't exactly allowing me time to recover. He fought just like I did, and he was bombarding me with blow after blow. I felt every punch and they continued landing thick and fast. I was swinging back, but to no avail. I managed to back away from him before he could put me down. I started fighting him from range, which gave me a little breathing space, but I was still very much under the cosh.

Once my eyesight had recovered (as much as it was ever likely to) I strategically rushed in at him sporadically, throwing hard and fast in short sharp bursts, before retreating. He was a big powerful bloke though and he seemed to absorb everything I could land. I felt weak, I had my sight back, but I hadn't regained my strength from his initial savage onslaught. He continued to come at me.

He was one hell of a fighter. Everything I had heard was true. His power was awesome.

Not only was I getting beaten I was being punished, and I wasn't used to it. If there had been a referee, he would have stopped the fight. However, it was a street fight, it wasn't about winning on points, fighting outside of rules is all about being the last man standing. I had always said that I would drink my own blood before letting a man beat me and that is exactly what I was doing, in fact I was almost drowning in it.

A couple of minutes in a street fight is a long time and I had been getting pummeled for about ten. For the first time in my career, I felt that it was only a matter of time before I was finished off. The thought of being beaten was already embarrassing me and picturing the Ordsall firm celebrating my defeat was eating away at me. Everything looked bleak and I was thinking like a beaten man. Suddenly Noonan slowed up and I heard an almighty gasp for air as he stepped back from me. That small action inspired me no end. It reminded me that he was just a man and I had never feared another man before, nor was I about to start.

Fuck your breather I thought as I rushed in on him throwing some hugely aggressive, hurtful punches. Those shots had a much greater effect on him than my earlier ones.

It was his turn to fight for survival, and he started trying to grab my shoulders to stop me swinging. There was no stopping me though, I wanted to put him through the hell he had put me through. I broke his nose with a punch similar to the first one he had hit me with. It wasn't just his nose that broke though, that punch seemed to break his spirit too. He continued backing away from me, but I continued my assault. He bent over trying to raise a hand to protect himself, but I lowered myself before launching an uppercut hard into his face.

There was nothing coming back after that, he was still on his feet, but he was exhausted, we both were. I grabbed his throat and tilted his head back, in two minds whether to break him or offer him an end to it all.

"Enough now?" I suggested. "Enough" he said, "you've beat me but it's only because you are fitter". His opinion didn't matter to me at that point. I turned and walked away, with my head held high. I launched a glare in the direction of Massey as I headed back towards the pub. There was no need for words, the look said it all.

I had two black eyes, my nose was split right down the middle and god only knows how many pints of blood I'd lost. I wanted to cry with the emotion of the victory. As I passed by Graeme, I gave him a little smirk, as if to say, 'how the fuck did I manage that'.

I consider that to be my best ever fight, although some folk that witnessed it, believed it was my worst. The fact that I was toe to toe with one of Manchester's greatest ever fighting machines and was inches from defeat yet turned it around, fills me with immense pride, even to this day. Fighters that got the better of Damian Noonan are few and far between. I realise that most who know me expect me to simply knock out everyone I go up against, but that can't always be the case, and a true fighter shows real spirit when he needs it most. It's all about your heart and desire when you're up against it in life. I showed mine that night. I also showed resilience, grit, strength and importantly on that occasion I proved I had the stamina to go the distance. There was nothing between us really except that I was the fitter man and in the end that was enough to make all the difference. It didn't matter that I had been knocked about a bit, I still won.

The only downside was that I hadn't taken the twenty-grand bet, as that would have been the icing on the cake.

A week or so later me and the wife visited our favourite Indian restaurant in town, for a quiet meal together. As soon as I pushed through the door, my heart sank. Sitting there bold as ever and surrounded by a table full of his entourage was Big Damien Noonan. I was outnumbered ten to one and by the looks of things, him and his mates were a few sheets to the wind, which meant anything could happen.

I had no choice but to swagger in like I didn't have a care in the world, deep down however I feared for mine and Jeanette's safety, if not our lives. No sooner were we inside, Damien rose to his feet and bellowed across the restaurant; "One Punch Doyley himself". I felt my pulse quicken, 'of all the fucking nights to fancy a curry'. "That man over there" Damien continued, "is the toughest man I have ever faced. He couldn't knock me out with one punch, but he gave me the fight of my life. Get him and his good lady a bottle of your finest champagne, in fact get our table a couple of bottles and we'll raise a glass to him too". I couldn't believe it, I was expecting to be attacked by him and his men, but I actually found myself being offered a bottle of fizz, courtesy of them - or so I thought.

I thanked him for his words and me and Jeanette continued over to our table, which thankfully was on the other side of the room. I felt I had to have one glass of the champagne, just to be polite. Jeanette made light work of the rest of it.

Damien shouted over to us again as him and his crew were leaving. Never the quiet type he announced for the whole restaurant to hear, not to mention with a huge grin on his face "I hope you enjoyed your drink Doyley". I raised my glass to him and nodded, grateful that they were leaving, and nothing had kicked off. It wasn't until we had finished our food and asked for the bill that I realised why his grin had been quite so large. The cheeky bastard had only told the waiter to put the 3 bottles of champagne onto our bill. I couldn't help but grin myself - typical Damien, larger than life and the outspoken joker through and through.

Chapter 14:

OPPORTUNITY KNOCKS

O ver the years my reputation landed me in plenty of tight spots, it has also, however, resulted in quite a few unique opportunities being presented to me. People often consider me to be a possible solution to a tricky problem - I became known as a bit of a 'fixer'.

After a hard week's work putting cannabis on my customers' tables, I was enjoying a relaxing afternoon with the family, when Jimmy, a friend and neighbor, knocked on the door. Jimmy was one of the most 'ready' kids on our road. One time he found himself in a situation with some lads that was only going from bad to worse, Jimmy felt backed into a corner and in an attempt to put an end to things he produced a gun. He claims to have had no intentions to use it until one of the lads he was threatening tried calling his bluff "how do we know the gun is real?" he stupidly asked.

Jimmy, feeling backed into a corner, shot the lad in his leg to prove it was.

I opened the door and saw my neighbor standing with a lad that looked like a proper posh knob. I frowned at Jimmy as if to say, 'how do you know someone like him?'.

Jim introduced me to his friend who was called Thomas. Thomas, who had a cracking shiner under his left eye, apparently wanted a gun. I found it quite amusing as he asked for it like it was just as simple as asking to borrow a cup of sugar.

"Forgive me, but I'm puzzled" I said. "Why would some private school graduate like you want a gun?" Again, just like it was the norm Thomas replied, "I want to shoot my business partner".

"I see, and why does your partner deserve to be shot?" I enquired. Thomas then told me how his business partner had caught him shagging the said partner's wife, so the said partner proceeded to punch Thomas all over the bedroom and out onto the street, leaving him with his black eye.

I said "fucking hell Tom, shouldn't your partner be asking me for the gun. Where I come from, you'd be very lucky to get away with a black eye for shagging another man's wife". Thomas told me he agreed, but explained it wasn't really all about the black eye, there was much more to the story.

He had designed a new invention which he and his partner invested their life savings into patenting and producing. Thomas had actually sold his house to find the funds and was temporarily living with his business partner and his wife. They were very close to reaping the benefits of all their hard work when Thomas was caught celebrating with the other bloke's missus and fucked everything up.

In no uncertain terms I told the pair of them that it was foolish to obtain a gun and even more so to attempt to use one. I explained that if by some miracle Thomas did shoot his partner, he would have been arrested before the sun set. Within minutes of being sat in a cell he would no doubt be crying and confessing all. Following that the police would also undoubtedly convince him to tell them exactly who had supplied the gun. All of a sudden, a few grand from a business deal would seem like a drop in the ocean compared to life imprisonment. Not to mention the gun supplier chomping at the bit to kill him as well. I invited them both into my house for a cup of coffee and explained an alternative solution that wouldn't result in anybody getting shot, and hopefully no jail terms. Intrigued, I then enquired about the invention.

Thomas told me about this water management system he had designed. It was basically a water saving device that was to be fitted above urinals in gents toilets. When a bloke went for a pee Thomas' device would sense their presence (through a motion sensor) and flush the water into the urinal 60 seconds later. As it worked on motion sensors it only flushed after use and the device saved litres of unnecessary water being flushed down the drains every day.

The old system simply had the flush activating on a timer mechanism, and therefore flushed every 20 minutes or so, day and night regardless of use. The old design was costing companies worldwide a fortune in water bills, not to mention wasting ridiculous amounts of water every day.

Thomas told me they were close to finishing their first contract at British Aerospace, which would leave them with £160,000 profit. As things stood, he couldn't finish the contract because his business partner had taken his keys to the office and wouldn't allow him back in. He had also taken his car keys and bank cards and had obviously kicked him out of his house.

Thomas' affair had left him with no home, no office, no transport and no money.

The business sounded good, and it looked like snowballing. It was forecast to make hundreds of thousands of pounds the following year, with the potential for millions after that. Thomas was the major shareholder but had agreed on a 60/40 split with his partner.

I negotiated a 50/50 split on his 60% of the British Airways contract, in return for getting his office and car back, telling his partner to stay away and assisting him in installing the remainder of the water management devices, so they could get paid.

I was earning good money at the time and didn't fancy going up and down the country fitting sensors to urinals, but I thought it sounded like a good opportunity for Graeme. I phoned him and explained the situation. He was happy at the chance of some extra cash and agreed to my proposal.

I told Jimmy to take Thomas to Graeme's house where he could stay for a while, while they finished the contract together. Graeme sorted out the finer details to ensure Thomas' business partner became Thomas' ex-business partner. With that taken care of Graeme, Thomas and Jimmy travelled the country over the following few weeks finishing the BA contract.

As soon as the job was completed, and the money was paid Thomas phoned the bank to release the funds. He was then marched down to the bank by Graeme three days later to collect the £160,000 (you could withdraw that much cash in those days, with just three days' notice).

Graeme and Jimmy eventually agreed to split £120,000 and Thomas took a smaller cut but was allowed to keep the company. It worked out a good deal all around, especially for Tom, but I told Graeme he was silly walking away from such a promising business venture and asked him to reconsider. Graeme needed something different in his life and that could have been his opportunity. He was more than happy with his cash though and I couldn't be arsed flogging a dead donkey, so I left him to it. I did actually consider investing in the company myself, but I had a lot on my plate at the time, so decided against it. Turns out it wasn't my shrewdest of business decisions however, as they are now fitted in toilets worldwide and Thomas will presumably be a multi-millionaire if he managed to keep his hands off married women.

One time I was in a gents having a slash when I looked up and saw one of the devices. I couldn't help but chuckle. As I looked to my left, there was a bloke standing next to me pissing, he was giving me the funniest of looks, which made me laugh even harder. The bloke zipped up and got out of there as fast as he could, God only knows what he thought I was laughing at.

With Graeme having some money to burn he asked me if he could invest in my cannabis business. I couldn't really say no and offend him, so I took his money and I got some of Jeanette's family selling for him around the Swinton area of North Manchester.

He had never earned money like it and couldn't believe the profits from cannabis.

As we were both earning good money, and as Graeme was a liability, I thought it made sense to give up the security business and concentrate our efforts into the drug game.

I suggested to Graeme that we sell our door firm, and his answer stays with me to this very day. "Heavens above Paul no, we're earning good money from the business". I strongly suspect however that he just didn't want to stop beating people senseless, and working the doors gave him ample opportunity to do that. It could have been because it gave him a chance to work his charms on the ladies, but I think that was probably just an added bonus.

After a while I stopped trying to work out why he was so keen on us working the doors, and just accepted that I was stuck with them and him.

I was concerned that our relationship was doing me more harm than good. I could manage Graeme, but on the whole he was an uncontrollable, unpredictable man. People were starting to show disdain towards me for standing by and allowing him to carry out his actions. Some even believed he was following my orders, but Graeme was his own boss when it came to acts of violence.

One night Graeme slapped a friend of mine across his face in a totally unexpected outburst. I asked him why he had done it, to which he replied, "Paul you're better off without him, he's nothing but a scumbag". I informed Graeme that I could and would pick my own friends and after a brief argument about the company I kept, we agreed to disagree. I could hardly believe that the one person who I thought could actually bring some serious heat down on me, was trying to guide me on choosing friends.

There was a person who had a worse reputation than that of ourselves. A despicable individual who ran an organised firm of gangsters in Bolton. He ruled with an iron fist and used fear and brutality to maintain his reputation as a man not to be crossed. His name was Billy Webb, and his gang were the first to sell class As on an industrial scale around the streets of Greater Manchester and Lancashire.

Following on from the kicking we had given to Baz's 'messenger' and our refusal to hand over the security of the Bolton nightclub 'Kiss' I was told to expect a visit from Billy and his boys.

One night, out of the blue I received a phone call from one of our doormen saying Billy and a number of his firm had turned up at Kiss and had kicked the shit out of another of our doormen. They then started helping themselves to drinks and even assaulted a few of the customers.

I told the doorman to pass on a message not to approach Billy or his men until we got there, and not to let him know that we were on our way. It took us half an hour to get to Kiss and I was surprised to hear that they were still inside. It would have been pointless trying to be diplomatic, it would have been seen as a weakness. The only option I was considering was to punish them and punish them like they had punished our guy.

Each one of my team had serious experience in unarmed combat, either professionally or on the streets. I was confident we could deal with them, but first I had to weigh up the situation before planning the attack. I peered in the club and saw Billy Webb standing in the middle of a pack of undesirables. Amateurishly they were unaware that we had already arrived. I knew we had the advantage. We could use the element of surprise.

That night there were six in our team. Me and Graeme who needed no introduction, our head doorman Raff, who was very well known throughout Bolton (especially so with the ladies). If anybody had ever done a calendar of doormen, Raff would be Mr. January and no doubt Graeme would have insisted on being February through to December.

We had two Pakistani champion wrestlers. Mo, who was legendary at the YMCA in Manchester. He once knocked a man out with a slap. The other was the doorman who would not be denied his revenge for the kicking he had received earlier that night from Billy's firm.

I instructed all the doors be locked, so no one could leave. Then I gave a little motivational speech to the lads. I said we were to go in hard and brutal. We needed to give the detestable bullies a kicking that they wouldn't forget. I wanted them waking at night in cold sweats, remembering how they had unsuccessfully tried to mug me off. As I was giving my instructions, I could see Graeme's smirk of delight growing wider. He looked like a kid preparing to go to the fun fair.

We had a very capable set of lads, but we were heavily outnumbered so needed to rush them quickly and efficiently. We agreed on our first six targets before we set off. After that it was a 'go with the flow' approach and basically just knock out anybody that hadn't already been done.

The battle was over inside of two minutes. We were impressive. Not one of Billy's firm landed a decent punch.

I later received information that one of his men had been carrying a gun. We had charged in on them that quickly, he had been knocked out before he was even able to draw it. Our attack had been brutal, effective and professional. Graeme being Graeme had gone overboard however and left several of them requiring hospital beds for a few nights. Needless to say, they got the message, *loud and clear.*

That Monday morning, I was arrested and questioned. The desk sergeant told me there was a ward at Bolton hospital full of patients as a result our battle in the club. The list of injuries was substantial. There was reportedly four cases of fractured skulls, two broken arms, a broken leg and multiple other serious ailments.

Graeme going that step too far had once again proved problematic.

Whenever a Category A prisoner is ever escorted anywhere off a Category A wing, he would be required to be handcuffed and escorted by two screws. Some of the more dangerous prisoners may be escorted by four or five screws and possibly a dog. I was starting to think that Graeme needed escorting by seven or eight screws and a pack of dogs every time he left the house.

As effective as our attack had been carried out, my arrest over it hit me quite hard. I was losing the heart for the door business. It was a burden that I really didn't need to have hanging over me.

A few weeks after that eventful night at Kiss, Billy and his firm had clearly recovered, and word got out that they were seeking revenge. Before long Raff was shot. Fortunately, he was only hit in the arm and suffered no more serious injuries, but it looked like Billy was intent on showing he wasn't running scared.

I found myself looking over my shoulder again. I thought he was going to become an additional thorn in my side, and I couldn't afford to be dragged into yet another drawn out gang war, especially as my truce with the Ordsall firm was still teetering on a knife edge.

Me and Graeme were close to finalising a plan to scare Billy off once and for all when we received a sinister and cowardly message. Word on that grape vine was that Billy was content with the shooting of Raff as his revenge and that me and Graeme would be taken care of by of good friends of his, from Salford.

It didn't take a genius to figure out which Salford firm Billy was referring to and if the threat was to be taken seriously, I realised another run in with Massey and his boys could be just around the next corner. I could only deal with that problem if it reared its ugly head though, so at that time I was just relieved Billy could be forgotten about - as much as you can forget about a sleeping rat anyway. Our employer's at Kiss were equally pleased to hear that Billy was no longer an issue as they were close to opening a new club in Bolton called The Temple. It was a fantastic place. A really beautiful set up, it even featured a waterfall inside. It was the biggest night club in the north capable of holding 2000 ravers. The security there was handed to us.

As soon as The Temple opened its doors it became known as a raver's paradise. Clubbers would be on Ecstasy, some dropping four or five a night. That in turn made the place a gangsters paradise. Big money was there for the taking, and Ecstasy would be their new gold mine.

The owner had spent far too much money to risk losing his license due to rifts between gangsters vying for position in his new club. I knew the place would attract people that I had grown up with, done time with or grafted with all my life. I have acquired a lot of friends over the years. From doormen to gangsters, football hooligans to drug dealers. I didn't need any introduction to half of Manchester's underworld, and I knew they would all be wanting to get in the Temple. My problem was that I couldn't lower myself to asking such friends and acquaintances to pay at the door, just to line some multi millionaire's pockets. I couldn't disrespect them in that way. For that reason, Graeme found himself on the front line yet again, and I found myself another pleasurable little place to work, out of the limelight, where no admission fee was necessary.

It was a high-class night club in Manchester, a great venue, full of beautiful girls and often some celebrities. Take That would go there from time to time, which had the girls going wild. There was rarely any serious trouble, and if there was, I ensured that it was swiftly nipped in the bud.

I even chatted up a beautiful lady there one night and took her out for a swanky meal. Now I've never really been the type of person for doing that, so the next day, proud as punch, I foolishly was showing off to Graeme. Me and my big mouth. Obviously being the womaniser that Graeme was, he decided he needed a piece of the action and wanted to start working there too. What had I done?

With both of us rarely working the doors in Bolton, the previous events from Kiss started to be forgotten as did Billy and his men. A few years later Billy was actually found murdered, lying in his own bed. Somebody let themselves into his flat and fatally shot him as he slept. The murder was never solved, but it was clearly very much a gangland execution.

Billy was another poor soul that never completed his journey in life. He paid the ultimate price for his life as a gang leader.

Chapter 15:

A TICKING TIME BOMB

Manchester was quite a quiet place through the week, so the bars were never that busy. Doormen are usually a lot more relaxed on letting customers in mid-week than they may be when it's busy at the weekend. One night I was inside the club, while Graeme was working the door with a colleague who coincidentally happened to look like me. A group of fairly tipsy customers, eight guys and two girls tried to get in. If I was on the door, I would have just let them in to get the place looking busy. Not Graeme, however. He told them they couldn't. One of the blokes wanted to know why, to which Graeme apparently barked "you've had too much to drink". The guy then said, "I used to be a doorman and one thing I didn't do was shout, because if I shouted you would know about it".

Those were the guy's last words for quite some time. Graeme, who always worked with his hammer head hidden in his hand (in case of any reprisals from our enemies), set about the man. The other seven all jumped in and they started to fight Graeme off.

They were simply no match though.

Graeme and his hammer head tore through all eight of them, and as was usual for him, he continued beating them until all eight were unconscious.

Upon hearing the screams from the girls, I made my way down from the office to see what all the commotion was over. I stepped outside just as Graeme was dusting himself down.

"What the fuck has happened" I screamed at Graeme. It was a rhetorical question really, so before even giving him a chance to answer, I said "go to my car now and wait for me, I need to get you out of here".

I drove us away before the police arrived. It was no great shock though when a warrant was put out for our arrest.

Graeme was arrested first and interviewed for eight Section 18s, Grievous Bodily Harm with intent. He was bailed to appear on an identity parade. After finding out Graeme got bail, I decided to hand myself in with a solicitor present.

During my interview I went no comment throughout. After a couple of hours of being interrogated the detective said, "we'll grant you bail until we can set up an identity parade". He then said, "thank you for your no comment replies Paul, at least you were polite".

I was slightly puzzled and asked if his remark was supposed to be funny. The detective told me that during Graeme's interview, at the end of each question he just glared at them like he was ready to attack at any given moment. "Is he psychotic?" the copper asked me. I laughed it off, but I knew him enough to know that actually he was.

Going on the ID parade I presumed I would be sweet because I had been inside the club for the entirety of the incident. Graeme's solicitor told him that the gentlemen - for some strange reason, didn't want to attend the parade but unfortunately one of the girl witnesses did. I heard Graeme's angry outburst from the far side of the police station. "That fucking bitch should be pissed on" he screamed. Out of all the hilarious things I've heard shouted out in police stations, that has to be one of the funniest. The shameful thing about it is that given half a chance he would no doubt have done it.

In those days you could choose your own identity parade. You could get anyone that looks like you, friends, brothers, cousins, anyone to stand alongside you. What Graeme did next was pure genius. He found out where the girl lived and to put the fear of God into her, he chose neighbours from either side of the girl's to line up next to him on the parade.

Once the girl realised that Graeme knew where she lived it was no great surprise that she failed to pick us out.

Although the ID parade was a success, we lost the door to the club, as well as two others in town as a result of the incident. Admittedly it was better than losing our liberty for 10 years for GBH, but those jobs were some of our better ones where in reality we should not have been getting involved in trouble. It was another case of Graeme's over absorbency bringing unnecessary heat on us. We just about kept the contract at the Inn of Good Hope, even though a lot of the customers stopped going in because of their hatred towards us.

After the relief of getting off had passed, I once again found myself feeling downhearted and deflated with regards to our security business. I'd been arrested twice for more than twenty serious assaults in a two-month period. Graeme's behaviour and temper was costing us. His explosive, psychopathic ways made him a ticking time bomb and, as his business partner, it was leaving me extremely vulnerable to spending another significant chunk of my life behind bars.

I started having nightmares about being doubled up in a cell with him, doing a life sentence. I needed to keep a watchful eye on him for my own sake as much as his.

Bars, pubs and nightclubs were starting to have security cameras fitted. The police fitted a top of the range camera at the Inn of Good Hope, with built in audio recording, which was the dog's bollocks in those days. I actually believe, contrary to what the police were saying, that it was put up to gather intelligence on me and Graeme.

One dark wintery Thursday night while working at the Inn, a car pulled up in the far corner of the car park. The men inside had their hoods up, so at first it was hard to tell exactly who they were. The voice that called out to me though I instantly recognised. It was Massey.

As I approached the car, I could make out the faces of the other men inside, amongst them was Dessie Noonan (Damien's brother) and Paul Flannery a very high ranking member of the Cheetham Hill firm. Gangsters who would have put fear into most doormen around the North. My main concern however was my psychopathic mate who had wandered up and was standing beside me.

Graeme's presence immediately made the situation tense. They disliked him more than they disliked me.

I am a grafter. I have always been a grafter; it's how I've made my money. When I say grafter, I obviously don't mean a nine till five, seven days a week kind of a guy. Clearly, I was not that. By grafting I refer to stealing, selling drugs, doing whatever I need to do to earn a dishonest crust.

The men in the car however were gangsters, thoroughbred gangsters at that. The type that had an army of followers, vying to trace their footsteps. They could give an order for somebody to be kidnapped, tortured or shot, and it would be considered done, no questions asked. Dessie was once, on a TV documentary, quoted as saying his family had "more guns than the police". Everyone found it hilarious, however it wasn't too far from the truth. That particular guy had an army of young lads willing to do whatever they were told, and he and his brothers were far from shy themselves.

On that particular night in the car park of The Inn of Good Hope it was Dessie that took the lead and was doing all the talking. He was speaking respectfully and calmly, but in an assertive manner. He didn't waste any time with pleasantries either and got straight to the point. He said "Graeme, Paul, we've heard that the owner of the Temple is being put under pressure by the police to let you boys go and that the door contract will be up for grabs. Well, we want that contract, so I'm asking you lads to step aside and let us have it. Now as we are all friends, I think that is a reasonable enough request, don't you?"

I knew that working at the Temple door wasn't worth falling out with these lads over, and I turned to Graeme to say that as we were looking at losing the door anyway, I would be happy not to stand in their way. When Graeme burst out with "no, no, no, I've given my word to the owner and I will not break my word. I'll be working the door at the Temple nightclub until the day the police say otherwise".

I was more shocked than the lads in the car with Graeme's outburst. Dessie simply said, "you have a little think about it and phone us in a day or two". To which Graeme replied, "I've already given you my answer, this discussion is over". The lad then stared at Graeme and in a very chilling tone said, "Graeme nobody knows what lies around the corner, you could be here one minute and gone the next". That was the fuse lit. Graeme started going barmy, screaming and shouting and jumping around. "Is that a threat? Is that a threat? Get out of the car if you want to threaten me".

Nobody was about to make the mistake of getting out to take Graeme on. They simply watched his raging tantruming, then looked right past him and asked me how I stood. Despite not agreeing with Graeme, I was his friend and business partner, which meant we stood together and would fall together therefore I was impelled to tell them as much. "I'm afraid I'm with him" I said, gesturing to Graeme, who was marching back and forth with steam coming from his ears.

Dessie raised an eyebrow at me as if he had expected something different and then said "very well. Stay lucky fellas" and with that they drove off.

I asked Graeme why working the Temple meant so much to him and how it was worth yet another fall out with a set of ferocious gangsters. To which he finally admitted to me that he had a share in the place. "Why the fuck didn't you just tell them that then, it may have changed things". "It's not their business what I do with my money" he said, and to be fair he did have a point.

For me it was just another kick in the balls that the door business was throwing my way. There was clearly going to be fallout from it, and I was getting a bit fed up with the monotony of it all. Every which way I looked; trouble seemed to be staring back at me.

That night on my way home from work, I kept glancing into the rear-view mirror, remembering Dessie's chilling words; "stay lucky fellas".

That weekend me and Tet were at Old Trafford watching United with the lads. As much as I love watching United, I simply couldn't concentrate on the match. I was expecting bother and the lads I was up against were not to be taken lightly. I had ordered an extra doorman for that evening at the Inn. Jimmy, who was an ex-boxer. He was a quick thinker and even quicker with his hands. Just the type of ally I needed. After the game me and Tet headed straight to the Inn.

Like a fool I was anticipating the pub would be rushed by a group of heavies. That's how it would have happened a few years earlier. I wasn't keeping pace with the changing times.

Gangsters had become gunslingers. Fisticuffs in the street was a fast-dying trade. I was much more a hooligan than a gangster and I had my trusty bat close by ready for what was to come.

The entrance to the Inn had glass doors facing the car park, beyond the double glass doors was a small set of stairs. At the top of the stairs were the toilets and a little area where we would usually stand. That night once I had warned everybody to be on guard and extra vigilant, then gone through the motions of preparing for the night ahead, I finally relaxed a little. As the clock ticked on, I even began to enjoy the evening.

As it wasn't too busy, I decided to have a sit on the stairs and read the Football Pink (the Manchester Evening News' football pullout). Not being the best of readers, I was totally lost in concentration, when suddenly I heard the sound of smashing glass followed by a woman screaming. I looked up to see the backside of Tet disappearing through the toilet door faster than I had ever seen him move. I then looked down the stairs to where the glass doors used to be, and I saw a car screeching off at speed.

At that point I realised we had just been shot at.

Alan and Jimmy had both taken two hits each. Someone in Heaven must have been looking down on me because there were bullet holes dotted around the stairs where I had been sitting, but I was totally unscathed. The incident was done in a matter of seconds and no sooner than I realised we were under attack, it was all over.

The adrenaline kicked in and the excitement followed. I was grinning from ear to ear. Tet came out of the toilets and said, "what the fuck have you got to be grinning about?" I didn't even have a response for him, my grin just got bigger, before it turned into a little chuckle.

I stopped laughing long enough to ask him what he had seen, and he told me that he noticed the car pull up at the front doors and he thought it looked a little moody because the passenger had his hood up. The car's window went down, and he had seen enough. It was at that point his intuition kicked in and he ran for cover. "Well thanks for warning me" I said. Tet put his hands up, tilted his head to one side and said "please". Basically, meaning fuck you, it's every man for himself.

At that point I started to laugh again. I was like a giddy kid experiencing a sugar rush.

Later that evening it dawned on me how totally unprepared I had been. I was reading a paper with a bat by my side, idly waiting for some of Manchester's most feared criminals to come after me.

What was I going to do, throw my bat at them and deflect the bullets with my copy of the Football Pink?

After tending to Jimmy and Alan and having them shipped off to hospital, we watched the CCTV footage back to see if we could get anything from it. There was nothing of any use. I did see one of the funniest things that I ever saw in my life though.

A woman came out of the toilets just as the first shots were fired. Graeme grabbed hold of her instantaneously. Rather than flinging her to safety though, he lifted her up in front of himself and used her as a human shield while he ran for cover. You could see the horror in the poor woman's face. She looked like she was having a heart attack.

"Fucking hell Graeme you could have gotten her killed" I said. To which Graeme simply asked, "Would you prefer that I was shot Paul?"

All in all, it was a funny night. The gunmen would no doubt have been fuming if they realised what great entertainment, they had provided us with, obviously one downside to it all was my good friend Jimmy getting shot. After making a full recovery though Jimmy soldiered on, and even he saw the funny side of things, admitting that it would be a great story to tell his Grandkids.

Graeme's friend Alan obviously got shot too, but If I'm honest I wasn't too concerned about him. In fact, I thought it was a bit of a shame the bullets missed his head. Alan turned out to be a despicable bloke. A year or so after the shooting he badly beat up his girlfriend and then the horrible bastard threw her through a first-floor bedroom window-unopened. He got what he deserved in court though - twenty years at Her Majesty's pleasure.

The day after the shooting my phone was ringing off the hook. I received what couldn't have been much shy of one hundred phone calls in the morning alone, all from friends and family, wanting the gory details. There was obviously only really one story to tell, which was how Graeme had shielded himself with the petrified woman.

Unsurprisingly nobody who actually knew Graeme was surprised to hear it, and everybody found it equally as amusing.

The police were all over me again, like shit on the walls of a dirty protest. Anyone would have thought that I was the shooter. I got pulled over three times in one day alone that week.

On the Saturday morning they raided my house searching for weapons. One copper said, "you had better tell me straight Mr. Doyle, is there anything in this house that shouldn't be here" To which I replied "yeah, you fucking lot".

My laid-back demeanor clearly annoyed them and one of them ordered that I be cuffed and put in the van. As they were doing so, I asked if my handcuffs could be put on a bit tighter, as my hands hadn't quite turned blue. With that I was shoved inside and slammed against the cage headfirst. None of it was bothering me though, I had nothing to hide and the fact that they were so infuriated by me, only made my smile wider.

Obviously, they didn't find any weapons at my house, as I had been expecting the dosey bastards all week.

I was taken to Manchester police headquarters at Chester House. Unbelievably I was put into a room and asked if I wanted a cup of tea or coffee. I think my jaw must have hit the ground. I was puzzled, one minute they wanted to cut the blood supply to my hands and the next they wanted to be mates with me.

Several senior officers sat around me, trying to make me feel uncomfortable. One asked "How do you feel about your friends being shot?" I didn't reply because I was still unsure what it was the horrible bastards actually wanted. The copper continued going on with himself, saying that they knew in the days running up to the shooting I had had some type of meeting with a gang of men in a car. He wanted to know what the meeting was about. I said, "it was no meeting". To which the idiot copper asked; was I scared of repercussions from the men in the car and had they threatened me. I asked him why he thought my friends would threaten me. To which he replied seemingly frustrated "We know the men in the car aren't your friends and we've got intelligence indicating that you've been having trouble with them over door rights at nightclubs. If you cooperate with us by telling us they threatened you, we can have them off the streets and up on charges of conspiring to murder you before you have time to finish that cup of coffee. If, however you choose not to cooperate, we will shut your security company down for good. The choice is yours Mr. Doyle".

I found their tactics disgraceful. It would have brought shame to me and my family name if I had cooperated with them, and they knew it. With my head held high I told the copper to go and fuck himself. I was thrown out of the police station with my self-respect still intact, but the police, true to their word, closed down our security business with immediate effect.

They knew very well that I would never grass, and they had clearly already made preparations to shut us down. That same night they had other security firms working our doors. Each of our pubs and bars had a squad van parked outside for the duration of the night, in case of reprisals. The police had shown their true colours. They were as bent as us criminals. I should have sued the bastards for illegally stealing my business.

Me being shot at resulted in the police punishing me, basically because they couldn't catch who had done it. Deep down I was quite relieved. I knew the net had been closing in on us and I don't think we would have lasted the course if we had stuck to our guns for much longer. Running the business had become an uphill struggle, and the destination was looking increasingly like me ending up back in jail or in a box.

The time had come for another meeting with Manchester's Mr. Big.

Massey told me that the shooting hadn't been ordered by him, which I did believe, and I marked his card's about the underhand tactics of the police. We both had a bit of a laugh about it, especially when I told him about Graeme and the human shield.

It was nice to have a catch up with him like the good old days, without any of his ogres breathing down our necks. After a drink, we went our separate ways and we wished one another good luck.

Chapter 16:

WHEN ONE DOOR CLOSES...

F or the first time in years, I found myself having boring weekends at home and it felt wonderful. Through the week I was working at my yard, keeping one eye on my reclaim business and the other eye on my brothers as, aside from our Mike, I wouldn't trust any of them with our own mother's purse. The yard was often a meeting place for me and my friends to discuss the movement of drugs. I had one hell of a busy phone, but it was just street level stuff. I had desires to be higher up the ladder, where the big money was made.

It had become very difficult for me to keep up with the high demand for cannabis. Most dealers were having similar problems, apart from one or two mancs and one particularly busy Scouse pal of mine called Kenny.

Due to the amount I was moving I got to know them all very well. Young Kenny was a bit of a whiz-kid, very sharp and good looking. He made millions from his links to Holland. Due to those connections, he could buy and sell cannabis a lot cheaper than anyone else.

He was a slippery sod and we got on well and credit where credit is due, he trusted me and my honest mug. For that reason, he would lay on large amounts of cannabis for me to pay back once I had sold it on. It worked well for us and continued to do so for many months. It didn't stop me from pestering him for a piece of the action in Holland though. I knew I was banging my head against a wall; he was having none of it and I couldn't blame him.

Unexpectedly one day, he came down to see me at the yard looking for a favour. He was saying his friend in Holland had a problem and asked if I could help resolve it.

My mind started looking into the future and my eyes lit up. I knew it could be a chance to get one foot in the door in Holland. Naturally, I told him if I could help I would. I asked what the problem was.

He told me that an English guy who had been working with the Dutch, had gone over to Holland to meet with him and his Dutch boss. The English guy ended up buying 200 kilos of cannabis and had 200 kilos 'laid on' (to be paid for after they were sold). However, since the guy had been back in England he had not been in touch, nor had he been contactable. The Dutch boss didn't know if he had been ripped off or if the English guy had been arrested. In those days, the Dutch gave the English customers fantastic deals, so it was unusual for a customer to rip off his supplier.

I asked Kenny for the English bloke's details. He didn't have an address, but he knew his name was Peter M…Known locally as 'Fat Pete' and that he owned a skip company in the North-East. I personally thought it sounded absurd that a professional drug dealer would lay on that much cannabis to another dealer, without knowing exactly where they lived.

The deal in those days though was whatever cannabis you paid up front for, it was standard for a supplier to lay on the equivalent amount again. It seemed that paying for half upfront, stood you in good stead to earn the supplier's trust and credit.

In England it was the era of the hooligan. Hooligans up and down the country had started selling drugs and were responsible for a growing chunk of criminality in the country. Priding myself on being a hooligan I knew almost everyone that was worth their salt in their respective areas.

I got straight on the phone and rang a fellow hooligan from Tyneside. I told him that I had a slight problem and asked if he could help me resolve it. I told him I was looking for a major cannabis seller going by the nickname of Fat Pete, and that Fat Pete had a skip-yard in Tyneside. My fellow hooligan was happy to offer his services and said he would ring around and get back to me within the hour.

While we were waiting for some information to come through, Kenny began telling me how tough Fat Pete was supposed to be, and some of the tales he had heard about him.

After about forty minutes my friend phoned back saying there were two Pete's who were fairly major cannabis dealers. One was living in Sunderland the other in Newcastle. He also warned me that the Sunderland guy was an extremely hard man, and not to be taken lightly.

He gave me both of their details and I thanked him for his generous efforts.

He only had Pete from Sunderland's phone number. Obviously I couldn't phone him, just in case he did another bunk – so it was going to take a trip up North to get to the bottom of the AWOL Pete and the missing cannabis.

I knew I had impressed Kenny already, by narrowing the search down to two people in under an hour, with only a nickname to go off. I clearly couldn't take it any further however without agreeing on some sort of a payment. As I had already proved myself more than capable, I managed to negotiate quite a lucrative deal. However, the hard work was still to be done.

I would have been a total fool to have gone alone, so I offered a share of the money to the one person I knew I had to take along with me. The one person who always gave me the extra courage I needed when the odds were stacked against me. Going into unknown territory required Graeme. I also took a weapon just in case I needed to swing the odds that bit further our way. Kenny, somewhat nervously, asked me my plan. I told him it was simple; go and see the guy in Sunderland.

"You said Pete's tough, well my pal said that Pete in Sunderland is very tough, so by my reckoning Sunderland Pete sounds like he may well be our guy.

"When we catch up with him you can clarify if he's the right Pete or not. Hopefully, he is, and we can put him on the phone to your Dutch friend and they can have a nice little chat."

Kenny looked worried. "What could go wrong?" I said, giving him a little smirk. Obviously, I knew full well that we were going into the unknown and an awful lot could go horribly wrong.

We arrived at Pete's house in Sunderland at about 5pm. Noone was home and there was a 'for sale' sign up on the drive. We carried on to his skip yard, and yet again nobody there. I had no option but to phone him. He answered and I told him we needed to speak over a very serious matter. I explained that I had a Dutch friend and I believed he owed my Dutch friend a large amount of money. I told him I was at his skip yard, and I was with a bloke that would be able to identify whether or not he was the person we were looking for.

"If you are the fella then we need to discuss the matter, if you are not, then I will offer my sincere apologies for wasting your time and we will leave you be".

Pete went barmy, yelling all sorts down the phone at me. In a roundabout way he told me he didn't owe anybody any money therefore he had no intention of meeting anybody. I explained to Pete that I completely understood his position, however as I had spent hours driving up to see him, I wouldn't be going anywhere until I had. "If I have to wait outside your house, the one that's up for sale, that has the lovely hanging baskets and the bay windows, then I will do that until somebody gets home".

My approach seemed to go down like a weighted vest in the ocean. Pete got extremely aggressive and started demanding to know who I was and who had told me where he lived.

I was getting a bit bored of listening to his rantings though. "I'm trying very hard to be polite to you Pete, but you're making it difficult. I've had fuck all to eat which is very annoying at the best of times, but on top of that you're yelling at me like some kind of army general and have shown me no respect whatsoever. All I'm asking for is five minutes of your time to help solve a problem, now will you please stop your yelling and do me the courtesy of meeting me in person".

Finally, Pete agreed. We arranged to meet at his skip yard.

Pete's yard was in the middle of waste ground that stretched for miles. If there was to be any trouble, no one would ever need know about it. He had us waiting there for over an hour and Graeme was beginning to get irate.

I phoned him back saying "Pete we're in Sunderland today. I assume you're getting a firm together, which I have no issue with, what I do have an issue with however is you keeping me waiting, so will you hurry the fuck up".

The cocky bastard simply replied "shortly" and hung up on me. I could have killed him for that. I hate rude twats and he was starting to appear very much like one.

About a minute later we saw cars driving towards us, and a few of them at that. Fat Pete was in a hundred grand soft top Mercedes, looking every bit the smooth cunt. He pulled up alongside us with his soft top roof down and glared at us. Seconds later we were surrounded by four other vehicles, all full of menacing looking thugs. As he stopped, I asked Kenny if he was the gentleman he had met in Holland, to which he, whilst looking close to shitting himself, replied "no".

I was just about to give Pete the good news, when he started shouting "who gave you my fucking address and who the fuck do you think you are coming for me?"

"Don't go getting me fucking annoyed Pete, you're not the person that owes the money, so as far as you're concerned the matter is over. I said I would apologise to you and I am a man of my word, so I'm sorry for wasting your time".

Pete continued ranting and was becoming even more aggressive and abusive. I'd had enough so I interrupted and said "Pete all your firm around us now tells me you're a capable bloke, and you're no doubt prone to handing out a beating from time to time but believe me when I say those days are long gone. Now I don't want to spend the next twenty years staring at a cell wall, just because you can't accept an apology. So, for the very last time, I'm going to tell you that I'm sorry for wasting your time, and then the ball will be in your court as to what happens next".

I got my weapon out and held it by my side for all to see, in the hope it would bring the situation to a close, and then I continued; "So Pete, will you accept my apology?"

For the first time Pete gave me a smile and a wink. He said, "we're all gangsters at the end of the day", then he waved away the other vehicles - much to my relief.

I said all the Hollywood gangster bullshit like "Have a nice day" and "Be lucky", then we jumped in our car and started out to Newcastle.

I was quite pleased with myself for remaining so calm and professional throughout. Pete had really tested my patience, but I had stayed cool and not allowed his attitude to bother me. I'll hold my hands up however, Pete looked a very powerful individual and would no doubt have been a tough Geordie nut to crack.

I looked in the rear-view mirror as we were driving off and I could see my little scouse buddy physically shaking. He was clearly out of his depth and just wanted to get home. Graeme being Graeme saw no danger, he just saw red. He had been ready to spring into action the whole time. I think he was a little disappointed that nothing came of it all. He would not have had the diplomacy to deal with Pete, he would have exploded like a firework if somebody had spoken to him like that.

Although Kenny wanted to go home, we still had a job to do, and I had no intention of travelling back just to make the same trip a day or two later. We pulled in for a quick drink to quench our thirst and he got himself a bit of 'Dutch' courage in the form of a straight double vodka. Our next destination was Pete number two's house.

An hour or so later we arrived at the address and I knocked on the door. To my delight a very welcoming Geordie lady answered. It was lovely to meet someone so friendly. Pete's wife invited us in and made us some coffee. She even sent her kid out to the chippy for us.

She broke the news that Pete had been arrested and charged for conspiracy to supply cannabis. She confirmed all the details of the Dutch guy and told us when Pete was due in court. Really the good lady couldn't have been more helpful. We had all the information we needed and half an hour later we were on our way home with full bellies. We hadn't upset nor injured anybody, and we didn't have some Geordie gangster vying for our blood. We did have the answers that we were looking for however, so on the whole the trip had been a success.

The further down the M1 we got, the more the colour returned to Kenny's cheeks.

If only we had gone to Newcastle Pete's house first. I took the opportunity on the drive home to quiz the scouser on everything I could think of regarding the Dutch drug business:

'How do you get the money to Holland?'

'Does every supplier double the amount if you pay the first half upfront?'

'How do you get cannabis into England?'

The questions flowed all the way home. For me, the journey wasn't long enough, however the colour seemed to have yet again drained from his face by the time we dropped him off. Graeme had been very quiet during the ride back. He also seemed to have been intently listening to everything that was said.

Once the Dutch guy had checked out Pete's wife's story, he then did quite a remarkable thing. He actually sent over some money to help her and her kid through what would clearly be a hard time for them. Obviously, he sent us our money too and that was the last I heard from either of them for a little while. Until one day out of the blue Kenny phoned me asking me how long my driver was going to be because his driver was at the meeting place with the cannabis.

Somewhat puzzled I took a moment before replying, then enquired "who had ordered the cannabis?" To which he replied, "Ashy did on your behalf, 40 kilos wasn't it?"

After a little chuckle to myself I regrouped and told him that I didn't know that Ashy had put an order in and I had recently received 40 kilos from another source. I said to him "when your driver meets with Ashy, make sure he gives him fuck all and tells him to phone me right away."

I knew full well as soon as I heard Ashy's name that he was going to rip them off, but I couldn't grass him up. Ten minutes later Ashy rang me, calling me some very unfriendly names however nothing I hadn't been called a million times before. I was nearly wetting myself with laughter. The thought of him rubbing his greedy hands together, thinking he was getting a big pay day, only to discover that I had rumbled him at the eleventh hour. I pulled myself together and told him not to drag my name through the mud with his nasty little games and with that I hung up on him, still grinning to myself.

My laughter was short lived though as a month or so later I received a similar phone call asking me when I would be paying for the 50 kilos that I had had.

My heart sank. Ashy had done it again and he'd used my name again too.

At that time 50 kilos was worth around £75k. It would have been the easiest bit of graft he had ever done. Realising what had gone on I told Kenny that it was in his best interest to come and see me. In the meantime, I phoned Ashy and this time I wasn't smiling. I went berserk asking why he had ripped him off especially after I had told him not to. He had stuck me right in the middle of it with respectable dealers. Ashy's response was "fuck 'em". He said that the scouser wanted ripping off for being such a slippery cunt.

I suggested Ashy gave the 50 kilos back, but he said he couldn't even if he wanted to as it wasn't even him that had organised the rip, he was simply the driver.

"Well, who the fuck organised it then?" I bellowed at him. His one-word response made my heart sink. "Graeme".

Fucking brilliant. I knew then that Kenny and the Dutchman had no chance of getting anything back. Graeme took a dislike to my mate as soon as he met him. I think he was jealous of him being a young upstart who was already well on his way up the ladder.

Still cursing Ashy, I told him that he or Graeme had better call them up and confess what their intentions were and make it perfectly clear that it had fuck all to do with me. Ashy said it would be a pleasure to tell the cocky fucker that Graeme had had his stuff away.

When Kenny finally came to see me, he looked mortified. Yet again the colour had completely gone from his face, the poor sod actually looked ill.

Associating with me seemed to be taking its toll on him. 'You wanna try being me' I thought to myself.

He explained that he had just received a call from Graeme saying that he would be keeping the 50 kilos because he blamed him for nearly getting us killed in Sunderland by Pete and his boys, and above that he also wanted another 50 kilos or else he would hunt him down and then it would become a hundred kilos more.

When relaying this to me he actually had tears in his eyes. I had to do my best not to laugh. What a pair of cunts Ashy and Graeme were for making a move like that on the poor bloke. The only good news (from my point of view) was that Graeme had made it very clear to him that I had nothing to do with any of it. Obviously, I knew what was coming next though; "Can you help me please Paul?"

I said "listen mate I'm sorry but I'm going to be straight with you. You're talking about the biggest psychopath Manchester has ever seen, it's going to be nigh on impossible to get anything back from him. Let me sleep on it and I'll get back to you".

Overnight I pieced together a beautiful plan, one where I could rise from the shit smelling of roses and with a combined effort, we could get the lost money back. I met Kenny the following day and told him we could recover the missing money, but it would take a couple of months. I said, "As the Dutch guy is your friend, and as I went out of my way to do him a favour, it would be nice if he returned the favour". I said I would be willing to pay for 50 kilos, if the Dutch guy would lay on the same amount, and once I had sold the 100 kilos, we would split the profits. Doing that just a couple of times would recover the lost money and leave me quids in too, I also promised to bung Kenny a few quid for his troubles, but importantly he would save face with the Dutch. On top of that I promised him I would also stop Graeme going after him or another 50 kilos.

Backed into a corner, there were very few other options available to him. He hadn't got that far in the business by being stupid. He was fully aware that I'd seen an opportunity and snatched it, but he also knew I was probably the only man on the planet with a chance of getting through to Graeme. If he didn't take me up on my offer, then he would end up with Graeme preying on *him* and most probably everybody he had loved.

He made one request and that was our deal was to have nothing to do with Graeme. Obviously I agreed and the next day I handed over £35k for 50 kilos of Holland's finest cannabis.

A single kilo in Holland cost £700. Once in England a wholesaler could get between £1.5k to £1.7k for that same kilo. The transport back to England would cost £200 per kilo. So, on top of my £35k, my 100 kilos cost me £20k in transportation. Without any hiccups my £55k would pull in £105k. After paying the outstanding £35k (for the 50 kilos which were laid on) I was looking at £70k profit.

Seventy grand was an unbelievable amount of money back in the nineteen nineties. It quite quickly became clear how my little scouse mate had become such a young self-made millionaire. There was great money to be made at every level of such an operation. I had friends doing armed robberies at that time for half the amount the transport man made, and he was the lowest earner in the chain.

It took little over three weeks from sending my initial £35k to Holland until the time I collected the final bit of money from my customers back in England.

What a result. I was delighted. I had three bags of cash ready for Kenny to collect. One was the money I owed the Dutch guy for the 'laid on' 50 kilos. Another was to contribute to the deficit after Graeme and Asy's little scam, and the third was a further £35k to start the process again.

The third bag was the significant one for me, that third bag indicated a step up in my criminal career. That third bag was the start of a new era in my life, and I was completely fucking buzzing at the prospect.

After several successful operations, the little scouse git gave me some bullshit story about how the transport man had quit, saying he had earned enough money and didn't want to push his luck. There was apparently nobody to replace him, therefore no more trips and subsequently no more drugs.

The money that Graeme and Ashy had scammed had been long since recovered, so basically, I was given the elbow. I felt like letting Graeme loose on the slippery little cunt.

The silver lining, however, was obviously that I had made some great money, and more importantly I'd acquired a good level of understanding about how the drugs business worked in Holland at that higher tier. I knew that was the level I needed to be operating at. I had to find a new connection and fast.

Chapter 17:

"TERRY'S DEAD"

Ant Farnworth was one hell of a colourful character, often seen speeding around Manchester in his soft top, 911 Porsche, usually with a 10/10 bird by his side and usually with her tits out for all to see. Some people considered him to have the perfect job, taking photos of half-naked women for a top selling newspaper. For that reason, as well his charm, his good looks, and also as he had plenty of cocaine on him at all times, that he was happy to share, he always seemed to be surrounded by an abundance of beautiful women.

He once starred in a porno film, which landed him one of his nicknames; 'The Porn Star'. His other nickname was 'The Snowman' which the ladies liked to call him.

Ant would only ever go to high class clubs and bars, often with his best mate Robin Reid. Robin, better known as Robbie, was a world middle-weight champion boxer, once known as the best looking boxer in Britain. Ant and Robbie were a pair of party animals and wherever they went friends followed. The girls swarmed around them like bees. The two of them were well known as a team and there aren't too many swanky gaffs in the country that they haven't partied in. Robbie didn't need any introductions, being a world champion boxer, and Ant was far from bashful when it came to mingling with the stars.

Going out with them felt like I was escaping the violence of Manchester and I knew I couldn't have invited Graeme along. Firstly, he would have got a thrill out of scaring the shit out of 'the spice boys', and secondly he was extremely jealous of Ant. Ant in turn felt very uneasy in Graeme's company. In fact, the only time I ever saw him looking uneasy was when Graeme was around.

There was one exception to that though. One time Ant came to see me, while Graeme was with me, but on that occasion, he wasn't the source of Ant's discomfort.

We were sat enjoying a lovely meal in a popular establishment in town called Johnsons. I was surprised to see Ant and Robbie turn up, especially seeing Ant, who usually looked a million dollars with his fancy clothes and jewellery, looking more like one of my brothers - a Salford scruff bag.

Realising there was a problem I asked him what was up?

At first, I couldn't get any sense out of him. He was talking at a hundred miles an hour, all frantic and rambling. I ordered him a drink to calm him down and once he had he stopped shaking he began to make some sense.

Ant told me that he had paid a girl from Salford to model for him. Halfway through the shoot her boyfriend stormed through his door, beat him up and stole his jewellery. He then demanded £15k in cash and said if he didn't get it, he would be back to kill him. At that point of the story Graeme burst out laughing "That's hilarious" Graeme hollered, holding his stomach to stop him from spitting his mouthful of pasta all over the table. Ant looked like he was going to cry.

I asked who the lad was, and he said the fellas name was Terry Farrimond from Salford, but he didn't know anything else or have his phone number. He informed me that Terry wanted the money to be dropped off at the Salford McDonalds car park at 3pm later that day, and that he would be waiting in a black BMW.

"You're in a bit of deep shit," I told Ant. I'd heard of Terry and knew he was a dangerous character whose threats shouldn't be taken lightly. "It's a problem that won't just go away, so it needs to be resolved," I said.

Most of my life I have mixed with gangsters like Terry, and I know how they tick. He wouldn't give a flying fuck about a street fighter like me or a psychopath like Graeme or even a world champion boxer like Robbie. He wouldn't have any fear of anyone who could throw a punch because he lived and worked in a world of guns. He wouldn't be capable nor stupid enough to go toe to toe with us, but he simply didn't need to.

I offered to meet Terry instead and promised to keep it diplomatic. I thought I would simply offer him an apology on Ant's behalf for having taken photographs of his naked girlfriend without his permission, whilst trying to assure him that there was nothing sexual in it. Ant has seen a thousand fannies and it was just a job to him. For Terry's inconvenience I thought I would suggest that he keep the jewellery but inform him that Ant hadn't got fifteen grand to give him.

I believed it was a fairly amicable solution. Asking him for the jewellery back would have been foolish as it would have undermined and provoked him.

We all went down to the McDonald's at 3pm. We were sitting around chatting when I saw a black BMW pull up across the road. I got out of the car and started to walk over to Terry to offer him my solution. Someone in the car obviously recognised me, and before I got close enough to speak Terry wound his window down and shouted, "I'll show you that". Then with two fingers held like the shape of a gun, gestured firing at me. The car then sped off.

Brilliant, I thought, so much for best laid plans.

The situation had clearly deteriorated, and I was now in the firing line, quite literally. Figuring that Terry would no longer give a fuck about Ant (until he had dealt with me anyway) I had to make

179

my next move pretty swiftly. I made some calls and managed to get Terry's parents' address.

Me and Graeme visited their house, and his father answered the door. Politely I asked him if he knew where Terry was. He informed me that he may be at his sister's house, and he offered up her details to us. I then gave him my phone number and asked him to tell Terry to phone Paul Doyle, if he saw him before we did. Graeme then added "Or the next time you see your son he'll be in a body bag'". I glared at Graeme in absolute amazement and disgust. Why the fuck did he have to say that? I quickly apologised for Graeme's remarks and told him that he had nothing to worry about, and with that we left.

The only person home at Terry's sister's was a TV aerial man. I asked if he'd seen Terry and he said no. I asked him if he would do me a favour and pass on a message from us. In a flash Graeme grabbed the bloke by the scruff of his neck, pinned him up against a wall and hit him flush in the mouth with a big right hand, clearly breaking the poor bloke's jaw. I pulled Graeme away from him immediately. Occasionally when we ask for 'a message' to be passed on we demonstrate the message, so there are no crossed wires as to our intentions. In this case however the poor guy was simply a member of the public who didn't even know Terry or his family. The situation was going from bad to worse, and I was starting to wonder if Graeme was purposely trying to cause more trouble for Ant. If he was, then he was obviously overlooking the fact that I was also in it up to my eyeballs. I had had enough. I called it a day and told everyone we'd catch up the following morning.

That night I decided to chill out with my family, it had turned into a stressful day and I simply wanted to put my feet up and forget all about it. As I was doing my best to put the day behind me, the phone rang. Massey was on the other end saying he was with Terry and would I have a word with him. Terry was clearly a little shook up and asked me what was going on. Firstly, I apologised for Graeme's behaviour and assured him that when we set out looking for him, I hadn't intended on things turning out how they had. I then finally got a chance to explain that Ant was a professional and he had no sordid intentions with Terry's missus. I told him that I understood how he felt and that he had every right to keep the jewellery. The money wouldn't be paid however, as Ant didn't have it.

Luckily, Terry was actually one of the more understanding, dangerous criminals that I've come across and he was prepared to forget about the fifteen grand on the condition that Ant stayed well away from his missus. I gave him my word and that brought an end to it, I could go back to selling cannabis and Terry could continue robbing banks, happy in the knowledge we didn't have to keep looking over our shoulders (no more than normal anyway). As for Ant, he didn't need to worry about owing a violent gangster £15k and the lucky fucker was free to continue taking pictures of naked women too…. just not Terry's.

A job well done, or so I thought.

The next morning Ant and Robbie came to my house. Ant had tears in his eyes. I presumed he had had a sleepless night worrying about everything.

I was just about to tell him to unclench, because the matter was resolved when he started blubbering like a baby. "Why, Paul why?" he sobbed "Why did you do that? There was no need to kill him. We're all going to end up rotting in jail". To say I was puzzled would be an understatement. "Have you had cocaine for breakfast?" I asked, "I am totally clueless as to what the fuck you're going on about".

Ant started to get hysterical and said, "everybody's talking about it". "About fucking what Ant?" I shouted. "You're starting to get on my tits now, so just spit it out".

For the second time in as many days, my peaceful day went drastically downhill.

"Terry's murder" Ant said.

I had to make myself a coffee to get my head straight. "Terry's dead, how can that be?" If Ant was right, we could well end up rotting in a jail cell.

Without knowing more about what had actually gone on, everything seemed to point to us:

What Graeme had said to Terry's father.

Terry's friends in the car recognising me and presuming that I had a gun.

The TV aerial man getting his jaw broken.

Massey was the only witness to prove that me and Terry had cleared the air, and what judge in their right mind would believe Massey - Manchester's most prolific criminal - if he was to say that Terry had phoned me and cleared the air - but from Massey's telephone, not his own.

I knew straight away we would all be getting arrested for Terry's murder. The only thing I could do, unbelievably, was to tell the police the truth. I told Ant and Robbie exactly what had happened and that I had nothing to do with Terry being murdered. I realised just how bleak things were when I could see that even they didn't believe my story.

Graeme decided to visit London for a little look at the sights. At best he was going to get nicked for GBH. Robbie was arrested, as was Ant, who was dragged out of bed in his leather underpants.

I handed myself in with a solicitor.

Ant and Robbie were arrested for conspiracy to murder. I was arrested for murder.

We were all put in cells next to each other, which was a common ploy by the police, as they hoped criminals would talk about their case while they were waiting, and the police would listen in.

Just before my first interview I heard a detective say to Robbie "We know neither you or Ant would murder anyone but that evil bastard in that cell there would". They clearly wanted to pin Terry's murder on me.

In the interview room I asked the detective why he had said that to Robbie. He looked into my eyes and said, "Because we've been waiting for this for a long time, and we've got you now Doyle". I couldn't help myself and I barked back at him "Fuck you, you bent bastard, you know it wasn't me you cunt".

After five interviews they started to become downhearted. My responses stayed the same every time. How could they change when they were the truth? The coppers realised they were getting nowhere but weren't ready to give up. They took me to court to request more time to interview me. They would have loved to have put me away for a very long time, just to get me off the streets. Even when their extended time ran out, instead of letting me go, they moved me to Preston police station over a stupid driving offence. It was all mind games to try to break me.

Upon arrival at the station there were two old coppers sat at the charge desk. One asked me if I would like a coffee before I got put in the cell for the night. I told him that would be lovely and one of them then brought in not only my coffee but also some biscuits. He sat down next to me and asked, "Did you kill the guy Paul?" Before I could respond the other copper started laughing. He said "Jesus I've seen the lot now. We've had our best detectives on him for days and he's not budged an inch, and you think you're going to get a confession with a cup of coffee and some Rich Tea biscuits". Even I started laughing. The poor old bloke huffed and puffed a little and walked out with his tail firmly between his legs.

Whilst in the holding cells at court the next day, waiting to be called up for my alleged driving offence, a bloke came in who looked and smelt every bit like an undercover copper. He tried to make conversation with me, asking me what I'd been arrested for. I told him I had done some serious damage to an undercover copper who was trying to set me up. Seconds later the cell door opened, and he was pulled out. It's the oldest trick in the book, put an undercover copper or a police informer in a cell with you then the twat would say you had confessed all to him.

After court I was set free. The police had held me for days, but they had nothing. I walked out of there a relieved man, nonetheless. I have known many people that have been stitched up for crimes they never committed, and it was by the grace of God that I wasn't added to that list.

Eventually after breathing heavily down my neck for the following few weeks, the police finally turned their attentions to somebody else over Terry's untimely death. I believe someone is still in prison for his murder today and unfortunately Terry goes on the list as another young man who never completed his journey through life. My heart went out to his father. I wish I could have taken back what Graeme had said to him that day.

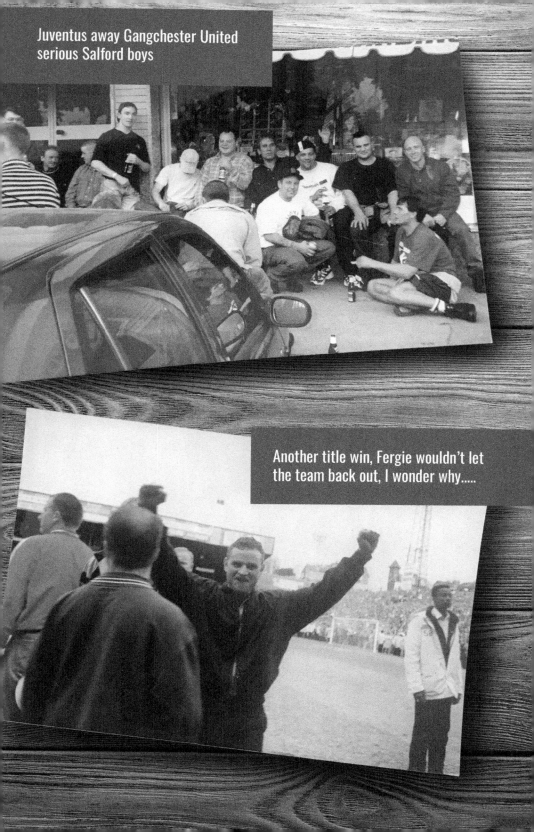

Juventus away Gangchester United serious Salford boys

Another title win, Fergie wouldn't let the team back out, I wonder why.....

Graham (far right) joining Salford's unwashed on a jolly

Night out with the original wing commander (Utd's real top man)

A lovely Jewish family get together

No need to pay for security
when you have pals like mine

Alex Polanski (left), notorious Manchester hard man and a very clever friend on the right

I don't know who gave me more grief, Jeanette or Graeme? RIP pal.

A lot on my mind.........

Chapter 18:

GOING DUTCH

had a great working and personal relationship for many years with somebody called Tom. Tom is a businessman-come-criminal. He's an exuberant character who's always willing to add a little bullshit to his 'real life crime' stories for added effect. The truth is though he has been involved in a lot of serious organised crime and knows some seriously organised players. Deep down despite his criminality he is a lovely guy and actually a bit soft. Occasionally when I told Tom some of my own genuine stories - which tend to involve a degree of violence - he would come out in a sweat just picturing the scene.

He is a very clever man and the best in the business at identity theft. If you want a bent mortgage Tom's your man. A fake passport, a driving license, be it in your own name or someone else's, see Tom. Big time drug smugglers throughout Europe use him to set up warehouses in England. The man could fraudulently set up just about anything you could desire.

Setting up a warehouse isn't simple. You need to have a company that has been trading at least three years and is VAT registered. It needs bank records in the form of a business account. That all needs to be set up in somebody else's name (which is where the identity theft comes into play). Setting up such companies is not cheap, and it could take up to six months to complete.

Once up and running such warehouses could be used to send merchandise to. Inside the genuine cargo would be your hidden extras, guns, drugs, money etc. Shipments would often be sent from Holland to a British recipient company, that should be based outside of hotspot areas such as London, Manchester or Liverpool. Those great cities are red light zones for customs officials to look out for. The legitimate cargo shouldn't be too cheap and it's handy to know what's selling well at the time of transport, that helps to put the odds in your favour for getting the shipment safely through customs. Tom offers all the advice and logistics as part of his excellent service.

Graeme came around to my house one day all excited saying he had landed us a job from Tom. The job was for a big-time drug smuggler in Holland. The Dutch smuggler wanted us to go to Kent to scare a bloke (who owned his own car sales business) into coughing up £200k that he owed. The car salesman had 'bailed' £200k worth of drugs (taken them on loan) and had not coughed up the money in the agreed time. The Dutch gangster had asked specifically for us because he had heard of our reputation in dealing with such matters. The proposed offer was that we got £12k up front, just to scare the shit out of the guy, and if he paid the £200k we would get another £40k. Those figures were well above the going rate in the nineties and it sounded too good to be true. Graeme was adamant, however, that it was legitimate and said Tom had the first installment waiting for us.

"OK Graeme", I said, "let's go round to Tom's and get the £12k, but I bet you he comes out in a cold sweat if we mention the additional £40k".

When we arrived, I was surprised to find that the job appeared genuine. Tom gave us £12k the minute we got through the door, as if it was fuck all. I was impressed, but I couldn't figure out why this guy was prepared to pay way over the odds for us just to scare somebody. I put it down to the guy in Holland being minted and not understanding the going rate in the UK.

I got straight into Tom for some more info on the contact in Holland. I also asked him if he could get the contact to sort us out with some cannabis. Tom said that his friend had already expressed an interest in meeting the pair of us, but he wanted this job done first. No wonder Graeme was excited, I became excited too. There was potential for a nice little bit of business and all we had to do was scare some car salesman into pissing his pants, for £12k that was already in our pockets.

As horrible as it sounds, I am experienced at putting pressure on people to do things that they really don't want to do. It's just routine for me, it had been my bread and butter for years. Me and Graeme both had a gift for that kind of work, and if I'm honest we often found it good fun. So, couple that with a decent payout, along with a potential new source for Dutch cannabis, and you can understand why I found myself smiling from ear to ear as we left Tom's house.

Driving home Graeme asked me when we should go. I said, "tomorrow at 3am", to which Graeme raised an eyebrow. I told him I was taking a lady friend to Old Trafford for the United match, so I needed to be back sharpish. Graeme smirked, winked and agreed.

We set off in Graeme's car at 3am the following morning. It took us three hours to get there so there was even time for a nice bit of breakfast before we took care of business. Upon arrival at the car forecourt, we were greeted by a young lady who told us her boss/the owner would be arriving in 30 minutes. We told her we would just take a look at the cars on offer until he arrived. There were lots of them too. Many nice Mercedes and BMWs. I spotted a red BMW that I fell in love with right away.

Half an hour later the owner arrived as promised and came rushing over to us, convinced he had the first sale of the day, before he'd even sat down. He introduced himself and started with his smooth talk about the cars. He asked us if we had seen a particular one that we fancied. I said "Yes, I like the look of the red BMW on the forecourt, so can we go into the office and have a chat". He took us inside, along with some other smooth, bullshit talking salesman and he sat down behind his desk. I said, "right lads let's not talk about the car just yet". I then pointed to the owner, telling him to knock the smarmy fucking smile off his face. He opened his mouth to speak, and I told him to keep it shut at all times, while I was talking.

"You owe my friend in Holland some serious money" I continued. Then I gestured to the other guy and asked who the fuck he was and if he owed any of the money. No surprise - he said he didn't and that he was just a salesman. I told Graeme to bitch slap him because I didn't like the look of him. Within seconds the guy was bent over in a corner pleading for Graeme to stop slapping him. Being soft hearted in my old age I told Graeme to leave him for the time being and ordered the little cry baby to dry his tears and get me a nice coffee with two Sweetex, before I unleashed Graeme again.

The bloke who did owe the money had already gone as white as a ghost. I turned to him and said, "I've come a long way to see you". He attempted to speak, and I violently barked at him "how many times do I have to tell you to shut your fucking mouth. The next time you interrupt me I'm going to kill you, right here in this office - do you understand?" He sheepishly nodded his head.

I told him we had come because of the money he owed. "You haven't been answering the phone to our friend in Holland. It's a dangerous game you're playing. If I had my way, I'd kill you now but the guy in Holland wants his money back. Now I'm going to ask you a question and before you answer me, if you give me any bullshit story, or ask for time to pay, I'm going to tell my good friend here to put you in a coma, and it doesn't stop there. My friends around the corner will come in here and take you away to some nearby scrubland, where I will finish you off with a bullet to the brain. So, believe me when I say that the only answer I want is a very simple yes or no".

I gave the guy the scariest look I had in my locker and stepped forward so that my face was inches from his. "Are you going to pay what you owe for the fuckin drugs?"

He squeaked "Yes" in a heartbeat.

I turned back to Graeme and asked him to phone our imaginary lads that were waiting around the corner and tell them they could head home. I then told the guy who was now sweating profusely to "call our friend in Holland as soon as I leave and tell him the good news. That being that you're still alive and are going to pay up".

I then sat back down in my seat and as cool as a cucumber said, "but before you do that, let's talk cars".

I told him that if we had taken him off to the scrubland and killed him, we would have been paid a lot more money by our mutual Dutch acquaintance, so by my reckoning he owed us a favour. I politely asked him if he would get me the keys to the red BMW on the forecourt along with the necessary documents, while I drank my cup of coffee, and then hopefully he'd never have to see us again.

Graeme looked sick as he watched me speeding off towards the M1, in my new £28k BMW laughing my head off. It was the perfect car for me to take my young lady friend to Old Trafford in.

The next day me and Graeme went to see Tom. He paid us the remaining £40k and told us that the Dutch Mr. Big was more than happy with what we had done and wanted to see us both in Holland. He had in fact already paid for our Business Class flights to Amsterdam and a five-star hotel for two nights. Tom said it was well worth us taking him up on his offer as it would be right up our street. I had been meaning to go over to Holland to see if I could buy cannabis anyway and everything pointed to this guy being the right man to buy it from. It seemed a little odd for him going to such great expense to get us there, however as things looked like they were falling into place nicely, me and Graeme thought no more of it and emphatically agreed to go.

I asked Tom what the Dutch guy was like and he informed me he isn't actually Dutch, his name is William and is a man not to be messed with - the type of bloke that you only get one chance with. I gave Graeme a look as if to say 'oh here we go again, another so called untouchable'.

In my mind the aim of the trip, if all else failed, was to buy 50 kilos of cannabis and hopefully get another 50 laid on (like the deal I used to get from my previous Dutch supplier). Obviously, I was looking forward to meeting William too though, as I wanted to hear what he had to say.

We arrived at the hotel, and whilst we were checking in at reception, I spotted a man watching us. He was well built, 6'4" wearing an expensive looking, lightweight suit. He looked like a smart businessman and I gave him a glare as he headed over to us. "Hello gentlemen, I'm William" he said. "I presume you two are Paul and Graeme?" Graeme replied "Oh hello William lovely to meet you. Yes, I am Graeme and my good-looking friend here is Paul". Both of them started laughing, I'm not sure why. William seemed taken aback by Graeme, particularly with the way he spoke. He had received a welcoming glare from me and a load of posh 'Queen's English' from Graeme. What a bizarre team we made.

William was stylish. He was spot on and up to date with his fashion sense and he exuded confidence. He gestured for us to take a seat in the lobby, where we had a coffee and a little chin wag. William made an immediate impression on both of us. He was quite unique, but I couldn't work out how. He was friendly and witty, but something was a little bit different about him. I tried to get straight to the point and find out what we were doing there, but William said he didn't want to talk business just yet. He said he wanted to get to know us a bit first. He arranged to return to the hotel an hour later and take us to a wonderful, quiet restaurant where we could talk more over a lovely meal. He finished his drink and left us to go to our rooms to get ready.

Something was rousing my suspicions about William, but I couldn't put my finger on it. I'd only known the guy for five minutes though, so I put it down to me being out of my comfort zone, and away from my own circle of people. Graeme on the other hand was buzzing with William. He didn't think it was strange that he had gone out of his way to get us to Amsterdam, or that he had paid us over the odds to scare the guy in Kent. Graeme said I was paranoid. He was right, I'm always paranoid. I believe that being a criminal you've got to be paranoid. You have to expect the unexpected at all times. My mind ticks over at a million miles an hour some days.

William picked us up from the hotel in an £100k chauffeur driven Mercedes, looking even more sleek and suave than an hour earlier. As we left the lobby, he regally announced "Today gentlemen we will dine at the best restaurant in Amsterdam". Graeme looked like he could have wet himself with excitement. He had already been taken in hook line and sinker.

Once inside the restaurant we sat down at a table where two other guys were already waiting for us. Both men were Dutch and around 30 years old. William introduced us and explained that we had come from Manchester hopefully to agree on some business. He said that we were friends with Tom and had helped him get the money back from the car salesman in Kent, as we had quite a talent in that type of business. He then started to explain that me and Graeme could sell a lot of cannabis around Manchester and throughout the North of England. The two Dutch men nodded along in acknowledgement to everything that was being said. It was my turn to nearly wet myself with excitement. William seemed to understand exactly why I had boarded that plane and went straight for the kill by putting the wheels in motion.

He turned to me and said, "We have a transport system going to the North West of England every two weeks". I was almost disbelieving of what was being said by that point. I was so impressed; I must have looked like a nodding dog. William knew his game. He was good. "When the transport gets to the warehouse" he continued "it unloads, and we give you three missed calls at the office". "What office?" I amateurishly asked. They all smiled then William said "you go to a public phone box and give us a call from it, so we have that number. That public phone box is then your office for that drop. Once that phone box has had three missed calls in a row, you send your van to the warehouse and pick the drugs up. It's all very nice and simple Paul".

I nodded some more and smiled.

"Now this is very important," William emphasised "As soon as you and Graeme receive the drugs, you will be responsible for them". I asked what quantity of drugs we were talking about to which William replied "450 kilos of cannabis and 250 kilos of speed amphetamine".

I made no verbal response, but my heart started to beat that fast I thought it was going to explode. This bloke was about to make me and Graeme responsible for 700 kilos of drugs worth over £1 million. I was away with the fairies. Numbers were whizzing around in my head. I was trying to do sums, work out profits. I could barely concentrate when William interrupted my thought process.

"You will have two weeks from receiving the drugs until you need to pay for them".

Back in 1992, 700 kilos of drugs was an enormous quantity. I hadn't even begun to think about how long we would get in prison if we got caught. I turned to the other two Dutch guys and said, "I'm not being rude, but could we have two minutes alone with William".

We walked out of the restaurant, so I could feel the fresh air on my face. Then I composed myself before turning to William. "Jesus Fuckin Christ", I said. "We've come over here to see you thinking we may be able to land a deal for 60 kilos of cannabis, half upfront, and you want me to put my name to over a million pounds worth of weed and wizz. I wasn't expecting this at all. I could have a good go at selling the weed in that time frame but as for the speed, all I've ever sold was a couple of kilos here and there. A head's up on your master plan might have been nice".

William started laughing. I was puzzled. I hadn't intended to amuse him. "Compose yourself Paul. What we do is go back inside and tell the Dutch guys that you can happily sell the drugs if not more". I started to feel that puzzled I could have fallen over. Had he not listened to anything that I had just told him?

"I will sell the speed for us Paul, all you and Graeme would have to do is drop it off for me. The cannabis will be of such a high standard that it will start selling itself". Me and Graeme looked at each other. Graeme appeared as bemused as me. He hadn't spoken for the previous five minutes.

"Trust me," Willaim said, and putting his arms around the pair of us, guiding us back into the restaurant.

I walked back to the table attempting to put a genuine smile on my face, and said to the Dutch guys, like a robot, "We can sell that, if not more". The words were falling out of my mouth. "I will get an address to a warehouse from Tom, and you have my word that two weeks after receiving the drugs I'll give Tom all the money for him to process for you. But please", I continued like a pro "don't send me any rubbish gear". The Dutch guys smugly exhaled and said, "we have the best cannabis in Holland and we make the best speed ourselves here in Amsterdam - it will all be top quality".

"Well, my friends", I said "we will take your word on that. Let's hope you can get the drugs to Manchester so I can do my work". I reached across the table and we shook on the deal. Graeme looked completely dumbfounded as to what was going on, then awkwardly smiled at me, as if to say, 'Paul I hope you know what you're doing'.

The two Dutch guys said, "let's hope we do long business together". They stood up and said their goodbyes to me and Graeme and went outside with William for a chat. When William returned, he had a new bounce to his step. He was clearly a very pleased man. "I'm going to make you two millionaires," he beamed. "The Dutch are sending the drugs before the end of the month, so let's order some champagne to celebrate". Right away I said I would just have a coffee, but William refused that. "No Paul tonight you're having the finest champagne and a fantastic meal and it's all on me". He shouted across the restaurant "Get me and my friends the finest champagne and the best steaks in Amsterdam and at the double good sir"

I couldn't help but laugh. I didn't want to let the side down either, so I indulged in the champagne too. It was the first time I had been drunk in years. I had known William for all of a couple of hours and he had me agreeing to over a million pounds worth of drugs and drinking champagne. The man clearly had a way of getting what he wanted. My paranoia seemed to dissipate in his company.

In reality and with the gift of hindsight what William had done was manipulate me and Graeme into a very large deal without allowing us any time to really consider it. William had secured a top result out of the two Dutch guys. They were laying on a ton of drugs every two weeks, which we later found out, was earning William three million pounds a month (back then you could probably have bought Manchester City for that amount of money). The person responsible for all the drugs though was essentially me. Graeme was still too wet around the ears to be handling anything more than a few boxes (kilos), so I had all the hard work to do.

I had to arrange picking the drugs up from the warehouse, then splitting them up and distributing the cannabis to my customers, not to mention dropping 250 kilos of speed to William's designated collection point. In those days no one paid for drugs up front, so you had to give your customers 10 days before going back to collect your money. I really had my work cut out. Fortunately for me, half of Britain wanted to get stoned in the nineties.

It had been a long day and the champagne was quickly having an effect on me. Graeme had pointed out that William was off his tits on coke, and he looked like he could have stayed up all night. The restaurant started to empty, and I was ready for bed. Eventually we decided to leave. William paid the bill which had crept to well over £2k. The restaurant ordered us taxis and we agreed to meet at our hotel the following day.

For William it was just another day at the office but for me it was the biggest deal I'd ever made. I was worried I may have jumped into the deal too soon. Had I done my usual thing of being simply too aggressive, as I am with everything?

There was no doubt in my mind that William had given me and Graeme the biggest chance of our criminal lives. He had opened the door to the Premier League of drug running and I had stepped through it without so much as a glance over my shoulder. I started telling myself that any career criminal would have done the same thing. I was feeling confident that I could sell the cannabis, so I got myself into bed and tried to sleep. The room was spinning though. The £300 bottles of champagne were coursing around my body and messing with my head. Eventually I fell asleep, still trying hopelessly to work out how many customers I had and who else I could sell to back home.

Chapter 19:

A WHOLE NEW WORLD

Despite a stinking hangover, I was still up bright and early. I'd spent that many years in prison during the course of my life, I was used to being an early riser. Graeme finally woke and we went down to meet William for a much-needed coffee.

William asked how confident I was that I could sell the cannabis. I told him I was, but we hadn't really spoken about prices and obviously the price had to be right. When he told me I would be getting the cannabis £300 cheaper per kilo than anyone else in England I felt my hangover start to lift straight away. He reiterated that he would have his customer lined up for the speed, before he went on to tell us that he had done his homework on the pair of us. William said he was aware of our connections across the North of England and had checked us both out prior to meeting us. "I had to make sure I could trust you", he said. "As I told you both last night, as soon as you receive the drugs you will be responsible for them and since meeting you in person, I am happy you will do as you have promised. I need to tell you something though...."

William paused and looked seriously at the pair of us. "I have not got this far in life by being a soft touch" he said. "If you run off with the drugs, we will find you and we will kill you. It's not nice for me to have to say these things, but I must make it very clear what my position is". He then reached into his jacket pocket and pulled out a polaroid. "This is how you will end up if you cross us". The image was of a person's head on a plate. The severed head had also had its nose and ears cut off. Looking at it I felt my hangover kick back in.

"Walk straight and we'll go a long way together, walk crooked and you will end up looking like a pig". I looked William right in the eye and said "I don't walk crooked nor am I scared of dying. Put your picture away, we get the message". William's response was cold and cool: "Paul I like you, I'm not scared of dying but there are a million ways that I would really not like to have to die". Me and Graeme both simultaneously laughed out loud. I actually wanted to stand up and clap. I put out my hand and once more we shook on our deal. The 'nasty' chat was over, and we got down to the finer details. I was however left wondering what type of man has a picture of a severed head in his wallet. I have a picture of my beautiful wife and children. I did start to consider how many psychopaths I was likely to end up working with during my lifetime.

William started explaining some working practices to us. "We use codes" he said. "You must learn them".

When dealing with such quantities of drugs it is obviously important to try to stay one step ahead of the old bill. The codes William and his Dutch crew used were simple but effective. For instance, when discussing money on the phone, for every thousand pounds you would just say £1. If it was £10k you would therefore say £10.

If you needed to pass on a phone number, over the phone or in writing, it would be done using letters.

Firstly you needed to agree on a 10-letter word, where no letter was repeated twice. For example, 'COALMINERS'. The C would stand for a 1, the O would stand for a 2, the A would be a 3 and so on. If the phone number was 08771 659 219 then you would write down SENNC IMR OCR.

If you needed to write down a debt list for a customer that owed you money, you would write the figure using symbols made up from the lines of a noughts and crosses grid. We used the letter Z as a zero:

$$\frac{1|2|3}{4|5|6}$$
$$7|8|9$$

So £250,360 would be UOZLCZ

I was taken aback by it all. It was a whole new world for me. It was like a re-birth in villainy.

Back in Manchester being a criminal had been getting dull and depressing. It was all about violence. Just because I had experience in the field, it didn't mean that it was what I wanted from life. I had grown fed up with it. The new Dutch adventure was much more exciting. William had obviously done his homework and realised me, and Graeme had already earned our stripes on the violent streets of Salford, Manchester and the North West of England, and he saw in us an opportunity to get his drugs out in droves without too much concern about being ripped off by anyone.

In the early nineties Manchester was really making a name for itself. It was more like Chicago in the USA than it was a city in England, newspapers had started to refer to it as Gunchester. There were over fifty organised gangs operating in and around Manchester and Salford. Moss side was more like the Ok Corral with shootings taking place on a daily basis.

The police couldn't handle the fact that gangs became more organised, more professional. It was a big problem for them. Manchester had overtaken Liverpool as the crime capital of Britain. The nightlife was unbelievable too, the best outside of London.

Over the years I had developed good working relationships with most of the criminal gangs in Manchester, which meant I could supply them with their cannabis. Just as importantly I had a lot of experience in dealing with high-ranking gangsters and my reputation meant I was respected by a lot of them. I also had countless football hooligan connections throughout the country and many of them were knocking out decent amounts of weed as well. William already knew all of this and he knew we were the right men for the job.

In the taxi back to the airport I remember thinking that it had certainly been a few days out of the ordinary for me and Graeme. I had been drunk for the first time in years, we had secured a multimillion-pound drug deal with two of Amsterdam's biggest cannabis suppliers, we had stayed in one of the countries poshest hotels without upsetting anybody and Graeme had gone almost a whole week without knocking anybody out. Not to mention the gruesome image we had witnessed of some poor guy's head on a plate. As weeks go, it really did stand out.

I was eager however to get back to Manchester. I had work to do, and I needed to get on with it as professionally as I knew how.

As soon as I got off the plane, I started phoning my customers, telling them that it was in their best interests to come and see me. The next day I had about ten meetings. Nobody could believe the price I could supply their cannabis for. The orders came flooding in, so fast that it was all sold before I had even received it. I couldn't have hoped for a better start.

Me and Graeme then went to see Tom to get the address for the warehouse. Over a coffee I was telling Tom about the meeting with two Dutch guys and the photo of the head on the plate. Tom said he had known the decapitated lad well before he met his bloody end. He also told us that William took the picture himself. I was shocked. "What kind of a man would do that?" I asked. Tom smiled and shrugged like he knew something we didn't. He again warned us not to get on the wrong side of William. I had a horrible feeling I had just stepped into a world of murderers and deeply troubled misfits. "Forget about all that murderous shit" I said, "I've promised my customers they will have cannabis, so let's sort the finer details, then give crazy William a call".

Tom came with us to phone William. We drove five miles out of town to an 'office'. Whilst I was on the phone to him, he informed me that the transport was on its way. William said he would phone back on the number we were using on Monday morning. "Three missed calls" he reminded us. "So, make sure nobody else uses that phone box".

We then went to the warehouse where Tom explained who we would meet when the goods arrived. Everything was starting to fall into place. It was exciting and really did feel like it could be a new beginning for me, with no more need for violence.

When Monday morning arrived, I sat on guard, outside the office extra early, making sure I didn't miss the calls, and also that nobody else got to use the telephone. When the calls came in, I had the feeling of a soldier going into battle. I felt determined, organised and prepared. I sent my driver to the warehouse and sensed it was going to be a special day.

An hour later I received a call saying the guy in the warehouse was going mad.

So much for being prepared. There were 8 pallets full of computer parts to dispose of. A Transit van was never going to do the job. I had to get a wagon and get down there myself as fast as I could. All of a sudden, I felt out of my depth again. How stupid had I been thinking the drugs would simply be ready to load into a van. I hadn't considered how disguised they would need to be to get through customs. The only place I could go through 8 pallets of computer parts and sift out the drugs was back at my own salvage yard. It was far from an ideal situation, but it had to be done.

It took well over three hours just to get the drugs out of the boxes. Then I had to count and double count to make sure the numbers were right. I had 70 sport bags ready to put 10 kilos into each bag. At the time I had a cracking tipper truck. To all intents and purposes, it appeared to be simply any old pick-up truck and you wouldn't know it had a tipper on it. I had a secret compartment under the bed, so once the tipper was up, I could hide three sports bags at a time inside, which meant that my driver could drop 30 kilos to each customer. 30 kilos was the perfect amount - You never put all your eggs in one basket just in case something goes wrong. If a customer was paying up front however, they could have as many kilos as they wanted.

By the end of the day all the cannabis was gone. It's quite incredible how much work is involved in ensuring the British public can sit back and have a nice smoke of an evening. I had no time to sit back and relax though. I had to get William's share of the speed to a safe house and the remainder down to a contact in Birmingham, all before getting back to the yard to burn the computer parts, leaving no trace of how the drugs had been smuggled into the country.

At the end of what was a very long day, I finally breathed a heavy sigh of relief. It had been an emotional rollercoaster, but it had eventually worked out right.

News soon spread about the quality and quantity of the drugs that I could get. Lots of my old friends were envious but it was my time to shine, and they just had to grin and bear it. A few days after my first haul I went to the office to phone William. I was ready to boast about how well things had gone and tell him I couldn't wait for the next lot. He, however, wasn't in the mood for listening. Something was clearly wrong and he demanded that me and Graeme got over to Amsterdam right away. "I can't explain now, but it's vitally important that you get over here" he said. I told Graeme, and he was thrilled to be going back. I was more concerned about what it was that he needed us for so urgently.

As soon as we landed in Amsterdam we were picked up by William. He immediately gave us both a handgun and began driving us to some small town just outside Hilversum in Northern

Holland. On the journey there he explained that he was in the middle of a drugs war. I was sitting in the back of the car going completely under. Just as it was looking as though I could get away from a life of violence, I found myself being driven to a war with a gun in my hand, and what made it worse was that it wasn't even my war. I was in Holland for fucks sake. I was never one for going to church but I had a horrible feeling that day that somebody up above had chosen a path for me, and I would not be able to escape from it. During that car ride across Holland, I started to resign myself to the fact that I would never get away from a life of violence. However, as I was about to get into a gun fight, I realised it wasn't the best time for me to be getting all emotional and philosophical. I needed to toughen up and more importantly show no weakness.

When we arrived William simply told us to watch his back. "If anyone makes a move, shoot them" he said. I had to laugh to myself. I'd been in the country for an hour and I was already being asked to shoot some cunt.

There were six Moroccan guys waiting for us in a room of a warehouse and William started arguing with one of them straight away and the situation became extremely tense- it was playing out like something from a movie. I tried to hold back my excitement, but when one of the Moroccans glared at me with a face full of hatred, I found myself raising my gun and pulling the trigger before I had even thought it through.

A classic shootout followed. I was walking forward like I had a bulletproof vest on. They were shooting as they were running. I surprised myself - nevermind William and Graeme. I walked over to the first guy that I had shot. He was lying on the floor crying, begging me not to kill him. I was stood over him with the gun raised when William shouted, "Paul let's go before the police come". In that moment I snapped out of my trance and I was back in the real world. It was as if madness had taken over me for a brief spell, but during that spell, however brief it was, I had wreaked havoc with a handgun. It appeared I had accepted who I was and I wasn't going to get away from it. It actually felt liberating.

We scrambled into William's car and he drove off as quickly as he could.

"What the fucking hell was that Paul?" Graeme yelled at me in a slightly less posh tone than I was used to hearing from him. William laughed and said, "Fuck it, it's done now and they had it coming to them anyway". He then said we would have to stay in Holland for a little while in a safe house, until things calmed down.

When we got to the safe house we settled in and William began to explain the troubles he was having. He told us he had killed one of the Moroccan gang members the week before and that everything had spiraled after the killing. Over the next few days and after a few more discussions with William I began to realise that the world we had entered into was far from a pleasant one. Nobody could be trusted. Everybody was wearing diamonds but they were all vicious thugs deep down. I was starting to get depressed again at the thought of all the violence. I was clearly at a point in my life where part of me wanted to turn my back on it, but I had unwittingly opened the door to even more of it and that still excited me. I didn't know which way to turn.

After three days in the safe house I told Graeme I had had enough and wanted to go home. I needed to get back and prepare to collect in my drug money anyway. All my life I had dreamt about getting to the top of the criminal underworld, imagining it to be glamorous. It was turning out to be a case of 'be careful what you wish for'.

On the fourth day I set off home. Graeme stayed on to watch William's back. They had another meeting with the Moroccans a few days later. It was in a cafe in a department store by Amsterdam Square. Such a busy public place was the only way that they could ensure no guns would be brought to the table.

Chapter 20:

TRUE COLOURS

Back in Manchester all I did that week was count money, I must be the only Jew to ever say it, but it did my head in, it was relentless. I had never seen so much money. It literally took me all day to count. I drove the cash over to Tom's the next day, where the bastard made us count it again. Luckily, he had cash counting machines, which made life a whole lot simpler. Once he was happy it was all there, he organised sending it to William.

The second load of computer parts came in. This time 800 kilos of cannabis. William told me that as the amount was increasing, they had decided to separate the shipments of cannabis and speed. One week the cannabis would come in, the following week the speed would arrive.

Again no sooner had the cannabis arrived it was gone. My customers' demands were increasing. They were all starting to ask for more. The second delivery of speed was apparently not raved about quite so enthusiastically, but that was fuck all to do with me, so generally everybody was happy.

Graeme was loving life in Amsterdam as William's sidekick. God only knows what those two were getting up to on a daily basis.

After my second lot of money came in for the cannabis, I again counted it up and paid Tom a visit. Upon arrival Tom said we had to go over to Amsterdam to meet William and the Dutch guys. He knew no more than that but we were booked on a flight the next day. The money coming in was obviously great but hopping on and off planes to and from Amsterdam was already starting to become a bit of a ball ache.

On the flight over Tom was telling me all sorts of stories about William; how he had killed at least 30 people, how he would often make his victims suffer, torturing them if necessary, rather than just giving them the privilege of a bullet. I told Tom I thought it was difficult to believe, but the severed head on the plate had been an eye opener. He then said something quite disturbing to me. He explained that William was not in it just for making money. He said he loved the life, the violence, the killing, the power. He got a buzz out of it all. The more drama the better.

Tom basically described William as a cold-blooded serial killer, who lived for what he did. He also said the police in the UK were well aware of him and wanted to talk to him about at least one murder on British soil.

Again I could feel the frown lines on my forehead. Something just wasn't right about all this. 'What is it that I'm missing?' I thought to myself. I suspected something with William was awry on day one, but never imagined it on the scale that Tom explained it to me. Surely he was exaggerating the facts, probably more of his bull shit stories. I couldn't be sure what was true and what wasn't, but my defenses were up and I was not about to start taking any stupid chances.

The day before we arrived Graeme had received the keys for his own apartment in Amsterdam central. He was happy as Larry over there. Myself and Tom had been booked into a hotel by William. I however insisted that me and Tom went to see Graeme before going to the hotel.

Upon arrival at Graeme's swanky Amsterdam pad I pulled him to one side and insisted he got me a gun and furthermore I wanted it every time I visited, from the minute I arrived until the minute

I left. Graeme could tell how serious and concerned I was, so he set off immediately and carried out my request. Me and Tom had a coffee and waited for him to return. I didn't step a foot outside the apartment until Graeme was back and I had my handgun tucked neatly inside my jacket. Tom and I then got a cab to our hotel. On the way I told Tom not to breathe a word about the gun to anybody else and assured him that it was just because of what had happened with the Moroccans the last time I was in Holland.

No sooner had we arrived at our hotel, I spotted the two Dutch guys sitting in the bar area. Clearly they were waiting for us. We went over to say hello, then Tom disappeared off to check us both in. The Dutch guys were obviously businessmen, pure and simple. They just wanted to make money and have an easy life. As soon as Tom had left us alone, they started talking to me about William and expressed some serious concerns that they had about him, mainly regarding his level of violence and the risks that it could bring to their business operations.

"Paul, we know you are doing all the work selling the drugs. We also now believe that we can put our trust in you" they said. "I told you I was a man of my word" I replied. The Dutch then suggested they did business directly with me and cut William out.

Suddenly it dawned on me that there was a strong possibility I was being tested. William could have asked them to say all that to find out if I could actually be trusted. In a split second I made my mind up and I started to laugh out loud. "Come on fellas, do you want me dead" I said. "I can see you are concerned and I can understand that but I cannot screw William out of the deal, any more than I would try to screw you gentlemen over".

My gut instinct told me that the offer was genuine and they wanted William out of the way, but it was too much of a gamble, even for me to take. I quickly moved the conversation along and told them that the speed hadn't been as good the second time around and the first load was much more like what I needed. They informed me that they knew it would be shit as it was no longer off them, it was from the Yugoslavs. They seemed surprised to hear that it was news to me.

I then realised why the arrangement had changed and one week I would receive the cannabis, the next week the speed. William had lied to me. At that moment William and Graeme arrived and the conversation came to an abrupt halt. While William was talking to the Dutch, I was quizzing Graeme about what he had been up to in Amsterdam. Graeme told me one or two crazy stories, including how he had met the boss of the Yugoslavian mafia. He said the Yugoslav boss had asked him and William to collect a million pounds for him.

I discreetly walked Graeme out of ear shot and relayed some of the stories I had been told about William. "Yes, they're all true" he jovially replied. "William told me the same stories himself".

"We're drug dealers" I said to Graeme, "not killers. I'm not happy about all this".

I suggested Graeme kept a very close eye on William. My words seemed to fall on deaf ears though, as by this point Graeme was so excited by Amsterdam and fooled by what William had brought to the table that he couldn't see anything untoward.

"Let's not mess things up just yet, hey Paul" he said kind of reassuringly.

William, Tom and the Dutch went off to a hotel room for a private meeting that didn't concern me and Graeme, leaving us sitting in the bar. While we were there a lad called Pete walked in. Pete was from Birmingham and I knew him as he was selling a lot of the speed for William at that time. Pete joined us and we chatted whilst waiting for the meeting upstairs to finish.

The Dutch guys came down first, they said their goodbyes and told me they would see me again soon and asked me to think about what they had said. It was all I could think about. If it had been a genuine offer then me and Graeme no longer needed William and his murderous ways. For the time being I knew I needed to keep it to myself though.

When Tom and William joined us we all went off to a very high class wine bar. William ordered two bottles of champagne. I refused any and ordered a glass of coke. He asked me to have a drink with them but again I refused. I told him I would watch their backs while they enjoyed themselves. I did like William but I was very unsure about how much we could trust him. He had been very good to me since the day we first met, but for some reason I had an urge to put a bullet in his head. I couldn't explain it, but I knew if I had any champagne it just might have happened - after all Amsterdam was clearly a playground for drug dealers and murderers, where anything went.

As had previously happened the day began to drag. The more William drank, the more coke he snorted and the more bolshy he got. Eventually he started bragging about the murders he'd committed and how untouchable he considered himself. Graeme seemed to be lapping it up. He was roaring with laughter at every joke that he cracked and even applauded at some of the claims William made. I found his manner entertaining but I didn't respect him for his alleged murders and his life certainly wasn't the life I wanted for myself or for Graeme, regardless of the money.

After several hours we made our way to a restaurant for dinner. William burst through the doors like a man possessed and demanded the best table in the place. We were seated in a great spot with a lovely view out, and before long we were tucking into a fantastic meal. All the while however William, Pete and Tom were snorting huge lines of cocaine straight off the dinner table in full view of everybody and anybody.

The restaurant owner eventually came over and sheepishly said "I'm sorry, but if you want to snort coke gentlemen, could you please do it in the toilets, so our other guests don't see". Right away I could see the anger build in William's face and he erupted into a torrent of abuse. "I've spent thousands in this restaurant and will be doing so again tonight. I asked for the best table this evening and you've put me on this one, not the one up there which you know is my favourite". William pointed to a slightly raised table that had already been occupied when we arrived. He then screamed for the other diners to be moved before he moved them himself.

Next to our table was a fish tank which had lobsters in it. Customers could choose the lobsters they wanted to eat from the tank. William started plucking lobsters out of the tank and hurling them at the people around the top table. It must have been terrifying for the other diners, most of whom ran out of the restaurant as fast as they could. None of them made it out faster than Tom though. He had gone completely under when the lobsters started flying around the room and vacated the premises as quickly as his little legs would carry him, probably fearing William may kill somebody.

Being the sober one I felt a sense of responsibility to intervene, but the sight of Tom sprinting out of the place gave me the giggles and I could only sit back, watching and chuckling.

Things then went from bad to worse for the owner, because not only did he have the most aggressive gangster in Amsterdam destroying his business reputation, he was then met with a demand of £50,000 and told he had 24 hours to cough up. William said it was no more than the amount that he had spent in his restaurant over the last month. To further rub salt in the poor bloke's wounds, Graeme, who was bubbling over with excitement, stood up and dropped the guy with a big right hook. He was actually laughing as he punched the guy. It was a Graeme that I had never seen before. Being around William had already started to have an effect on him.

At that point I stood up and ushered everybody out. We went to a bar around the corner where they indulged in more champagne before Pete started saying he wanted some ladies.

'If you want ladies Peter, then we shall have ladies" William roared, before getting up and leading us off to a high-class brothel where he was a member.

Inside the brothel there was a large room with a fancy bar, a huge TV screen and lots of beautiful women. I have never been one to go with working girls, it's just not the way I am. I simply ordered another glass of Coca-Cola and sat watching the girls doing the catwalk on the big screen. William, Pete and Graeme ordered a girl each and went through some doors to another room.

After a minute or so a girl came over to me asking what she could do for me. I said, "nothing thanks I'm just waiting for some friends". Then another came over, then another, all asking the same shit. It had been a long day and it was about two o'clock in the morning, so when the fifth girl came over I told her to "fuck off and leave me alone". The next thing I knew a bouncer came over asking me why I wasn't with a girl. I politely told the guy I was just chilling, waiting for my friends, with a drink I've paid over the odds for, and that I simply don't want a girl.

"You told one of my girls to fuck off" he said, "so now you can fuck off outside and wait there".

I was that fed up of being pestered I simply reached inside my jacket and pulled out the handgun that Graeme had gotten for me. "Is this what you want?" I barked at him in a very menacing way. Screams rang out and within seconds William and Graeme came bursting back through from the other room (Graeme just in his pants and William stark bollock naked).

They had heard the commotion and William rushed at the bouncer screaming for him to get away from me. I slipped the gun back inside my jacket.

Once the bouncer realised that I was one of William's friends he apologised instantly. He then turned to the working girl and slapped her across the face, saying "You silly bitch keep away from this man, he said no".

I ended up feeling sorry for the girl and I gave her a wedge of Dutch guilders as we were leaving. It was a good job I was sober or else I may well have shot him for slapping her, never mind the way he had spoken to me. All in all it had been another crazy day in Amsterdam. When I said it was a playground, believe me it was. Anything went back then. It was an eye-opening City.

The next morning, at breakfast, I asked Tom why he had run off. He told me he didn't want to be there when William killed the owner. I assured him that the bloke had survived, but he would be waking up to a £50,000 headache. Tom believed he had gotten off lightly.

That day I asked Graeme when he thought he would be coming home, but he said he was sticking around to collect the million pounds for the Yugoslavian mafia. After that he might have a few days back in Manchester. I knew Graeme had fallen in love with Amsterdam, but I feared that the two Dutch cannabis dealers were right about William and there may well have already been an operation on us over there, even in those early days. He asked me to stick around and help him and William, but I didn't want to be involved in that side of things. I wanted to get back to selling cannabis in the UK, as we had originally planned.

Before leaving for the airport Graeme told me he was going to arrange for a friend of his, Irish Jerry, to go over to Amsterdam to assist him in watching William's back. William clearly needed watching, as he was making lots of enemies. Irish Jerry was a good friend of Graeme's. He was an ex-boxer, and a pretty tough bloke. I told Graeme to make sure Jerry was on the ball though, because I was worried he may have bitten off more than he could handle, in protecting William. "We'll be fine" sniggered Graeme. "Not as efficient as me and you, but Jerry is a good second choice". I thanked Graeme for the compliment and me and Tom flagged down a taxi to the airport. The whole trip had been no more than William wanting to splash some cash and show us all who was boss. I wasn't overly impressed that I had been dragged along.

Back in England things were much more settled. It was good to be on home soil again. I certainly felt a lot more relaxed back in Salford. I spent a lot of time in 'the office' on the phone to William or Graeme. Some days I would have to phone them five or six times. Then all of a sudden for three days neither myself nor Tom heard from them nor could we get hold of them.

Tom was pulling his hair out with worry, presuming they had been arrested. On day four I got a phone call from Graeme saying he was returning home but he would say no more over the phone. He asked if I would pick him up from Manchester airport that afternoon. I detected something in his voice that I had never heard before. I was curious to find out what had gone on and where he had been for the previous few days, so naturally I agreed to pick him up.

As soon as Graeme walked out into the terminal I saw a changed man. He could barely raise a smile and was visibly distressed. I asked him what was wrong and why they had gone silent for so long. All he told me was that he had collected the million pounds from the guy who owed the Yugoslavian mafia boss and he simply wanted to come home.

He then said he needed me to give him £80k out of the money we owed William for the current batch of cannabis. "Willaim told me to get it off you when I got home. It's my bonus", he said.

"Okay Graeme, sure" I said, "I can get it for you on the way home". Graeme hardly spoke another word to me during the entire half hour journey. I asked him how collecting the Yugoslav's money had gone, but he refused to tell me the story. He simply said, "It's been the maddest few days of my life, but I don't want to go into it now". I could see the anguish in his face. Something was clearly troubling him but I decided not to push it further. I gave him the £80k, but he still seemed downhearted. Something very serious had obviously gone on. I chose my words carefully because Graeme was behaving oddly. As he was getting out of the car I said, "I can see something is haunting you, are you OK mate?" He gave me a look like I had never seen from him before, then simply turned and walked into his house.

I started piecing things together. I figured there was a good chance William had involved Graeme in one of his sick torturous murders. They must have killed the guy to give up the million pounds for the Yugoslav boss. I felt compelled to get to the bottom of it so I drove straight over to Tom's house. I told him about the £80k and how upset Graeme was. I asked him how likely it was that William had to kill the guy for the money. Tom confirmed it was extremely possible, with a sort of defeatist look on his face. He didn't really want to speculate without knowing more though.

A few days later Graeme had relaxed a little and I suggested we went shopping to spend some of our hard-earned money and to get a smile back on his face. During our day out he told me exactly what had happened. I actually physically gasped in horror. What they had done to that poor man was about as nasty and as cruel of a thing as I had ever heard in all my life. He told me that William had tortured the bloke for two days until his body finally gave out.

For William it would have been almost routine, for Graeme however, it was a game changer. It was a whole new level. Graeme said that he felt it was far too risky for him to go back to Holland.

That weekend Irish Jerry also arrived back in the UK. He said I needed to give him £25k of William's money. He also told me that Pete (William's speed dealer in Birmingham) had gone missing. I called William, from the office, on the Monday morning. I had to confirm the arrival of a new shipment of cannabis. Deep down I was fuming with him, but I still had to deal with him on a daily basis, so I played it cool and simply told him I had given the £80k to Graeme and another £25k to Irish Jerry. William replied with an arrogant remark, stating "I treat your friends like they're my own sons". I felt a rage inside me and a desire to snap the arrogant cunts jaw, but I just ignored the comment and continued to discuss business. I ended the call as soon as our work discussion was over.

I had just received a ton of cannabis and 500 kilos of speed for William was due a couple of days later. The value of the speed alone was over £1million. William's man was lined up to collect the speed from me and I was going on about selling my cannabis as usual. Later that week I saw Tom and I ended up totally erupting on him. I felt he was partly responsible for Graeme and Jerry being used by William. He knew all about William long before we ever met him. I demanded that Tom tell me everything he knew about him. I needed to understand why William was so out of control and why he seemingly killed people for fun.

It turned out that there was a lot to tell.

In a nutshell, when living and working in the Costa Del Sol, William had ripped off a large, organised Spanish drug gang to the tune of £1million. He then went on the run from them and ended up living in Amsterdam. He quickly utilised some of his contacts and set up some big business deals with some Dutch drug smugglers. Once he had proven his worth yet again in the narcotics game, by moving some vast quantities of drugs he got working on building himself a small army of protectors.

He needed a gang of dangerous men to keep the Spanish drug lords from killing him, and that is where we came in. Because of our reputation as violent men, mainly due to the door wars in Manchester, William had paid us over the odds to visit the car salesman in Kent and essentially do what we did best, scare the shit out of him. He had then flown us over to Amsterdam, paying for our plane tickets, five-star accommodation and top notch cuisine, simply to impress us and entice us into his world. It was extremely clever the way he manipulated us. He was pulling the strings and the lure of us making such big money clouded our judgement, as did the trust that we had had in Tom.

William wanted to show his enemies in Spain that he had his own firm that were prepared to kill.

News had spread quickly about my midday shoot out with the Moroccans and Graeme and Jerry torturing and murdering people was the icing on his cake. William had reached his objectives. To all intents and purposes he had established a villainous gang of murderers that were protecting him and to all intents and purposes, we were it.

At having all of this confirmed to me I told Tom I had had enough. I asked him to pass a message on to William that once I had collected the money for the cannabis I would drop it with Tom as usual, but I wanted nothing more to do with him. I never have been, nor ever will be, a 'gun for hire' and I wouldn't go around killing people to save some other cunt's skin. I told Tom in no uncertain terms that I was disgusted with him for leading us into a world of savages and murderers, and especially for vouching for William, as he had done.

Having a little rant at Tom, as well as telling him I would no longer work with William was enough to make me breathe a sigh of relief. I knew to expect some kind of a backlash, but in that moment I didn't care. It felt like I had made the first steps to restoring peace in my life, not to mention restoring some kind of order to Graeme's already disturbed mind.

William is to this day one of the biggest serial killers ever born in the UK. You need to be looking at the likes of Harold Shipman to surpass the number of deaths he is accountable for.

His impact on criminality in Europe at the turn of the century was nothing short of astonishing. He manipulated people to help him on his way, then when he no longer needed them, or could no longer use them, he simply disposed of them. Often in the most brutal of ways imaginable.

He has moved tonnes of drugs around Europe, made and ripped off millions of pounds and been behind dozens of murders.

I have never been able to get to the bottom of why his path of destruction wasn't greater in England, but rumour has it that he was wanted for at least one murder and also for blowing up his ex-wife's house, so he fled to the continent.

I wouldn't describe William as a professional gangster, more of a professional killer.

At the time if I had told my friends in England what had been going on in Holland they would never have believed me. It was only because of what happened over the following few months that my stories became credible.

Chapter 21:

THE ULTIMATE DOUBLE CROSS

After my chat with Tom I was expecting a call from William, so I got myself geared up for it. However days passed and the call didn't come. A week or so went by before I returned to Tom's to drop off the money for the cannabis. He told me William had been arrested. He didn't know what for, but he asked me to keep hold of William's share from the cannabis sales, which amounted to two hundred grand. I agreed and left Tom with the rest of the cash.

In the nineties the Dutch police had a skilled unit known as the 'Snatch Squad'. They were a specialised force that worked alongside Interpol. The team would carry out arrests of high-profile criminals, gangsters, murderers and terrorists in Holland. Their tactics were to surprise you, throw a bag over your head and bundle you into the back of a van before you even knew who was snatching you. It was basically a legalised kidnapping. It was a major breach of your human rights that they just wouldn't get away with nowadays.

The beauty of it was that if you were 'snatched' you wouldn't know if it was the police or your enemies that had taken you and often people would start to talk as soon as they were in the van. If however you didn't start spilling your guts out straight away, you would be detained in a high security police station, in solitary confinement. You would be lucky to see a solicitor and could be held there for weeks without any contact with the outside world.

It later transpired that such a police unit had snatched William on suspicion of murder, a shooting in Holland and importation of drugs. To all intents and purposes that should have been the end of William. He was in deep shit. My amazement was beyond belief when I received a phone call from him a few weeks later.

Not only had the Dutch authorities granted him bail they had also deported him to Ireland after giving him the choice of country he wished to reside in.

William cut to the chase and told me that Tom had passed on my message, stating that I no longer wished to work with him. I told him that was correct and once I had given him the £200k that I owed him I didn't want to speak to him again. At that point William's tone changed "No no no Paul" he said. "You owe £1.7 million".

"No no no" I cockily replied. "I have already paid Tom for the cannabis, who in turn had paid the two Dutch associates".

William said he knew that but that he wanted the money for the speed. By that point I was confused and becoming a little bit pissed off. I responded by telling him to stop playing games and that as he well knew, the speed customer was his customer and his responsibility.

Then began his threats "If I was you Paul I would go and speak to Graeme and ask just what I am capable of. When you've done that, phone me back and tell me when I can expect my money".

I phoned Graeme and told him I was on my way to see him. When I got there I repeated the conversation I had. Graeme phoned William immediately telling him he was talking rubbish and asked exactly what game he was playing. William replied calmly saying all he wanted was the money that was owed to him. Graeme started to lose his cool and they got into a huge argument. Threats started to be fired both ways. I couldn't stand by listening any longer, so I took the phone from Graeme. I spoke in a more collected manner and told him that he knew we'd not had the money from his speed, the arrangement right from the start had never changed, he dealt with the speed, I sold the cannabis. "The Dutch have been paid for the weed, and the speed is your responsibility, so fuck off with your mind games because they won't wash with me". William simply replied by saying "the owner of the speed will not be happy when I tell him you don't have his money Paul. Graeme knows who that is as he did some work for him. He is going to want to speak to you both". And with that he hung up.

I turned to Graeme and asked where the speed had come from. He confirmed my suspicions, it was the Yugoslavian mafia's.

My heart sank, as I realised what had happened. The Dutch police had confiscated all of his money, his houses, his cars, the lot. Then they sent him packing to Ireland penniless. Upon release William then must have had the £1.5 million collected for the speed, but kept it for himself, while making up some bullshit story to the Yugoslavs about us collecting the money while he was incarcerated and telling them that we were ultimately responsible for their money.

It wasn't long before I found myself receiving a call from the mafia boss.

He was going mad, shouting and ranting and raving at me. I tried to explain that William was responsible for his money and that he was stitching us both up. He was having none of it though. William was clearly his golden boy. It seemed that his powers of persuasion knew no bounds. He was screaming at me, telling me he wanted his money or else he would kill me.

The call was dragging on and on and we were constantly going over the same ground. I eventually started to get a little bored of his threats and couldn't help but respond with a few cheeky replies.

At one point he told me he was going to put me in a saucepan, to which I politely told him that I didn't think I would fit into a saucepan. He assured me I would - once he had chopped me up. I told him I thought that was a bit nasty.

It escalated to a stage where we were both talking such bollocks that it was almost comical. I bet it was the first time a Yugoslavian Mafia boss had tried scolding a Salford football hooligan. Especially one that had grown bored of listening. I don't consider myself to be exactly razor sharp but I certainly did that guy's head in with my quickfire witty responses, until the point where I excused myself from the 'telling off' and hung up on him.

It soon transpired that William owed more than just £1.5 million for the speed…by all accounts he had stitched Pete up in a similar manner. The major difference between Pete and myself and Graeme, however, was that Pete had already been punished for his supposed betrayal and was a missing person. God only knows what they did to that poor guy. What I am certain of though is that it would not have been deserved.

Obviously, I realised that the death threats were genuine and that Graeme and I could have been on borrowed time, but we didn't have £1.5million quid to give, so we had few options available to us. Also being extorted was never something that we were likely to take lying down. A few more days passed before I heard from William again. When the call eventually came he was asking for his £200k. "But I thought I owed you£1.7million" I flippantly replied. I then told him to tell the mafia boss we didn't owe him any money: "Tell him whatever the fuck you want to tell him, just make it clear that me and Graeme owe him fuck all, and then you will get your £200k" I said.

To say my words went down like a lead balloon would be an understatement. William flew into another rage, hurling more threats at me. My response again was to cockily excuse myself and put down the phone.

Every day for well over a month I received the most vile of threats. It was relentless. They were coming at me from all angles too. Every man and his dog seemed to be getting in on it. My phone was ringing off the hook. I had such a large number of calls from Yugoslavs that I almost considered getting a translator. I received calls from much closer to home too; Scousers, Cockneys, Brummies. I had a few Irishmen phone me who were actually harder to understand than the Yugoslavians. I decided against the translator as I figured it was probably better not knowing what was being yelled at me. I was living day-to-day, constantly looking over my shoulder. Not that I was likely to recognise my attackers anyway, but it was a serious burden to carry. The year was nearing its end but I honestly wasn't expecting to make it through to Christmas in one piece. I believe that the hell that I was put through as a kid is what prepared me for dealing with such stresses in my life. Without those early aged experiences in the reform schools I think I would have buckled under the pressure.

Me and Graeme did have a few things still in our favour, however. For starters we had £200k of William's which we could use as a bargaining tool, especially as he seemed such a desperate man. Also we had already proven we were up for a fight and capable of taking it all the way if necessary. I'd had a broad daylight shoot out in Holland and Graeme and Jerry had been punishing people for William over in Amsterdam. On top of that I had a hundred or more people that were loyal to me, loyal like soldiers. I had my brothers, my close friends, gang associates and I also had an army of football hooligans that would stand by me through thick and thin as they had done many times before on the football terraces.

I would be as ready as I could possibly be for whoever, whatever and whenever. I knew I couldn't let the threats dominate my life, after all I had a business to run. I was at my reclaim yard daily with close friends and colleagues. It was a busy time at work and that helped to distract me.

Having had no contact from the Dutch cannabis dealers since Tom had paid them for our final consignment, I presumed my name had probably been dragged through the mud by William and his friends in an effort to hurt me financially, when one day out of the blue that all changed. The phone rang and to my surprise I wasn't receiving a volley of insults and death threats, on the contrary, I was delighted to be hearing a friendly Dutch voice, that I recognised well, on the other end of the line. The Dutch guys were only ever interested in making money, and I had built up a good relationship with them. They genuinely had never liked working with William and with him being deported from Holland they had tracked me down to offer me a new deal working directly with them. I was buzzing. Finally a bit of good news after all the shit that I had been going through. I knew my customers would be delighted too. I had built up a great custom base and for the previous couple of months I had left them needing to go elsewhere.

With William out of the equation too, the profits to be had were mind blowing.

I was at my yard when the call came in, with two great friends of mine, Tet and Dylan.

Dylan is a giant of a man. 6ft 5in and 17 stone, a former professional rugby player who had many caps for Ireland. He is one hell of a sportsman and a very handy bloke to have around.

Tet is the modern-day Fagan, the ultimate thief. That shameless man has the skill set required to dip into your pockets, while casually discussing the weather with you, and relieve you of anything of any value. If ever one of his victims did rumble him, he would just say that he had a medical condition. He describes it as Tourette's of the fingers, claiming they have a mind of their own. Tet also claims to be a born survivor. That basically means if a situation ever gets too hot under the collar, he is the first to leg it, declaring 'every man for himself'. Tet is, however, always very good to have around and is prepared to get his hands dirty.

I said to the two of them that we needed to find Graeme and tell him the good news because I knew it would cheer him up. As the words were coming out of my mouth the phone rang again. This time it was Graeme himself. He was asking us to join him for a meal to meet some new friends of his. "Perfect" I said, "dinner is on me". So Tet and Dylan jumped in the van and off we headed to a restaurant in Manchester.

When we arrived Graeme was already sitting there with two blokes. I recognised one of them from around town, he was known as Billy the kickboxer and he was a smug prick. He had apparently been a champion kick boxer when he was younger. The other was a snidey looking skinny cunt who I didn't know, he called himself SAS Gerry. Straight away I took a disliking to him. 'Who would name themselves that?' I thought.

We sat down and everybody got introduced to one another, then straight from the off SAS Gerry began leading the conversation. It was a continuous ramble about himself and his contacts, about how tough he was and how many tough people he knew. Before long he was reeling off stories about his time in the army, portraying himself as a hero and bragging about his exploits.

For an adult man he was chatting on like a Salford juvenile. I've seen more sense spoken on the Jeremy Kyle show. I noticed while Gerry was going on with himself that the kickboxer was weighing me up. He either wanted my phone number or he was sussing up how to handle me if it kicked off.

I suffered 30 minutes of Gerry's fairy tales before I could take no more. As soon as we had finished our dinners, me, Tet and Dylan made our excuses and left. On the drive home all I could I think of was 'why the fuck is Graeme surrounding himself with such flashy, bullshitting cunts and more importantly why was he introducing me to them?'

Chapter 22:

A BIT OF FUN AT GALATASARAY

The following week 400 kilos of top-quality cannabis arrived as promised, from the Dutch, meaning we were back in business. Me and Graeme decided to go and see some of our customers and make sure they knew we were back on track and things would be continuing as before. Firstly Graeme drove us out to Warrington in his car for a meeting there with a contact that he had introduced me to. Stupidly Graeme parked up on double yellow lines. We were gone for about half an hour discussing business. As we were walking back to the car I immediately spotted a traffic warden writing out a parking ticket for Graeme. I kept quiet and continued walking, before diving into the passenger seat chuckling to myself about the fun that I knew was about to transpire.

Graeme spotted the traffic warden and started arguing with him. Then he snatched the ticket book off the guy and ripped up the lot. It was always a losing battle trying to argue with Graeme, he was too sharp for most people and if he thought he may lose, then the red mist would descend. I knew that if the argument continued it would progress from being a losing battle, into being a bloody battle and obviously we didn't need any unnecessary police attention while business was just about to take off again.

I saw Graeme's body language change, which I knew full well meant that he was seconds away from the point of no return. I wasn't keen on putting myself in the firing line but in an attempt to stop him from losing his shit I shouted out of the window, "Come on, let's go, we've got bigger fish to fry". My efforts were in vain though and the next thing I knew Graeme had the traffic warden by the throat, shaking the life out of him. Half-heartedly I tried again saying "let him go mate, let's just fuck off". By that time, the poor traffic warden was already shrieking for help. Graeme then bitch slapped him and let him go, but the fun was far from over. He jumped into the driving seat, clearly still in a rage, slapping himself in the face and ranting about the outrage of it all. Then just when I thought I had seen it all he drove the car at the traffic warden, sending him up in the air and on to the bonnet. Graeme started speeding off; 20, 30, 40 MPH. The traffic warden had hold of the bonnet just below the windscreen. He was clinging on for dear life. I could see the terrified look on his face. I wish I had had one of today's camera phones. The absolute look of horror could have been my screensaver. The only time any expression had ever come close was when he had used that poor lady as a human shield at the Inn Of Good Hope, whilst we were getting shot at. I couldn't contain my laughter; I was in stitches. I just about managed to stop laughing enough to tell Graeme to pull over before the silly prick got seriously hurt, to which he replied, "Yes Paul, I suppose you're right". He looked at me with a sick smirk on his face then slammed on the brakes. The traffic warden flew off the car and landed in a crumpled heap on the road. Graeme, still not satisfied, got out and picked him up, he bitch slapped him once more and literally threw him onto the pavement face first.

After months of death threats it really did prove to be some great unexpected entertainment for me. Unfortunately for Graeme though the car was in his name and it didn't take long for the police to arrest him. A few months later, after being found guilty at trial, he was sentenced to 30 months in prison. It wasn't nice seeing Graeme locked up, and he clearly didn't settle into prison life too easily, but on the plus side of it all, at least he was safe from William while he was in there. In one way it was a bit of a weight off my shoulders too, not having to worry about his actions on a daily basis. On the other hand, I knew to expect a rise in the threats and pressure heading my way. With Graeme locked up William and his friends saw it as an ideal opportunity to get to me. They figured I would be vulnerable and alone.

I had my work cut out with Graeme not being around. My reclaim business was booming and the cannabis was flying in and immediately straight out. I was turning over some serious money. I was hands on at the yard doing a lot of the graft myself, mainly in an attempt to keep my mind occupied, but also to keep a watchful eye over my thieving brothers.

One day I was in the middle of unloading a van full of stone flags, I looked as rough as dog shit, I was filthy and dressed in some scruffy work gear. A big fancy Mercedes pulled up on the yard without me even noticing. A cockney voice called out to me "Oi you, come here". I looked up and saw two heavyweights sitting in the merc. As I climbed down from the van one of them said "go get your boss, Paul Doyle". I knew they weren't the police but I had to ask to sound convincing. "Who should I say wants him, you aren't the police are you?". The bloke snapped at me aggressively "Just fucking tell him to come and see us now you nosey prick". "Okay, no problem, just give me a second" I replied. Their demeanor was exactly as mine would have been, had I been sent to pass on a message. I jumped into the driver's seat of the stacker truck that I had been unloading, and reversed it behind their car and across the entrance, blocking them in. I then innocently toddled off to the office like a good little errand boy.

Once inside I went straight for my gun, checked it was loaded, summoned the lads and walked back out to the Cockney idiots that had found themselves trapped in my yard.

I walked to the driver side window, leant in and fired a bullet straight into the drivers leg.

At the exact same time my friends dragged the other guy out of the car, dishing out a good hiding. I did the same to the driver shouting every name a Manc could give a cockney; Cunt, Prick, Twat, Mug, Slag, everything I could think of. "I'm going to kill you both" I said as we dragged them over to the office. The confidence had already drained right out of them. We were only scaring them, but it worked. They seriously started shitting themselves when Tet began taking their belongings from them, saying "You won't need these things where you're going".

They started squealing like babies. "We only had a message for you. The Yugoslavians sent us".

"I don't give a fuck what they have to say" I screamed as I started unloading left and right blows on to the pair of their rib cages. "I've told those cunts that I didn't take their money, and that's the truth". After I had released a whole lot of pent-up aggression I sat the pair of them up and told them it was their lucky day. "As you soft southern cunts are so shit at what you do I will take pity on you and let you see the light of another day. Fuck off out of Manchester and back to whichever shithole you came from, then phone your boss, and make it abundantly clear that I never took his money, nor will he get a penny out of me". With that my lads dragged them back to their car and dumped them in it. The inside of the car became almost instantly covered in blood and mud. Tet warned them they had a matter of seconds to drive away before their swanky Mercedes went up in flames with them inside. I moved the truck to let them pass and waved as they drove off.

That night William was on the phone calling us a "bunch of fucking clowns" for not killing the cockney wide boys. He was laughing down the phone at me, until I told him that the only person I was interested in killing was him. Fuck it I thought, I had nothing to lose, he was coming for me anyway, so I decided to see how he handled the thought of me going after him for a change.

The threats from the Yugoslavs started to dry up after our savage treatment of the Cockneys. It seemed that those useless southern faggots were able to pass on one message that day after all.

As the Yugoslavs backed off, William became more intense.

I presumed the mafia boss must have told him that the £1.5 million was being written off, as I had been a tougher nut to crack then they might have imagined. If that was the case though, that left William needing to get his two hundred grand back himself. The problem there was that my mindset had changed as a result of all the threats I had been receiving. As honest as I am when it comes to paying my debts, I had decided that William was getting fuck all off me. He had caused me untold amounts of stress by blaming me and Graeme for stealing the mafia bosses' money. As far as I was concerned William's £200k had become my compensation money.

United had been drawn against Galatasaray in the Champions league and I saw an away day trip to Istanbul as the perfect opportunity to briefly leave my troubles with William behind and enjoy some good old fashioned football hooliganry. As it turned out however, it was more of a case of jumping out of the frying pan and into the fire.

Being a hooligan was always more like a sport for me. It was pleasurable and fun and I was by no means the only person who felt like that. It was a real trend back in the day and it couldn't have got much bigger than Man United vs Galatasaray in Istanbul (especially as the home leg at Old Trafford turned out to be such a spicy affair). My phone had been ringing off the hook from fellow 'Barmy' faithful's that were desperate to go.

A Barmy is a hardcore United fan that would travel anywhere on earth and beyond to watch United. A true Barmy is that fanatical that if he came home one night and discovered Eric Cantona shagging his missus, he would probably start chanting 'Ooh Aah Cantona' and cheer him on to the finish, before asking for his signature on his wife's tits. United is simply the bee all and end all and when they do go to away games, all 'Barmies' become like brothers in arms.

In the run up to the game the media was playing it's part in getting both sets of supporters riled. The Turks had been putting flags up saying things like 'Man United, Welcome to hell' and it was making headline news back home. We knew we were in for an unmissable trip. Me and about 30 of the lads booked to go with a tour operator called UF Tours. We were joined on the flight to Turkey by another 200 Barmies and I had a few tricks up my sleeve to ensure things went anything but smoothly. Firstly I had packed my Israeli flag, which I intended to offer Tet to wear during the game. That dosey sod had no idea about the historic differences between the Muslims and the Jews (and nor would he care anyway). I figured that would be like a red rag to a bull.

We got the employee of UF Tours (who was put on the plane with us in an attempt to keep some sort of order) blind drunk before we were anywhere near Turkish soil. He was singing and dancing around like one of us. Tet obviously had one hand over the bloke's shoulder, and the other rifling through his pockets for anything of value.

When we landed in Istanbul we had designated buses, but to speed things up, four of us decided to get a taxi to our hotel. The taxi driver took us to the wrong place though and we ended up walking the best part of a mile through the streets of Istanbul in search of our actual digs. The atmosphere was palpable. Never mind the Galatasaray fans, we could tell that the regular Turkish Joe public hated us too. Finally we found the correct hotel and checked in, (with false documents and names, as standard). We unloaded our bags and headed back out to get a meal. We found a nice enough little place that didn't seem too hostile and we ordered some food. The people may not have liked us any more than we liked them, but the food was great. I had a plate full of flame grilled mixed meats and veg all for about a quid. While we were eating we saw two United fans being chased down the street by about twenty Turks. Ashy suggested helping them out, but the grub was just too good to leave and we figured there wouldn't be a shortage of action anyway, so we left them to it.

Ashy being six foot two and blonde stood out like a sore thumb in Istanbul. What made things infinitely worse for him was that during the first leg at Old Trafford, Peter Schmeichel (the six-foot 3 inch, blonde haired United keeper) had ruthlessly thrown a Galatasaray pitch invader off the pitch, and the Turks had promised revenge for that action. The day before the game we were walking around in a busy, bustling centre when I saw a fairly smart looking businessman with a Galatasaray scarf poking out from under his overcoat. I got his attention and pointed to Ashy, while telling the bloke that he was Peter Schmeichel. The guy snapped and started hitting Ashy with his briefcase whilst screaming obscenities about Schmeichel. In a split second another four or five Galatasaray fans joined in the attack. Me and Tet were falling over ourselves laughing, as Ashy set off backing down the street, with his hands up, protesting his innocence.

That night we went out in the town near our digs. There didn't seem to be too many options for places to go and there were virtually no women to be seen. We stumbled across one road with a few bars and restaurants. We were in a group of about ten or twelve and we settled in a bar. On the opposite side of the road, we spotted a similar number of United fans (that we didn't know) in another bar. Before too long they crossed the road and asked to join us. It had been getting a bit hairy where they were and some Galatasaray fans had started to gather. There was growing tension in the air and it seemed like one little ignition was all it was going to take to blow things right out of the water. We were discussing what we could do to stir things up a bit and get a reaction, when a young lad from Rochdale that was with us lifted the top of one of the English girls who was along for the ride, flashing her tits at the Turks and shouting "I bet you miserable cunts wouldn't even know what to do with them, would ya"

That was the spark that was needed. All hell broke loose.

The Turks started trying to get into the bar we were drinking in and their numbers seemed to be growing by the second,. We were trapped and had to resort to using bar stools, tables, glasses and bottles to keep them at bay.

After about five minutes of mayhem and a total trashing of the bar, two police riot vans arrived followed by two mini-buses. The police cut through the crowd and dragged us out of the carnage, before dumping us into the mini-buses. The Turks weren't deterred by that though and began attacking our bus, trying to tip it over.

We were taken out of town to a hotel where scores of other United fans had already been dumped. They, like us, were mostly covered in claret and had had their United shirts ripped off their backs. Trouble apparently erupted right across the city and we were coming off worse. Some of the Barmies had been whipped by the Turkish police, just to get them to run away from the Galatasaray fans, faster than they already were doing.

The police left us to find our own way back to our hotels, presuming we had learnt our lessons. All they actually did however was to bring a huge number of United fans together then leave us to it. We put our heads together and started to plan our next move. We hadn't got very far when a member of the hotel staff got into a row with one of the lads and for a second time things kicked off. The police had left us and this time we heavily outnumbered the Turks. The lobby was getting smashed to bits, the staff barricaded themselves in a safe room and I took the opportunity to empty the safe.

Police vans began reappearing, as did the locals. Hundreds of Turks were storming down the street towards us and we were in danger of being cornered yet again. I figured it was either get caught in the hotel and be sentenced to years in a Turkish prison for stealing from the safe or take on the crowd. In an instant I dived out of a window and headed down the street. Like I had done in Anfield a few years earlier, I tucked my head and shoulders in and ran down the street like Linford Christie on speed. I headed for the hotel where I knew Coco and some of the lads were staying. Luckily, the boys were there. They had also been battling in the City but had gotten away. I divvied up some of the money that I had stolen between the lads. It seemed like we had won the lottery, but that was because of the currency difference. It did turn out to be a few thousand pounds though. I filled them all in on what had been going on down the road and everybody was having a good laugh about the carnage that we were causing, when Coco suggested I take a walk back to the hotel to see what was going on. He suggested I went because I have dark enough skin to pass for a Turk and obviously because I knew the hotel's location. Being a nosey git I agreed.

I walked back towards the hotel and when it was in range of sight I stopped in a kebab shop, so that I could inconspicuously sit and eat while monitoring the fun. My plan rapidly unraveled as soon as my Manc accent came out, while ordering my food. For the second time in an hour I found myself running from an army of Turks, baying for my blood. That time I wasn't so lucky either as I ran straight towards some waiting coppers who nicked me for the safe theft.

I was fingerprinted at the first station, then shipped out to another for a photo, then taken to a third for questioning. At the third station they finally searched me for money. It was long gone though. I had already given some to some of the lads to help fund their trips and what was left I had shoved down the back of a seat in the first police car. None of that deterred them from locking me up for the night though.

I was thrown into a cell which was typical of something from a third world country. There were four men already sharing the cell, which had no beds, just scruffy mattresses on the floor and a toilet (which was really just a hole in the ground connected to a sewer), right in the middle of the room. The place stank and it felt like I'd gone back in time a thousand years, just being in there.

I started speaking with the blokes in the cell, and from what I could gather, from their broken English, they had all been locked up in there for a number of weeks and were surviving solely on bread and water. I started to shit myself about doing a stretch in those conditions.

It was a long night and the film Midnight Express was playing in my head through most of it. The occasional cockroach scurrying over me would interrupt my chain of thoughts. Fortunately, the police had nothing on me and couldn't prove I had taken the money, so the following day I was relocated to another station near the airport. I was delighted to see most of the lads already locked up there. We were all being held until our flights that night and none of us would be allowed to so much as watch the match on a tv screen. The conditions were far nicer than the dump I had spent the night in though and at mealtimes one of the boys was even allowed to do kebab runs for us all.

At roughly the same time as United were kicking off, we were put onto coaches and escorted by two armoured tanks to the airport. After sitting on the runway for a couple of hours everybody was handed back their passports and we boarded the plane. It soon became obvious that Tet and Ashy weren't with us and the pilot said we could only allow them a certain time to arrive or they would be left behind. None of us knew where they were or what had happened. For all we knew they were dead in a Turkish ditch. Just as the panic really started to set in, the pilot received news that the two of them were being ferried down the runway to the plane. The jammy sods had not only avoided being nicked but had even managed to get to the game. They were the only two of us that saw a ball kicked on that trip.

The game and the two day build up to it had made headline news back home. There was talk of United fans burning Turkish flags as well as looting hotels and bars. There were two sides to the story though and there was plenty of footage of Galatasaray fans wreaking havoc, not to mention some images of police brutality. The bitterness didn't exactly end when we all arrived home either. A few years later Leeds faced Galatasaray in the UEFA cup semifinals. Two Leeds fans were stabbed to death before the first leg in Istanbul. Four men were arrested for murder and Galatasaray fans were banned from travelling for the return leg at Elland Road.

Chapter 23:

BUILDING AN ARMY
– A Red Army

A s grateful as I was to have not ended up incarcerated in a shit hole of a Turkish prison cell, life back home was far from fun and games. William's threats became more and more intense and they were also getting closer to home. I heard on the grapevine that he was sending a firm of scousers down to attempt a hit on me. I received word that it was to be that coming Saturday, at Henry's bar in town. There was obviously a snide amongst us. Someone in my circle must have been passing information to him, as to where I was planning to be and when. I had made plans to go to Henry's bar that particular Saturday and William must have been made privy to that information.

I was beginning to see just how capable of a man he could be and how many contacts and resources he had. That said though a firm of scouse gangsters going into Manchester City centre, to carry out a hit on a busy Saturday night would be a big ask for anybody to pull off. I figured it was probably more mind games. I knew he was too smart to make a mistake like that. Don't get me wrong, the majority of people would probably have been running scared by his psychological intimidation, but I was far too experienced to be affected by it.

I saw his threat as an opportunity to show all of my enemies exactly how capable of an outfit I was surrounded by. I knew that I could use whoever had been informing on me, to inadvertently pass back a message of my own.

During the 1970s, 80s and 90s United's football hooligans had conquered almost every city in England due to the sheer volume of them prepared to travel on away days, following the scent of blood. It was very simply a case of strength in numbers and I decided to use exactly that policy. I put the word out that there was a firm of scouse gangsters coming to Henry's bar and it would be my blood that they were looking to spill. For all I knew it may well have been the case - even though I highly doubted it. I arranged to meet up with some loyal friends to discuss the threat. Obviously, the usual suspects; Ashy, Big Dylan, Tet and the lads that would work at my yard. Beyond them I arranged for some other fairly well-known figures around Manchester and Salford like Wayne, Benny, Teamo and Micky R. They were men that would all standby me in my hour of need, regardless of the possible danger to themselves.

We discussed what I thought William was up to, namely trying to use Graeme's custodial sentence to his advantage. I told them about the rumoured threat to my life and that I wanted to make a real show of force to act as a future deterrent.

Benny knew exactly what I was thinking and he agreed straight away to get the United hooligans out in numbers. Benny knew just about every member of the Barmy Army that was worth his salt and we were both well aware of what the hooligans were capable of. To say that they tread a different path to almost all other organised criminals wouldn't do them justice. They are literally lawless. When they are out on the town they can and will attack whoever confronts them and that includes other hooligans, villains, gangsters or the police.

Mentioning Scousers to hard core United hooligans, even today is a sure way to get their blood boiling. I knew the main players would turn out for it and with them backing me, alongside my own crew I knew we had more than enough '*troops*' to send out a strong message.

Benny produced the goods and by the Thursday of that week everything was set. He informed me that the United boys would be heading to Henry's bar straight after the match. I couldn't wait for the weekend to arrive.

After the final whistle myself and approximately thirty of my closest mates went straight to Henry's. We could hear the noise booming out of the place before we were within a hundred yards. "It's obviously a good turnout" I said to the others as we approached. I could barely believe my eyes when I walked through the doors though. There were well over a hundred lads ready to go to war with me and they looked hungry for blood.

A large number of the 'Cockney Reds' had turned up. Those guys played a major part in making United hooligans such a force to be reckoned with. I'm one of the lucky ones that has had the honour to fight alongside the Cockney Reds. They had a beautiful style about them when they went to war. They would follow behind their leader, Big Sam. Each member had such a confident swagger that it gave them a well-deserved air of arrogance. It was an intimidating sight for anybody to witness marching towards them.

As for Big Sam, the best way to describe him is as a big black warrior. He could, and often would fight four or five hooligans at a time. Having him and his men turn out for me was a real privilege.

I've met tens of criminal gangs up and down the country and I don't know one firm that would have been capable of dealing with the outfit that we had on show that night.

As I stood admiring some of the fantastic characters around me, I noticed two young up and coming Salford gangsters amongst the crowd. Remarkably they still stood out from the rest for looking extremely powerful and mean - Vinny Clay and Skimbo.

It usually took a riot van full of Rambo-cops to control those two when they kicked off. On one occasion Vinny was sitting on his doorstep enjoying a joint in the sunshine, entertaining some other members of a young Salford Firm, when unbelievably two coppers pulled up without any backup and with the intention of arresting him. Vinny was in no mood to spend such a beautiful day sitting in a police cell though, so in a snap decision he decided to take it to the coppers, both of whom sensibly retreated as fast as they could on foot, back down the street.

The crowd of onlookers cheered and laughed but Vinny didn't stop there. He returned to his house and disappeared inside. When he came out he was carrying a petrol powered still-saw. His little gathering of friends went wild as they witnessed him cutting the roof off the abandoned police car.

Vinny and Skimbo's appearances alone would have been enough to scare the crap out of most common folk. I was delighted to have them as part of the crew, standing by my side.

After an hour or so, with no sign of any scousers appearing, a lot of the hooligans started to get frustrated at the lack of action. They wanted scouse blood. Big Sam suggested going hunting for them. It was a lovely thought but what he didn't realise was that my plan was actually working beautifully. It was plain for all to see that I could put together a small army, and an angry one at that.

Aware that it was down to me to entertain the masses, I soon realised I needed to pull something out of the bag and give them a night to remember. I thought of a way of killing two birds with one stone. A couple of weeks earlier Teamo and his wife had been refused entry into a nightclub. Teamo started arguing with the doormen and one of them decided to give him a slap in front of his wife. Teamo outnumbered and embarrassed told them he would be back to take his revenge. The doorman mistakenly laughed at him and fucked him off. They had no doubt heard that sort of thing a hundred times before, but little did they know that Teamo was actually a well-connected individual and would be true to his word. The door firm was from out of town. The club owners believed outsiders were best equipped to control the security, after all of Manchester's historic door wars troubles. What nobody seemed to have accounted for was just how angrily a Mancunian may react to being slapped about by outsiders in his own city, not to mention in front of his own wife.

I saw the perfect opportunity for me to entertain my new army and for Teamo to get his revenge.

I'd been mooching around Manchester city centre, up to no good, since the age of seven. To this day I still know every back alley there is, I also knew there was a big difference from me creeping around the city unnoticed and a hundred hooligans doing the same thing. It was essential we moved discreetly to get from one side of town to the other undetected and I stressed to the lads that we needed a level of professionalism to get away with it. Nowadays there is that much CCTV around town that alarms would be raised left right and centre and in no time at all half of Greater Manchester's boys in blue would be out to intercept you.

Successfully we maneuvered our way across the city and came out of the final alleyway about two hundred yards away from our targets. Teamo proudly led the charge towards the doormen. I had to laugh when I saw the fear and sheer disbelief on their faces as we appeared out of the darkness, running directly at them. Unfortunately for them they received a heavy kicking that night, but in our eyes it was a well-deserved one.

The hooligans being a professional bunch knew when it was time to retreat. The two young Salford thugs, Skimbo and Vinny however were enjoying themselves so much that they continued to smash the place up. It brought back great memories from my early days as a street thug and for a few moments I stood back with a smile on my face and watched them. Eventually I had to spoil their fun though. They had turned out for me and I wasn't about to leave them to get nicked. I pointed out to them that the club was well and truly smashed up, as were the doormen, so it was time to leave before the police arrived.

The night was a big success all around, the Hooligans got a bit of action, the Salford boys enjoyed their demolition job, Teamo got his revenge and the outside door firm, to my knowledge, never worked in Manchester again. Most importantly my plan worked perfectly. I had made a massive statement to anybody who was anybody in or around Manchester's criminal underworld. I already knew that somebody would be passing the news back to William too.

The informant clearly didn't waste any time reporting back either. The moment I got home the mouthy prick was phoning me. He was ranting and raving at me once again, telling me he wanted his money, and threatening that he was going to remove my body parts and force me to eat them. I told him that I was bored of his constant crying and not for the first or last time I hung up on him and unplugged the phone for a well-deserved night's kip.

There's no doubt William had enjoyed being kingpin in the Costa del Sol, but in Manchester I had proved that I was more than capable of holding my own, whoever the enemy.

After my triumphant weekend, the police arrested two high ranking United hooligans that had been spotted out with me on the Saturday night. They took them into the main police HQ at Chester House and interviewed them to find out why I was running around the town centre causing trouble with United's hooligans. The lads informed them that I was a good friend and innocently asked why they shouldn't go on a night out with me.

The senior copper apparently warned them that my extra-curricular affairs went far beyond that of football hooliganism, and that they should stay well away from me unless they wanted to get caught up in a world that was a lot different to the one which they knew.

The police for once weren't too far off the money either, I had an idea in my head about introducing some of my most loyal football hooligans into serious organised crime. I didn't think it was going to be too hard either, given that most of them were already street level villains with very open minds and many of them had happily turned out to stand by my side in my hour of need. I had started to crave an army that my enemies would envy. A firm capable of slaughtering whoever dared to challenge us. I believed converting my fellow hooligans was the best way to achieve it.

My usual group of pals that congregated in and around town each weekend doubled in size virtually overnight. We already received VIP treatment everywhere we went, so with the added numbers we were becoming more and more noticeable. I'm not sure if the bar and club owners loved us or loathed us, but one thing was for certain, when we were out, their places were full of big spenders.

Manchester was a changing city. Regular wine bars were becoming swanky cocktail bars, pubs were changing from old men 'boozers' into trendy places that served better food and a wider choice of drink, attracting a nice mix of both men and women. Top chefs from around the world were opening restaurants. More upmarket clientele had started to venture into the city to experience it's nightlife. What they didn't expect was to be rubbing shoulders with us lot, but they were. Money was no object for a lot of us. Organised criminals aren't exactly known for being short of a quid or two. I personally was rolling in it.

Around the Deansgate area business was booming. Restaurants, pubs, wine bars and cocktail bars were raking it in and everybody wanted to be seen there. The problem we had was we stood out a little too much. We realised that we needed to at least attempt to smarten ourselves up in order to blend in with Manchester's new clientele - after all, in most bars we were treated like celebrities. Doormen would push a waiting queue aside while we walked straight passed and into VIP areas. It became common knowledge that we had most of the bars and clubs boxed off and the reason was simple; we had the power to do pretty much whatever we wanted and people knew that. I'd like to think that we were known for being respectful to other hard-working men and women. If they posed us no problems then we posed none to them. Anybody who stood in our way however would be dealt with in a very different manner.

People wanted to be seen with us. Individuals we didn't even know would tell doormen that they were part of our group so they could get some respect, not to mention get into places without queuing or paying. Word was quickly spreading that we were the boys to be seen with.

One Saturday night it backfired on us though. Dot (one of my pals) like a stupid twat invited his new girlfriend out with us, basically because he was smitten and wanted to impress her.

Dot was the straight member in our group. He wouldn't be capable of winning a fight against my grandmother, however when he got pissed he turned into a fucking walking, talking nightmare. Dot would threaten one and all and cause untold grief for the rest of us to sort out. He had an unbelievable gift of sniffing out loose women, in fact he was simply the best at rooting them out. His problem however was that the soppy cunt fell in love with every girl that ever so much as cuddled him.

Obviously, Dot's girlfriend had a great night out with us, she lapped up all the VIP treatment, but predictably the next day she also wasted no time in spreading her great news to the rest of our loved ones. That obviously resulted in all of us being pestered to death, to show our loved ones the same treatment. Like a shithouse I gave into Jeanette, even though I felt like crying. I knew taking the girls out on the town would be a major headache, I also knew that one weekend wouldn't be enough, and they would want the same thing every week. Some of the other lads caved in too and we were all well aware that that following Saturday had disaster written all over it. Dot had fucked it up for everyone.

We met the ladies in Henry's bar, after most of us lads had been to Old Trafford. We were all skeptical about what the night had in store and we dragged our heels getting across town to the bar. When we finally arrived we were greeted by the ladies telling us how they had been verbally abused by a group of young thugs that were in there. Ashy went over to give the lads a chance to leave in one piece. He suggested it was in their best interests to clear out because the girls they had been gobbing off to were out with Paul Doyle. The disrespectful young louts didn't take their opportunity and instead told Ashy that "Doyley's day is done, so you can tell him to fuck off too". Ashy returned and passed on the message. Before he had a chance to finish speaking, the table of young thugs got stormed and each one in their group was left unconscious in a pile on the floor. Ashy in his youth would have destroyed the lads on his own, however we were all getting a bit long in the tooth to be involved in unnecessary conflicts. With that thought in mind, the following weekend he brought out his nephew to watch our backs and deal with any future bull shit skirmishes like the one that night.

Ashy's nephew is David Tottan, a great lad who has now become a very well-known Salford gangster. Tottan is a new breed of villain. When it came to criminality him and his firm were far more professional than we ever were at their age. He was already known throughout the North West for heading a young firm of serious armed robbers. To say they were good at what they did wouldn't do them justice. It's alleged that his firm was that well equipped and organised, not to mention brazen, that they were known to have robbed two banks at the same time, because they happened to be on opposite sides of the same street. Pure genius!

Despite them only being young men, the police were rumoured to have a shoot to kill policy on them. That served as an indication as to just how dangerous him and his crew were considered.

Tottan's family lived on the same street as my mother and I saw him growing up from a young boy into a man. As you can imagine the area was full of criminals and like any good criminally minded neighbourhood in Salford, they had their own neighbourhood watch scheme - They would be sure to alert each other whenever the police showed their faces in the area.

At one time it became common knowledge that the old bill had started surveillance on someone in my mum's street and they were doing it covertly from a house opposite. One afternoon while myself, Ashy and Tottan were at Old Trafford, some young thugs apparently burst into the house wearing balaclavas and gave the undercover coppers a good hiding. The police were obviously never going to accept such a humiliation lying down and they decided to take revenge. Suspects were arrested and the whole affair ended up in court. The bent coppers stated that no balaclavas were worn and they recognised one of the attackers as Mark Early (one of the local residents). Poor Early received a nine year sentence which was outrageous, because I have it on very good authority that he did nothing wrong - He had definitely worn his balaclava during the attack.

With the likes of Dave Tottan, Vinny Clay and Skimbo joining us on nights out, we were able to relax a little more and enjoy ourselves, safe in the knowledge that some of Salford's most notorious youngsters had our backs. It was a marriage made in heaven. They educated themselves by watching us handle any sticky situations that arose and at the same time we relaxed knowing the youngsters would deal with anything more petulant that we no longer wanted to be involved in. Our weekends out became even more comical, more entertaining and sometimes (unbelievably) even more dangerous.

Manchester's police, namely their A Division, decided on a change of tact in tackling organised crime in the City. They started using 'heavy handed' tactics and they even began to broadcast their new approach on the local radios. They vocalised that they were going to be enforcing rights to stop and search, with an aim to reduce the availability of weapons on the streets by catching criminals carrying knives and guns. In reality some senior figure in the force had given the green light for a stop, search and if necessary beat, threaten and antagonise policy. They were desperate to get as many of Manchester's hardened criminals off the streets as they could and they were more than prepared to bend the rules to achieve it.

One of my oldest friends Coco was quite badly beaten up by some coppers one Saturday evening, on his way home from Old Trafford. Coco is one of the coolest people I know when it comes to his taste in fashion. He always wears the highest quality items and accessories. In the mid-80s when most football fans were knocking around in jeans and Doc Marten boots, Coco was wearing outfits costing anything up to a thousand pounds. God knows how much he has spent on clothes over the years. I've known him to fly to Italy just to buy a pair of shoes. He was by head and shoulders the most standout hooligan to be seen at Old Trafford. Unfortunately for him the police recognised him for the same reasons. He was an easy target that night and the cheeky fuckers even charged him with a public order offence after knocking lumps out of him.

At a similar time, a car full of us was driving into town when we hit a roadblock, it had been set up specifically to stop us. We were all manhandled out of the vehicle by some wannabe Rambo coppers, craving an arrest. First the car was searched for weapons when none were found their attentions' turned to us. We were shoved over the bonnet whilst searched. Once they realised their search was in vain, one particular lowlife cunt said to me "Doyle let's see how well you can take a punch". The sly twat then threw a huge right hand which landed sweet on my jaw. As difficult as it was to do, I refrained from lashing out. I simply gave the potato head a death stare that said it all. He had already got his answer anyway. Yes I certainly can take a punch, and his best (free) shot wasn't anywhere near enough to put me down.

Like most professional criminals I would rarely carry a weapon on my person, especially in and around town, with that said however I did have a one-inch knife on my key ring.

That weekend me and my pal Wayne met in a bar in town to start our night out. Wayne was a professional bodyguard for some of the United players. He's a well-known figure and a handy bloke. We'd barely sat down with a drink when I spotted the Rambo Cops from earlier in the week, heading towards the bar we were in. There was a good chance they were searching for me and the boys, so I decided it was in our best interests to leave before the bastards spotted us. We snuck off through the fire exit. Outside the bar two riot vans were parked up, unguarded. I decided to exact a little bit of revenge for the cheap shot I had taken. Using my one-inch knife, I stabbed holes into each and every tyre on the two vans, before casually walking off and waiting at the end of the street for the fun to start. It was hilarious watching the coppers pointing their fingers at each other and arguing about why nobody had stayed with the vans. It was one of those glorious moments that I'll never forget. It was only a small thing, but it was fucking comical to watch how pissed off they were. My pleasure didn't last long though as one of them heard our roars of laughter and the cheeky twat started shouting "Doyle you fat bastard, we'll get you for this". Admittedly I was carrying a little extra timber at that time, but it didn't hinder me too much when they gave chase as I still left them all for dead.

Some days later I was driving out of my close when an unmarked police car pulled me over. The devious prick said that my car was stolen. To which I replied, "are you pissed mate, it's a rental". The copper told me to wait while he checked it out. Seconds later a riot van full of more Rambo cops pulled alongside us. Before I realised what was going on I was being kicked and punched all over the place. The bastards showed me no mercy and left me in agony on the side of the road. I had a bust leg and my face had swollen up like the elephant man's. To rub salt into my wounds the original detective then came back over to me, as if he had seen nothing and said, "Good news Mr. Doyle, the car is not stolen and you're free to go, have a lovely day sir."

I realised that I was on a serious collision course with the Manchester police force. They clearly saw me and my associates as a real thorn in their sides and they were prepared to stoop to new levels to make my life as difficult as possible. Christmas was only a couple of months away so I had no intention of them fucking up my busiest period, or anybody elses for that matter.

Chapter 24:

WAYS AND MEANS

I t's common knowledge amongst drug dealers that every year the police try to spoil Christmas, by making as many drug busts as they can in the run up to the festive period. It works brilliantly for them because they get to finish their year on a statistical high, at the same time as ruining Christmas for the dealers and their families. They are not alone in trying to ruin it either. Some unscrupulous dealers see it as a time to steal from other dealers, just to put presents under their own tree. That time of year is often a complete ball ache for me, and for that reason I always made it my policy to finish grafting at the end of November, in an attempt to dodge any unnecessary headaches closer to the big day.

Before I 'laid on' any cannabis to a customer I would always talk them through the important rules that must be clearly understood. Whatever is laid on becomes the responsibility of the customer. If anyone steals it from them it is their own fault for not doing their job properly. The bill still needs paying or the consequences need facing. I was always firm on that, after all I wasn't running a charity. That being said I was usually prepared to offer a helping hand to get the drugs or the money back from whoever had committed the dirty deed.

There are many ways to solve such a problem, and that would depend on the details of the theft. Each case would be taken on its own merit. It may simply take a threatening phone call, or it might require a car full of heavies.

If the theft was down to one cocky individual, I would often send a 'scarer' to recover the debt. Most scarers are self-employed and charge about 40% of the total debt to recover it. For obvious reasons, a big powerful looking bloke with an aggressive demeanor makes for a perfect choice of candidate and I believe I know the best in the business - Big Ian Massey.

Ian stands at six foot four and weighs 18 stone. He has incredible punching power and fantastic fighting skills. As a schoolboy he was a wrestling, boxing and karate champion. He later graduated into a tremendous street fighter. In the mid1980s he proudly made Britain's most wanted list for armed robberies, eventually receiving a 14-year prison sentence, at a time when the prison system was at its harshest. Upon his release he decided to use his fighting skills as a bodyguard and debt collector and turned away from armed robbery. On one occasion four coppers were sent to arrest him. After putting Ian in handcuffs the stupid cunts thought it was their chance to give him a kicking. He still took down all four of the fools whilst handcuffed. Since that day they take chains whenever they attempt to arrest him.

When you combine Ian's height, weight, fighting skills and lawless attitude, the outcome is one disturbed machine, albeit with an excellent sense of humour. He is a great bloke and I would always enjoy paying him a visit. If nothing else it would be a good chance to hear one of his amusing stories. One day I took my mates Browny and Tet to meet him.

I said "Ian let me introduce you to my good friend Browny, he's salt of the earth. I'm not sure if we can trust this one though" I said as I pointed to Tet. Ian having a twisted sense of humour said, "You always have to be sure Paul", then he approached Tet and put his index finger on his forehead and his thumb on his chin, while staring into his eyes. He gave Tet's head what looked like a little jerk, but it was enough to leave him with a stiff neck. To this day he still refers to Ian as 'The Lunatic'. When it comes to work though Ian is very professional. He tries his best not to lose his head or react in anger. He would always make out he was doing the debtor a favour by saving them from an even stickier situation - which I think is a great psychological game to play.

That particular November I was recovering from my police brutality, looking forward to shutting up shop for the Christmas period, when I received news from one of my Birmingham customers that some, apparent big time, bully had stolen £75,000 worth of cannabis from him. I knew straight away not to send some bloodthirsty friends of mine to bring the guy back down to earth with a bump, because that probably wouldn't have gotten me the drugs or the money back. It was a significant debt which meant I required a professional touch. It was time to pay Ian Massey a visit.

I gave him all the details about this six-foot six inch, lone wolf who apparently came with a serious reputation. I obviously told him the size of the debt that needed recovering, which he was delighted about and gladly accepted the job.

Without one ounce of fear or concern he headed off to Birmingham the very next day. He drove down nice and early, to catch the guy off guard as Ian thought a six am wakeup call would do just the job.

Using all his experience he told the bloke he had travelled down early to catch him at home because he needed to inform him that his life was in danger. He told him that the ball lay firmly in his own court. I can either head back to Manchester and report back to the organisation that sent me, saying common sense has prevailed or I can report back saying it had not. The latter of the two would unfortunately result in you not seeing Christmas this year though.

The guy who was in total shock invited Ian in for a coffee to discuss the problem. That was a smart move on his behalf. Massey, knowing the door was still open to play mind games, requested, whilst putting on a pair of surgical gloves, "just one sugar for me and put mine in an old mug, as I will need to take it with me".

While the blood started draining from the big guy's face, Ian went for the jugular. He told him that the cannabis he had stolen didn't actually belong to the dealer he had stolen it from. He then explained to him that the organisation that actually owned the cannabis simply would not stand to take such a loss and the only reason they had sent him to speak to the guy was because it was near to Christmas and it wouldn't be fair to expect anybody to be going on the run at that time of year. Ian's experience and disturbingly menacing demeanour obviously had the desired effect on the bloke who paid half the money straight away and said the rest would be available in a week.

Ever the professional, exactly seven days later Ian returned to Birmingham and ever the big soft-hearted bugger, not to mention total head fucker, he did so with an early Christmas present for the bloke. Upon answering the door Ian handed him a puppy, saying that it was a gift for making the right decision and also a reminder to do so in the future.

Ian's methods were so original, that he got inside people's heads in a way that I never believed anybody else could. The man's successful record is proof that his psychological torment works wonders.

A couple of weeks after Ian's trip I received a knock at my door. It was the big Brummy himself. I had to arc my neck to look up at him, he was a huge fella. He put me at ease immediately though as the first thing he did was apologise for disturbing me at home, then he explained who he was and said he had come to ask a favour of me. I invited him and over a cup of coffee he relayed to me the whole story about Ian turning up and putting the fear of God into him. I couldn't stop laughing as he told me about his early Christmas present and how he had been unable to tell Ian he didn't want the dog, for fear of his reaction. He almost begged me to ensure Ian never turned up at his house again. He explained that the only reason he had taken the cannabis was because my customer had actually ripped him off for thousands of pounds over another drug deal. He went on to say that he had been the middleman for a Dutch organisation but after being ripped off by my customer, he had fallen out of favour with the Dutch. We ended up having a long chat which resulted in a very agreeable business arrangement for the pair of us.

The big Brummy went home delighted that day after I agreed to lay on 50 kilos of cannabis each month at a very competitive price. From what could have been a nasty situation everybody ended up smelling of roses. I landed myself a new customer, my Birmingham dealer had his debt recovered, Ian Massey received a substantial Christmas bonus and the big guy got a tasty new cannabis deal, that was better than the one he had before. God knows what happened to the puppy in the end.

By the mid-nineties drive by shootings had become the preferred way to carry out a hit. Times had changed considerably since I had started out as an enforcer and I began to believe that I was living on borrowed time. The way I saw it, it wouldn't be long before someone put a bullet in me. I figured I would most likely be targeted in one of three places; whilst I was driving my car, possibly at home or the down at the reclaim yard.

The yard offered me the most protection, as I always had a small gathering of streetwise friends and family members prepared to go to war with me.

Out driving I was vigilant. I always kept a good distance from the car in front, to avoid being blocked in and I spent more time checking my rear view mirror than looking at the road ahead. I had to concede, as much as I didn't want to admit it, I was most vulnerable at home, relaxing with Jeanette and the kids. For that reason I started to have a shotgun dropped off at my house every evening at 6pm and collected again at 11pm when I would retire for the night.

One evening as I sat with the family, I had one eye on the tv, the other looking out on to the cul-de-sac for any unwelcome visitors, when I noticed a BMW with blacked out windows pull up and park on the road. I told Jeanette to take the kids into the kitchen.

As I stood up to take a better look I saw a monster of a bloke get out of the car and start walking towards our house. The fella was huge, but seeing the size of him actually relaxed me, as it meant that he was more than likely wanting to beat the shit out of me, as opposed to blast holes in me. I opened the front door and before I could say so much as "kiss my arse you're not welcome" the cocky cunt had barged straight by me and was standing in my hall. To say I was in shock would be an understatement.

In a cockney accent he said, "Paul I've been sent by the big fella to discuss your debt".

In a very calm manner I simply said to him "Okay, well before we talk business I'm going to check that the wife is ok and tell her to stay in the kitchen while we chat". I walked off to the kitchen but brushed straight past Jeanette and picked up the shotgun. I stormed back into the living room screaming some obscenities at him, before ramming the weapon into his mouth.

The monster turned into a pussy cat, clearly fearing his time was up. Even Jeanette came running in behind me screaming at me to get a grip of myself. She didn't understand that I was merely playing mind games with him. I would never kill anyone while my children were in the house. My plan had worked though, he was petrified and Jeanette believing that I was going to blow his brains out, worked in my favour too.

After I finished giving him a good old fashioned 'telling off' for bursting into my house and disrespecting me and my family, I asked Jeanette to make him a cup of coffee so we could have a more sensible chat.

The cockney told me his name was Johnno and he said that William had asked him to collect the money that I owed. I informed him that he was putting himself in danger, because working with William would either land him in prison or in the mortuary (if his body was ever found). I explained that I didn't owe William any money therefore he would never get a penny out of me. I advised him to tread carefully and reminded him that if it hadn't been for Jeanette begging me to spare his life, he would already be a dead man.

Johnno left the house in a much politer manner than he had entered it twenty minutes earlier. He even gave Jeanette a couple of hundred quid for her inconvenience, and for being the voice of reason.

The next day I gave Paul Massey a call to enquire about Big Johnno, the cockney monster. Massey said he knew him because he had tried muscling into Salford, thinking he could tax some of the small-time drug dealers. He was swiftly warned to leave however or pay the consequences. The heat quickly mounted up for Johnno and before long he moved to the Stockport area, where he had a bit more success and became a well-known figure. Word spread about Johnno unsuccessfully trying to recover the debt for William though. On one hand it had shown my enemies that I was fully loaded and ready for conflict - even in my family home. On the other hand however it affirmed to them that if they were to pull off a successful hit on me, coming heavily armed was going to be their only realistic option.

Whilst driving to work one morning, I noticed two cars following me and as they didn't make any efforts to overtake or pull alongside me, I figured that they must have been undercover police. I immediately called Jeanette and told her that I thought the house needed 'a good cleaning'. The unmarked cars followed me all the way to the yard and then simply drove off as I turned in. Jeanette ensured me that the house was clean, but nobody came knocking. It wasn't until the following morning that anything occurred. However when it did, it did with a bang.

The whole of our cul-de-sac was blocked off by riot vans and an armed squad went through my house like a pack of wild animals. The warrant was issued because they had received information that I had a firearm. I knew the house was in order so I welcomed them in and told them to knock themselves out. Nothing was found but did we get an apology for our house being tipped upside down, did we bollocks. I was delighted to see them waste so many resources on a dead end though.

Somebody was leaking obviously information about me and I suspected William to be the likely suspect

Chapter 25:

NEVER PLAIN SAILING

I was adamant not to show any weakness to my enemies and I thought being a constant face about town was one way to prove I wasn't scared. I was geared up for a big night out, until an offer that I couldn't refuse came my way.

Ant (the porn star) called me asking for a favour, and what a favour it was. He asked if I would help him out in escorting some glamour models down to London to watch the Robby Reid world title fight. A hotel was provided and paid for as was a ringside ticket to the fight.

The girls were actually the ring girls that night (the girls holding up the round number in between rounds). "I'm sick of you always asking me for favours" was my response. "But as Robby is a friend I will go out of my way to take the ladies to London and sit ringside to cheer him on".

That Thursday my car got its first ever valet. As much as I had been looking forward to a night out in Manchester, I began to feel relieved to be getting away. I set myself a little challenge to make it through the full weekend without any trouble.

Saturday soon arrived and I could hardly contain my excitement. The girls were all beautiful and everything was set for a cracking weekend. My over exuberance did get the better of me however, because I stupidly swallowed two Es for the journey - and I was driving. If the M6 wasn't such a straight motorway I'm not sure we would have made it to London.

By the grace of god we did and as we entered the hotel I immediately delved into my man bag, which was full to the brim of freshly ironed £50 pound notes. Showing off I upgraded my room to the penthouse suite. I was determined to make a good impression on the ring girls and with a bag full of cash and a pocket full of Es I was confident that I had the winning formula.

At the arena, as promised I was ringside and sitting next to one of the ring girls. We had a bit of a giggle together but I was all excited by the boxing and spent most of the fight on my feet shouting advice at Robbie (like I knew what I was doing).

He was fighting a classy boxer called Thulane 'Sugar Boy' Malinga. I think Robbie took too much of my advice though because unfortunately he lost on points.

I was determined not to let it put a dampener on things, after all I was a few hours into a night out and none of the punches that had been thrown were at me.

Myself, Ant and the girls went back to the hotel to await Robbie's arrival. I headed straight to the bar and asked for the champagne list. There were seven or eight bottles on it and not being a drinker I was unsure what to get, so in keeping with me trying to impress, I ordered a bottle of each. As I was off my head on Es and surrounded by such beautiful ladies, I felt compelled to try my luck with one of them. I sat down next to the girl that I had sat with in the arena and I began feeding her some of my best lines. I gave her all the cheesy stuff and I chucked in a bit of northern humour. Things were going well.

Just as the ring girl excused herself to go to powder her nose, Robbie and his entourage arrived. They headed straight to our table. I'm not sure if it was due to the fact the other beautiful ring girls were with us or because there was that much fizz knocking about that we looked like we were shooting some kind of champagne advert.

The party really got underway and even I found myself swigging champagne whilst mingling with top promoters, trainers, boxers, bodyguards and glamour girls, not to mention my good mate Ant, who is always good for a laugh. I had forgotten about the young lady that I was trying to chat up and found myself having an intense conversation about the fight with an athletic looking guy who claimed to be Frank Warren's bodyguard. I said I felt Robbie had done enough to win because Sugar Ray Malinga had chosen to dance around and didn't really want to get embroiled in a proper tussle. The other bloke disagreed with me and was highlighting Robbie's downfalls. I began getting right behind my pal and ranting about how well he had done and that he deserved something more from the fight. I got a little carried away however and next minute Robin Reid himself broke up our chat. "Calm down Doyley" he said, "and give me a hug".

It was always great to see Robbie and I told him how well I thought he had done and what a great night I was having away from all the stresses of Manchester. We were just beginning to have a bit of a catch up when the room began to spin. Champagne and pills had caught up with me.

I was trying my best to concentrate on what Robbie was saying when I felt a tug on my arm. The ring girl that I had been chatting up was standing by my side with some suave cunt who was clearly trying it on with her. She asked me if I could do her a favour and get rid of him.

I was feeling far too pissed to have a verbal confrontation, so I played my trump card and landed a sweet right hook on his jaw. He went down like a sack of shit and my instinct was to finish him off, but I wobbled back myself and figured I had better sit down before I joined him on the deck. Nevertheless I was a hero, her knight in shining armour and she wanted me to take her to my penthouse suite so I could show her some more of my impressive moves.

I did go to my suite, but the only thing that I hugged that night was the toilet while my eyes spun around in my head. It wasn't the first time I'd slept in a toilet but it was the only time I'd paid £1000 for the privilege.

To say I woke with a hangover would not do it justice, I felt like someone had hit me over the head with every one of those champagne bottles I had bought. There were a few more sore heads that morning too. The glamour girls seemed slightly less glamorous as they snored their way back up the M6 in the back of my car. About ten miles from home I received a call from the wife asking how my trip had gone. Obviously, I had neglected to fill her in on all the finer details before I left. I said, "It was a very successful trip thank you love" to which she replied, "no doubt it was you fuckin pig". She then continued to yell at me about how I had been seen on national television on the front row for the fight with some half naked slapper under my arm.

I looked down at the phone in dismay, then simply turned it off. I knew I had no comeback and my head was far too sore to think of one. I knew I was in trouble and would have to face the music. A few hours earlier I had been having such a great time, thinking that I was going to end the weekend smelling of roses, then after a night hugging the loo and a phone call from the missus, all I could smell was the shit I was going to be in when I got home.

"That's the last time I'm drinking" I said to Ant.

Back in the real world of sunny Manchester me and the lads were being put under a lot of pressure from the police's A Division. Whenever we were in groups of 4 or more we were targeted for stop and searches and the usual verbal bull shit that went along with them. The problem I had though was there were rarely ever fewer than four us regardless of the scenario.

My attitude towards violence had definitely started to change in my mid-thirties, I was happiest when trouble wasn't rearing its ugly head, a lot of the buzz had disappeared as I had matured, however I was compelled to keep up appearances for my enemies to see, so I could continue to show I was far from defenseless while Graeme was incarcerated and due to recruiting so many of United's hooligans into the mix, my gang was looking as big and as intimidating as ever before.

Across the North of England, the criminal underworld were well aware that our firm had become a major force to be reckoned with. Enemies were reluctant to risk venturing into our city because they knew I stood strong. I had long since moved away from the doors and was happier in the less violent drug business. I became keen on stepping out of the limelight a little and wanted a break from Manchester's unpredictable nightlife.

One Saturday night, in a cocktail bar on Deansgate, I was having a conversation with three very classy ladies when one of them asked why I wasn't drinking. I told her that it was because I can drive if I'm not drinking (I failed to mention that I got more pleasure being off my head on Es). She seemed to think it was great news and suggested I drove us all to a new club near the airport so we could carry the night on there. How could I refuse, I thought to myself. I told them I'd have to sneak out, otherwise my friends would insist on joining us and they would no doubt spoil our fun of getting to know each other.

The moment I drove into the club's car park I could tell the place stood out, mainly due to the swanky cars parked up, but also the clientele queuing to get in. The girls walked to the back of the queue but, having been a figure about Manchester for the previous twenty years I knew the head doorman so I walked to the front of the line and had a brief chat with the bouncers. One of the gentlemen went to the back of the queue to request that the girls joined me in the VIP room.

As a show of respect I went straight to the bar and gave the bartender money for three bottles of champagne for the doormen. I asked her to give them the choice of either the money or the champagne at the end of their shift. The three ladies I was entertaining couldn't believe that they were introducing me to the club, but I had ended up introducing them to the VIP area, where some well-known celebrities and footballers were already enjoying themselves. They were also bewildered by the amount of people that were letting on to me as we walked through the lounge.

I remained modest and told them that it must have been mistaken identity and I was being confused for somebody else, but they could see my insincerity and lapped it up.

At the end of a delightful night and without the slightest sign of trouble I believed I had had a right result. Not only with my new girlfriends but also with Kell's nightclub. I had found a new venue to relax and enjoy myself and I knew it would be amongst people that were far less likely to have a vendetta against me than those in our usual haunts.

I sneakily crept off from the lads, halfway through the following Saturday night and returned to Kell's again, this time on my own. As before I received the VIP treatment from the friendly bouncers. After getting myself an orange squash and putting a healthy tip behind the bar for the doormen, I stood in the corner of the VIP lounge watching everybody enjoying themselves, while I was happily coming up on ecstasy. I had another lovely night out. I mingled with a few acquaintances that I knew there, and I had a some nice chats with the bartenders and security staff. I felt as chilled out and relaxed on a night out as I had in a long time.

As I climbed into bed that night, I found it amazing that I'd been out two weeks on the trot without so much as a sniff of violence. Surely, I had found my new watering hole. I was determined to behave myself and continue to reap the rewards that Kell's had to offer me.

The next weekend as I approached the entrance to Kell's I noticed a different set of doormen working. I knew them because they worked at Old Trafford under Ned Kelly, who ran the security for Manchester United.

I had a friendly chat with the doormen and asked where the lads were from the previous two weeks. They told me the other doormen had been sacked because they had refused to bar me. I felt very guilty for their job losses, they were both decent men who were good at their jobs and had not deserved it. I asked who wanted me barred when I hadn't had a single ounce of trouble in there, to which they replied that it was the owner, who had a disliking of me.

As we were talking the doormen quickly ushered me inside as the owner had just driven into the car park. I had a look and noticed the suave cunt driving a black soft top Mercedes.

No sooner had I got into the VIP lounge, Ned Kelly came over to me explaining that the problem was the owner had heard of my terrible reputation for being involved in trouble. I informed Ned that I had been in for two weeks in a row and not had one single issue. I also assured him that I was hoping to keep it that way. Ned promised to have a word with the owner on my behalf and asked that I just tried to stay low key again that night.

I wasn't convinced about Ned putting a good word in for me, so I thought it was probably my last night in Kell's. To my delight I spotted the owner at the bar of the VIP lounge just moments later. It was my time to play mind games with the snide cunt and I made a bee line for him straight away. "I believe I don't have to introduce myself to you, because you're well aware of who I am. In fact, I heard that you sacked some very good doormen for letting me in here last week. As you can see your new doormen haven't knocked me back either and if they ever try to, I will hold you personally accountable". I went on to tell him that I knew the number plate of his very swanky, black, soft top Mercedes and could easily pass it on to a friendly bent copper I knew, who would then be able to inform me of the keeper's full identity and address. Even though I was bullshitting, the shit house folded. He must have thought I'd done my homework, with me knowing about his black Merc. I finished by telling him that I intended on spending all evening in the VIP area and if Ned Kelly and his team, or the police came to speak to me it would indicate to me that there was clearly an issue. "Now can I expect any problems this evening?" I asked.

Extremely apologetically he asked me to pardon the mix up and told me that I was welcome anytime as his guest. "Please allow me to get you a glass of champagne" he said.

I felt like applauding myself. It had been a Hollywood gangster style performance, and I had convinced him that I would hunt him down if I needed to.

For the next month or so I was having a delightful time with my newfound friends, but the lads had started to ask questions as to why I kept sneaking off early on a Saturday night. Some of them even thought that I had a mistress on the go. I was doing my best to deflect and dodge the questions, but I wasn't foolish enough to believe I could keep it up for long.

One night a doorman came over to me while I was in the Kell's, saying there were five lads asking to speak to me at the entrance. My gloriously untroubled nights in there had come to an end. Reluctantly and with my head hung in shame for lying to the boys, I gave the doormen a few quid and introduced my mates to Kell's VIP area. They clearly loved it, but we stood out like sore thumbs. The following Saturday a ridiculously large number of my firm joined me in there with their wives and girlfriends. Again, I stood alone in the corner watching everybody enjoying themselves. The difference that night however was I was standing there alone to hide the tears in my eyes.

It would be wrong of me to suggest that any one of my friends had not supported me through thick and thin. They have all been street warriors themselves and I am immensely proud of one and all. Each of them has been there at some point or other, ready to lay down their lives for me, as I have with them. I have led them into many battles, I have encouraged and even reveled in their hooligan, thug-like behaviour and I have enjoyed every minute of it, but the truth of the matter was that our behaviour had been disgraceful over the years and we had reached a point where something had to give.

Don't get me wrong, Monday to Friday and Saturday afternoon at the football I still wanted to be surrounded by my lunatic buddies, behaving as menacingly as we wished. Between the hours of 9pm and 5am on a Saturday night however I needed them to change their ways if we wanted to remain regulars in Kell's nightclub. Kell's after all was the best place for us to mingle, be it with top premier league footballers, celebrities, the rich and famous or even just the lovely ladies that were always close behind such folk. For that reason, I sat them all down one afternoon and we discussed making some adjustments. Put simply we had to behave.

When Kell's closed its doors for the night, most of the regulars from the VIP lounge would make their way through to the four seasons hotel, which was on the same complex. Believe it or not, the majority of the customers in the hotel bar after 3 o'clock in the morning were professional footballers. We would obviously never embarrass ourselves by falling at their feet, but we enjoyed being in the crowd. The footballers were none too bothered by our lot. Our worlds were miles apart. I was a street kid who had lived on every wing in Strangeways at some time or other, and most of my mates had similar backgrounds. There aren't too many millionaire premier league footballers that you would expect to relate to us. That being said it never seemed to stop me from asking if any of them had any spare Es at 3 in the morning, when I was off my nut.

Millionaire footballers generally seem to like mixing with other millionaire footballers, or at least other millionaires. There are always some exceptions to the rule though. Some top players that I've been fortunate enough to meet are very nice to Joe public. They can, after all, come from all walks of life and some of them know how hard the working class can have it. I'm not just being a biased red when I say this, but the nicest successful footballers that I ever met were the young Manchester United Class of 92. I believe the simple reason being that they were mostly from working class families and had grounded upbringings and in my opinion the friendliest of them all has to be David Beckham. He always had time for the likes of us. In fact, he gave Jeanette a fair bit of his time. They seemed to get along well. During one of their little chats Jeanette told David (or 'Becks' as she liked to refer to him, when she was showing off about knowing him) that we had a Rottweiler. He informed Jeanette that a Rottweiler is a pack dog and said it would be much happier if we got another one to keep it company. Naturally, that week I bought another rottweiler - after all who am I to argue with David Beckham? Beckham was impressed to hear that we had followed his advice and bought another Rottweiler. His next bit of advice for me was a little stranger. He said that I should spit in the dogs' mouths to let them know who their boss is.

So that following morning, nervously I sat the dogs down and spat in both of their mouths. I was half expecting to lose the end of my nose for my troubles, but remarkably it worked. Both dogs' demeanors changed almost instantly. They were much more responsive to me and if anything, they seemed to look at me more fondly.

Not being happy with my own dogs being at my 'Beck' and call, I began to experiment. Whenever I visited any of my friend's houses. I would spit in their dog's mouths when no one was looking. Nobody could ever understand why all their dogs seemed to love me more than them. Whenever I returned to their houses, even if it was months later, the dogs would still jump all over me and submit to me like I was the leader of the pack. Some of my mates weren't too impressed that I had more control over their pets than they did, but unfortunately Beckham hadn't shared his words of wisdom with them, so it was tough luck.

I briefly contemplated carrying out the same test on some of the beautiful ladies in Kell's but I figured it probably wouldn't have ended too well, so I decided to leave that one for Beckham to try first. I imagine there are plenty of starry-eyed women out there that would be happy to oblige him.

One weekend my mate, Five Star Keith (Keith invented his own nickname of Five Star, because he would refuse to stay anywhere other than five-star hotels or eat in anything but the best restaurants) arranged a big catch-up weekend with some of his friends. Keith is no stranger to Manchester's nightlife scene. He had been hitting the bars and clubs in town for as long as I had. He certainly needed no introduction to the club owners, or the doormen for that matter as he is a self-made millionaire who was not shy about splashing his cash. Outside of our firm Keith developed a much deserved fan club up and down the country. He is an affable bloke and always seemed to make new friends wherever he went.

A gang of lads from Lincoln travelled up to join Keith on his night out. The Lincoln lads were a firm of highly respected criminals and hooligans. Most of whom had travelled the length and breadth of England testing themselves against other hooligan outfits. Their main lad was big Mark. Mark's a very powerful lad, a throwback from the good old days where fighters would go toe to toe and the best man won. He was a real tough lad with a strong heart. Another of their top boys was a guy who was years ahead of his time. Smokey was an international drug smuggler and was making huge sums of money from importing, long before I had even considered it.

I knew all the Lincoln firm well, they were a great bunch to hang out with. Whenever they came up to Manchester you could guarantee there would be fireworks.

That particular night we hit the town in numbers and had a ball. Later we made our way to Kell's and again we had a brilliant laugh. By the time it was closing and we moved across to the four-season hotel it dawned on me there had been no trouble all night. I was impressed, if not a little surprised. Just as I was beginning to beam with the pride that I felt about myself and the lads' new and improved behaviour, I pushed open the doors to the bar area of the Four Seasons hotel and discovered an almighty scuffle had broken out.

The bar was full of Manchester City footballers, which didn't go down well with the die-hard reds from Lincoln. We were used to seeing the City lot and usually just ignored them and let them be, after all we had to live alongside each other and it would be pointless for us to shoe them in every time we bumped into them (fun, but pointless). Our Lincolnshire friends however felt differently, they weren't used to seeing them out and their blood collectively boiled. They saw supporting United almost like a marriage, it was a lifelong commitment, and they set about proving it by rushing the City players, attacking them with beer, wine and champagne bottles. It wasn't a particularly sporting attack but I had to raise my glass to the show of passion. Watching it gave me quite a buzz too.

There was a bit of a downside to the attack, from our point of view, because the City player that took the brunt of the beating and was actually hospitalised, was a born and bred Salford lad. He was another example of someone from a working-class background who had done well for himself. Like any true Salford lad he never pressed charges. The fact that he didn't was obviously not enough for the incident to avoid making headline News though.

The News of the World read: Footballer Terry Phelan, assaulted by thugs wielding champagne bottles. The article went on to tell how the thugs were all believed to be Manchester United football hooligans and were all dressed from head to toe in black attire.

Reading it made me smile from ear to ear. More so in the weeks that followed as other football hooligans started to refer to us United hooligans as 'The Men in Black'.

A line from another paper also made me laugh. It read how 'police questioned customers that were there at the time of the attack, but each one said they had been in the toilet during the incident'.

Ned phoned me that week and asked what had happened. I had no choice but to tell him the truth…. "I didn't see a thing, as I was in the toilet".

People often jump to their own conclusions when they first meet me.

They look at my appearance, they hear my speech (I have a slight speech impediment which results in me sounding a bit like an American mobster) and they make a snap judgement. Obviously, my reputation precedes me and further fuels their negative opinions.

I have occasionally been known to use some folks' assumptions about me as an opportunity to have a bit of fun with them - more so when I've had an E and I'm feeling mischievous.

Sometimes I'll tell gangster stories, which are partially true but with some bullshit added in to spice things up a little. Or I may let share a few ideas I have about how to pull off audacious crimes.

A few weeks after the Terry Phelan incident, I was sitting in the VIP lounge with Ned Kelly, a couple of regulars and some other footballers, generally just having a chin wag and enjoying my night, when the discussion turned to crime and one of them, being a pissed up, nosey fucker, asked me if I had ever murdered anybody. I was initially pretty pissed off with the line of questioning. As a criminal, that is something you would never ask another, especially if you didn't really know them. I decided however to have a bit of fun with the cheeky fucker.

"In answer to your question, I have been arrested, but never convicted of murder, therefore I am not a murderer" I said. I purposely said it that way because, firstly it was true, but secondly it was obviously controversial. Without allowing anybody any time to interrupt me I continued "I won't discuss with you any crimes that I have committed, because if you were to pass my words on, you could land me in a lot of trouble, and if you did that, then the chances of me becoming a murderer may increase. What I'll do instead is let you all in on a little secret. It isn't about what I've done, but is something I was considering doing, and it affects some of you around this table". They all fell silent and a collection of ears pricked up in unison. A couple of them even leant right in to hear my big reveal.

"Now I must stress that since I've become friends with Ned, I've put a stop to this plan".

Ned looked at me as if to ask What the fuck's going on here Paul? "Now as you're all well aware" I continued "I have an army of somewhat undesirable men that are willing to stand by me to the very end if necessary. Most are hardened criminals and all of them are keen to make a quick buck. Well some months ago we had a meeting with numerous other iconic Manchester criminals, to discuss a plan that had potential to make us all rich overnight".

By the time I had finished giving them the introduction, they were all mesmerized. I considered stopping there and screaming BOO, just to see who jumped the furthest. I didn't though, I actually went on to tell them about a plot we had concocted to send both Manchester United and Manchester City football clubs a list of the addresses of all their players. As well as a second list of local establishments, such as Kell's, amongst others, that they often frequented socially.

Along with the lists was to be a demand for protection money, to ensure no harm came to their Premier league stars when they were out and about.

Just imagine the dilemma United would have found themselves in if we had started breaking the legs of their class of 92 players. It could have changed football history books for a start, but also no elite professionals would ever want to join United again. (Not many were that keen on joining City at that time anyway, but that's besides the point.)

"Consider the rise in the insurance premiums" I continued. "They would go up tenfold. Surely it would be better paying us off rather than taking the risk" At that point Ned butted in "You would never get away with it, you'd be arrested".

"Quite possibly Ned" I said, "I have been arrested many times before though and a court would have to prove beyond any reasonable doubt that I committed the crime and let's not forget this wouldn't be my first rodeo".

They all bought my story hook line and sinker. I got up from the table and patted Ned on his shoulder, simply saying "I'll leave you chaps to think that one over".

I could see a mixture of anger and frustration in his face, but some of the footballers looked more like crying. They were clearly giving it some thought. I could barely refrain from bursting out laughing.

The truth behind the story is that I had seriously considered it as a plausible idea. The bull shit behind the story though is that I never actually floated the idea around amongst any other gangsters and it never came close to transpiring. I couldn't have done that to my beloved United, regardless of the money and City didn't have many good players anyway.

I do believe that that mischievous little anecdote ended up backfiring on me, as a couple of weeks later I was given a tip off, from a reliable inside source, that the police had an operation on me and my firm and were closely monitoring our behaviour in Kell's.

Within weeks of my tip off, new, super modern, 'the dog's bollocks' type security cameras were fitted on the ceilings in Kell's, they were extremely advanced for their time. It was still long before every Tom Dick and Harry had CCTV in their homes. The cameras were video and audio and one just happened to be positioned directly above where our group congregated in the VIP lounge. They also installed some in the Four Seasons hotel.

One of my long-standing friends at the time was Sully. Myself, Sully and Coco were dragged up side by side in the Reform schools and formed close bonds.

Sully could get into most women's knickers just with his good looks. His romances never used to last too long however because poor Sully had a dark side. I believe it was caused by his terrible childhood in the system. An upbringing like that would have a negative effect on anybody and later in life Sully developed a drug problem.

In the earlier years after being released from our respective Borstals and prisons, myself and Sully often carried out raids together. We hit jewellery stores around Greater Manchester and made quite the team - as we were both thieving little cunts.

At the end of one Saturday night, me Sully and another mate of ours, Big George, ended up in the bar of the Four Seasons. The place was busier than normal, largely because Andy Cole was having a birthday celebration with a few of his friends. The champagne was flowing and Cole and his gathering were clearly enjoying themselves.

At some point during the night me and Sully bumped into him coming out of the toilet and Sully who was a few sheets to the wind said to Cole "My friend bet good money on you to score today, but you kept fucking missing. Do you need it on a plate or something?"

At that moment I stepped in between the two of them and told Andy Cole to take no notice because Sully was drunk.

A couple of hours later as the place was beginning to empty Sully, unprompted shouted over to Cole "Hey Andy the night's nearly finished, it's a shame you can't finish".

With that Cole went crazy, shouting "What's your fucking problem?" Sully argued back that he supported United week in week out and that Cole never scores, "that's my fucking problem" he said. Cole took his comments right to heart and whipped his jumper off to have it out with Sully "Come on then" Cole was shouting, he was ready to go there and then.

I held Sully back while George and the doormen tried to calm Andy down.

One of his friends said Andy, come on you're a professional footballer not a fighter. Cole shouted over to Sully "I'm not playing football tonight though".

Sully was equally up for it, so I reminded him the police were recording his every move on their new security cameras. With that he looked up to the ceiling, then fetched a bar stool. He climbed up on the stool and ripped the camera down, before whipping out his cock and pissing all over it.

Sully's behaviour was painfully embarrassing, but it really wasn't anything out of the ordinary for our lot and I have to admit finding it hysterically funny at the time. For Andy Cole it may have been the kick up the arse that got his United career off the ground, as he following weekend he scored a hat trick before obviously going on to become one of United's most successful goal scorers of all time and a legend at Old Trafford.

Unfortunately, Sully's future was far less successful. He didn't live long enough. Sully died from a drug overdose and became another poor soul who died too young.

Strangely in all the years I considered Sully a true friend, I only ever knew him by his nickname.

His real name was Anthony Sullivan.

My Saturday's became fairly routine, they started with a fry up at home with the family, before heading out to meet the boys. We would usually gather at about midday (earlier if United were playing away) and start our hunt for opposing football hooligans. After a good battle I would watch the game and enjoy a pie or two, before leaving the ground and heading into Manchester city centre to start our evening out. Most the lads got pissed up while I munched my way through ecstasy pills. Sometime before midnight we'd set off to Kell's and end our night in there. There was a predictability about it all but for me it was just what I needed after a hard week at the office. The fact a blood thirsty serial killer was breathing down my neck, made it even more important for me to have one day a week where I could just kick back and relax.

Although we'd had a pretty successful start to our time in Kell's there had been more and more incidents creeping in that were putting us in danger of being barred. One of the recurring themes seemed to be upsetting the footballers. In the space of just a few months Terry Phelan and his pals had taken a beating, I had scared a table full of them into believing that there may have been a conspiracy to demand protection money, in order to prevent local gangsters from crippling them and then Sully had ruined Andy Cole's birthday celebrations with their little dispute.

I was mindful of our behaviour deteriorating again, but old habits die hard and the night that Dwight Yorke made his Old Trafford debut things kicked off again. United's newest signing scored twice that day in front of 50,000 delighted United fans and the party began there. Kell's was particularly busy that night and when Cole arrived with his new strike partner, the place began to buzz. Yorke was getting a lot of attention, in fact, he was literally being mobbed by well-wishers. He could barely take a piss without being harassed and quite possibly the attention was too much for him because he was very rude to a lady friend of mine when she approached him and introduced herself.

"Hi, you may know my husband" is all that she said to which Yorke rudely replied "How exactly would I know your husband" before barging passed her without another word.

She came back over to our table and explained what had happened.

I couldn't believe it. I glared over in Yorke's direction and Cole caught my eye.

After the Sully incident he was a little wiser as to what we were all about and I think he realised Dwight had ruffled some feathers. Cole grabbed him by the arm and took him to one side for a word in his ear. A minute or so later Yorke came over and asked the girl if she would accept his apology and a drink. She was too classy to say no, and luckily for him the incident was put behind them. United player or not Yorke got off lightly, because rocking up in Manchester and treating people with such disrespect is a punishable behaviour, especially such a lovely lady friend of mine.

Later that night Yorke bore witness to exactly what could happen when friends of ours became victims of disrespectful behaviour. I was making my way over to Ned Kelly's table to say hello when a fight broke out behind me. I had more than a suspicion it was going to be one of our lot, so I immediately U-turned to investigate. I was right, and it was my mate Mick right in the middle of things. Surprisingly, Mick was being punched all over the place virtually without responding. Usually he is a match for any man, but there was this young professional footballer who was easily getting the better of him. I had a gut instinct that something wasn't as it seemed.

Some of the customers saw it as great entertainment and one in particular was encouraging the fight. It was another young footballer from Man City and he was telling people to stand back and leave them to it. I felt I had to do something though because Mick was taking a pasting.

As Ned was watching the whole thing and because the attacker was just a youngster, I didn't go in all guns blazing. I simply dragged the lad away from Mick and said, "Fellas you know that this isn't how you should be behaving in front of ladies". I then grabbed hold of Coco and told him to get Mick cleaned up in the toilets before we all got barred.

Coco took Mick to clean up the blood, which we had presumed was coming from his face, as he had clearly taken a lot of punches. Whilst in the toilets though Coco found a large piece of broken glass sticking out of Mick's neck. He had been stabbed. Coco came storming out of the toilets raging, he was going absolutely berserk and screaming "Where's that cunt gone, where is he, where is he". Coco wanted revenge for Mick's cowardly attack but somebody had obviously realised the danger the lad was in and had snuck him out of the fire exit. Coco started to vent his fury on the City footballer who had been shouting for people to leave them to fight.

I was yelling at Coco to tell me what the fuck was going on. In the middle of kicking the shit out of the guy, Coco shouted "the bastards stabbed Mick". A couple of ladies rushed off to the toilets to help Mick while me and my mates started knocking holes out of the rest of their crew. The footballers and their friends were getting knocked all over the place. It was carnage. There was a good bit of retribution taken that night in what must have been an eye opener for Dwight Yorke. I imagine he realised how close he had come to being on the wrong side of us. Welcome to Manchester Dwight.

After some investigating of our own we found out the lad who had stabbed Mick actually played for Stockport County. Forty plus hooded lads paid a visit to County's training ground that week. Half the players ran from the pitch terrified as they saw them approaching. One of the heads of the gang spoke with the coaching staff and explained that unless compensation was paid to Mick, Manchester would not be a safe place for any of their players to be seen.

The message was obviously understood as Mick received £40k.

The whole affair made me think back to my earlier conversation with Ned and the footballers. Demanding protection money from big clubs could well have been a lucrative career move.

Chapter 26:

LURED TO AN HORRIFIC DEATH

Graeme was due to be released from prison, so I contacted his girlfriend to see if she wanted me to pick him up and drive him home. She said they had already arranged to spend some time together in London, so she was going to pick him up herself. She asked if I could drop off Graeme's money at her house beforehand. I thought the request was odd. If I came out of prison and someone was handing over two hundred grand, I would want to at least show my appreciation before I went anywhere.

I knew prison had taken its toll on Graeme though. He was very different from me and many of my other mates, and he saw prison very differently. He hated everything about the place, from the stench to the regime. I figured a few days in London might lift his spirits and he would come back ready to carry on where he had left off.

After a couple of weeks away Graeme eventually came back wanting to discuss his future.

I told him that business was steady however I felt the police were possibly closing in on me over a few different things. Firstly the drugs business, secondly all the nonsense regarding William and thirdly me and my newly developed army of hooligan gangsters.

My attitude to it all was simple, box clever and try to stay one step ahead but if the worst happens, then it is what it is, we crack on with our prison time and come out fit and fresh. It was after all the career I had chosen and it came with the territory. Graeme's attitude was completely different though, which was amazing really, considering not too long before his sentence he had been carrying out all sorts of atrocities in Amsterdam that the majority of hardcore criminals wouldn't even contemplate doing. He clearly felt that going back inside was the worst outcome for him personally and he was weighing up his options.

I kept telling Graeme that we needed to address the major ongoing situation we had hanging over our shoulders - namely William, before one of us ended up dead. He blankly refused to even discuss it though. He was happy enough to continue making money from the cannabis (which I had been putting all the work into) and pretend that everything else would just sort itself out. Graeme appeared to be somewhat of a changed man. I wondered if he could have been the first man to be rehabilitated by the system. As far as I was concerned though William was the most devious, manipulative, not to mention evil man on the planet and I knew full well that at some point he would make another move on one, or both of us.

Graeme started spending more time with his new found friends SAS Gerry and Billy the kickboxer. I made it clear to Graeme that I didn't like nor trust either of them, but he told me that he wasn't exactly a fan of some of my mates, but as he didn't keep banging on about it he asked me to respect his decisions. Deep down we understood each other, we were from different walks of life, but me and him worked very well together and we were good friends, so there was no point upsetting the apple cart. We were there for each other if necessary and that was important. Graeme still had his investment in The Temple in Bolton and from time to time he would put in a shift on the doors there.

Late one Saturday night I drove onto my close to find Graeme's car parked up outside my house. I knew he was in some kind of trouble and would be wanting advice. Before I even got out of the car I could see he was covered in blood. I figured it wasn't likely to be his own and so I asked him what it was he had done. He explained that whilst at The Temple two groups of lads had tried to get in. The first group he allowed in, the second however he refused entry. It turned out the two groups were together and both lots began arguing with the doormen. Graeme told me he had led the way in launching both sets of lads out, but when the other doormen returned to their jobs, Graeme decided he wasn't content and gave a few of them a little bitch slap, but nothing major. The lads however didn't take it very well and found his actions humiliating. They decided to take revenge - oblivious to the fact they were dealing with Manchester's hardest psychopath.

An hour later they returned, tooled up and confident of exacting revenge. It didn't however pan out quite as they were hoping. Single handedly Graeme not only knocked out all five of them but to add insult to injury he also bit a chunk out of the main aggressor's cheek as well as biting the tip of his finger off. Right there lay his predicament, he couldn't claim self defence due to the damage he had inflicted and Graeme was well aware of the trouble he was in.

Not wanting to stress Graeme out more than he already was, I told him that if the lads had the mindset to attack him, tooled up, there was a chance they were criminals themselves therefore unlikely to press charges. I gave him a change of clothes (that didn't exactly fit him) and advised him to go away for a few days, keep his head down and hope things blow over.

The police turned up at Graeme's house a couple of days after the incident with a warrant for his arrest. They would have known that he was one of the only men around capable and prepared to inflict such damage, fighting alone against five men. His solicitor arranged an appointment for him to be interviewed. There's always a chance of bail with a half decent solicitor present but in those days without one you were usually fucked.

Down at the station it became apparent that the only person pressing charges was the lad who had his cheek bitten off. Graeme made a no comment interview but the police took his bite sample, which was sent to the lab for testing. Apparently no two bite marks are exactly the same, therefore a clear bite mark could prove to be almost as definitive as a fingerprint. Graeme's future was looking bleak but he was granted bail for 8 weeks.

That month proved to be a busy time for me, I was organising our next shipment of cannabis, while allowing Graeme a bit of free time to relax and enjoy himself, just in case his days as a free man were numbered. Little did I know then but it wasn't just Graeme's liberty that was at risk. As much as I detested Gerry it was nice to see Graeme getting back to his old self and he seemed to be doing that with him. Apparently he was on a winning streak with the ladies too (as he put it) bedding four or five a week. I would catch up with him daily to discuss our drug enterprise, but we weren't seeing too much of each other aside from that. He would bang on about Gerry more and more every time I saw him. One day he started talking about some beautiful apartment in a picturesque town in the Costa del Sol. One of Gerry's close lady friends owned it and was happy to welcome him to stay with her.

He went on to tell me he was considering jumping bail and moving over there.

Once again I voiced my concerns about Gerry, but it fell on deaf ears. I thought he seemed overly eager for Graeme to go out to Spain and suspected he wanted to use him as an enforcer over there. Gerry was brainwashing him with talk of golf, beautiful women and training everyday outside in the sunshine. Something wasn't sitting right with me but there was only so much I could say. Graeme had asked me to stop complaining about Gerry and I had to respect his wishes. He was a big boy anyway and I knew he would make his own decision.

A few days passed without hearing anything from Graeme before he called in to see me at the yard to tell me his mind was made up. He was as giddy as a big kid, bragging that he would be staying with some old madame who ran a high-class brothel, and how he would have his pick of women when he was over there. I was disappointed with Graeme's decision to go, I thought it was reckless with the history we had in Europe with William and stupid to go on the run. Obviously, we believed William was wanted by the Moroccans though and wouldn't be showing his face in Spain for a long time, but we knew he had many connections and Graeme was not the kind of bloke to go unnoticed. The psychopath in Graeme left him with no sense of fear however and the prospect of running into William's henchmen didn't faze him, furthermore he was adamant he didn't want to go back to jail. I argued that he should accept his punishment and do his sentence. I believed having it hanging over him would affect his happiness and stop him from being able to return home. He wasn't interested in listening, there was nothing I could do or say to change his mind. As crying about it isn't exactly my style, I instead took him for a farewell night out in Kells.

During our night out I was enjoying a pleasant chat with one of the most beautiful women you could wish to meet, a very classy lady who's not short of a few quid either. Every smooth sod in there had tried their luck with her at some point or another, but to no avail. Me and her got on well though and she always seemed comfortable around me. That particular night she was telling me about her tennis lessons when an idea popped into my head. As it was Graeme's farewell night I thought I would do him a favour and introduce them.

"I'm with a pal of mine tonight who could have been a professional tennis player" I said. "I think you think you might like him". "Paul you know I'm not easily impressed", she replied.

I did at that point consider telling her about the time I poked a 20 stone bouncer in the eyes and had him at my knees, crying like a baby. It was Graeme's night though so I continued to sell him to her instead. "He's a good friend of mine and it's his leaving do, why don't you just say hello".

I called Graeme over and introduced them to one another, before leaving them to it while I went to mingle.

Within an hour they came over together to say their goodbyes. She winked at me as if to say "Thanks, I am impressed". I did briefly question what I had done setting her up with him, knowing what an animal he could be in the bedroom. She might be quite a goer herself though I thought, after all they say it's the quiet ones you should look out for.

When I caught up with Graeme the next day he was in a very jolly mood. He said they had had a great time together. He also said that he wanted to treat some of the lads to a barbecue at his house before he left. I pointed out that it wasn't exactly barbeque weather, but he insisted.

He asked me to invite a few of the boys but was adamant that everyone should park their cars at the end of his street and to be quiet, so as not to disturb his neighbours. I was very puzzled by it all, Graeme usually didn't give a fuck about upsetting anybody, so why be so arsed about neighbours he was moving away from, and why would he have an evening time barbecue in the middle of February. Regardless, I put the word out and I went along with my brother Mark.

When I parked my car we were met by one of Graeme's friends who told us to go straight into the back garden and not to make a sound. He said there was a surprise instore for us but it was imperative that we were silent. Now as everybody knows, on a dark night, if you have your lights on in the house you can't see outside, however everybody outside can see clearly into a well-lit room. When we got into the garden the first thing I saw was about a dozen of Graeme's friends standing in front of a table full of drinks and sandwiches, staring through the patio doors into the house. The lads all had great big dirty grins on their faces, so I turned to see what they were looking at. To my horror I saw my tennis playing friend from Kell's, legs akimbo while Graeme was shagging her on the dining room table, with an array of sex toys scattered around the room. I had to laugh, but I did feel very sorry for the poor girl. She obviously had no idea that she was being gawped at by a bunch of Graeme's pervy pals. I refused to stay and watch, but shamefully my brother Mark refused to leave. He said it was great entertainment and wanted to watch the full show. Later that night he phoned me to say that after Graeme had finished *making love to her* he opened up the patio doors, while she still lay there naked, to the rapturous applause of his crowd. I couldn't believe he could be so cruel and I felt terribly guilty for introducing them.

Days later Graeme set off to Spain in search of a brighter future than the one he was in for back here. SAS Gerry went with him to make sure he settled in okay at the hooker's villa.

After a little while of them being over there, Gerry took Graeme to see some Moroccan drug lord who offered them tons of cannabis at an unbelievable price. He phoned me and told me about the deal. I immediately said it was very unlikely to be genuine, but I would make a call and see if it sounded at all plausible. I rang a very respectable cannabis dealer in Barcelona. He confirmed to me that it was not even possible to buy cannabis in Morocco at that price, never mind sell it, that meant it was either a con or it was shit stuff that they couldn't get rid of.

I rang Graeme back and told him what my pal had said. I also told him that I had no desire to change anything anyway, because business was running smoothly with the Dutch firm and furthermore I didn't want to work with Gerry. Graeme said that he felt he owed him and asked me if I would do him a personal favour of meeting Gerry upon his return to Manchester (which was later that week). Reluctantly I agreed, even though it was a hassle I could do without.

We arranged to meet at a pub near my house. When I got there I sat outside in the beer garden, for some privacy. Gerry soon arrived and went to the bar for drinks. When he came out he sat uncomfortably close to me, which I wasn't the least bit impressed about - it even crossed my mind that he might be queer. I put it down to the sensitive nature of the intended talks and tried to forget about it.

Gerry led the conversation. "Paul, we all have a chance to make a large amount of money" he said, "but cards on the table, we're depending on you. I know Graeme has already told you about our meeting with the Moroccans. We can sort the transport, so the final piece of the puzzle is you distributing it over here". I told him the price for the cannabis is far too cheap, so I believed the stuff had to be shit and I wouldn't be able to sell shit stuff. He said, "We all know what the price should be but this particular Moroccan is one of the biggest suppliers of cannabis in the South of Spain, he is also a genuine friend and that is why we're getting such a great deal".

I was starting to let down my guard a little, Gerry was very convincing, he didn't seem like such a prick when he was on his own either. Perhaps he was just a show-boater, I thought.

He asked if I was capable of selling a large quantity. I told him "At that price I could sell ten tonnes a month without breaking sweat". I was exaggerating, but Gerry lapped it up and told me that the Moroccans would be delighted to hear that.

"My friend will need to meet you in person though Paul. He has one or two questions to ask you and it is important for him to look you in the eye, to see if you are trustworthy. He is a great believer in his own ability to read a man by looking him in the eye".

That sounded odd to me, but I thought it may just have been a cultural thing, so I did no more than raise an eyebrow. Gerry then continued, saying "He has already paid for your flight to Spain and has arranged for you to stay in his favourite five-star hotel in the Costa Del Sol".

I had a sense of Deja vu, William had used exactly the same tactics when he arranged for me and Graeme to visit him in Amsterdam. The deal was sounding too good to be true and my suspicious, paranoid, criminal mind started churning at 100 miles an hour, evaluating the situation.

I was puzzled as to why a drug lord would lay on millions of pounds worth of drugs based solely on trustworthy eyes. It just didn't make sense to me, there was something amiss, but I couldn't put my finger on it and the profit margins were starting to lure me in.

While my mind was accelerating into overdrive I found myself gazing down, deep in concentration. Without realising it I had focused my eyes directly onto Gerry's wallet. He had placed it between the two of us on the table. After a few moments of being consumed in deep thought, I realised I was actually staring at a badge on the wallet. I had not spotted it earlier, but the badge stood out a mile. It was ridiculously big for a wallet of that size. All of a sudden the reality of it all hit me, I was being recorded. The badge was that out of place that it had to be a transmitting device. That was the reason he had placed it on the table right under my nose and that was why he had sat so close to me. Gerry had to be an undercover copper.

My mind went blank for a few seconds. I couldn't believe I had put myself in a predicament like that. I was desperately trying to remember everything I had said, so I could attempt to unpick it. 'I could sell 10 tonnes a month without breaking sweat'. It had only been an off the cuff remark, but it was looking like it could be a costly one. I wanted to give myself a slap to the face.

I raised my head and put my forehead right up to Gerry's and glared at him with a look of sheer evil. "Can you read a man by looking into his eyes?" I asked. Gerry looked puzzled. "You can never judge a book by its cover" I then said. "Do you really believe I could sell 10 tonnes of cannabis a month? You must be fucking mad, I don't even touch the stuff, so don't waste my time with your stories of a Moroccan drug lord, five-star hotels and sun tans in the Costa Del Sol, it means nothing to me". With that I got up and left.

I got into my car and drove straight to the nearest phone box. I rang Graeme to tell him we were being set up. He told me that I was being totally paranoid and he thought I needed time to reconsider things. I insisted to him that I was right and I didn't need any time to reconsider anything. We began to argue back and forth, but my points were falling on deaf ears.

I'll never forget the way he ended that conversation with me "There's no talking to you sometimes Paul, I'll phone you tomorrow" he said and with that the line went dead.

I headed home where I sat in my chair and had an hour to myself deep in thought.

Was I wrong?

Was I stupid to think Gerry was working for the police?

Why would he get Graeme out of the country if he was?

I knew something wasn't right. If it wasn't that he was an undercover, then why on earth would he record our conversation?

Maybe he was a police informer I thought, or maybe he's working for somebody else.

All of a sudden, like a lightning bolt hitting me, everything became clear. Gerry was working for William.

He must have been. My feelings of Deja vu were bang on the money. William was trying to lure me to Spain, and he had already got Graeme there. His manipulative skills had come into play once more. Gerry had been used to trick Graeme into moving over to the Costa Del Sol with the notion of women, sunshine and a new life (without a prison sentence hanging over him). He knew I wouldn't have gone over there for those reasons though, so he then used Gerry to trick Graeme into getting me on a plane. William knew promises of tonnes of stupidly cheap cannabis from a Moroccan drug lord would more than likely spike my interest.

All William had done was sit back and pull the strings while that snidey twat SAS Gerry carried out his dirty work. I escaped a very close call by spotting that badge, but I knew Graeme was in grave danger. For over an hour I tried calling him, constantly calling time after time. It was just ringing out though, there was no answer. The evil pair must have realised it wouldn't have taken me too long to work out what they were planning and the last thing they wanted was for me to scupper their plans by informing Graeme his life was in big danger.

After an hour or more of calling I knew deep down that they had already got to Graeme. I kept trying his phone just in case he was still angry and blanking me, but I knew. I also tried calling Gerry's phone but that was switched off. Gerry was more than likely on his way to Spain by that point, to finish off the job he and William had been conspiring, for God only knows how long.

William must have been furious that I'd slipped through the net, which probably wouldn't have boded too well for Graeme and was no doubt why they acted so quickly in finally getting to him.

According to what I have heard since that fateful day, they instructed the madame he was staying with to drug him, then while he was passed out, some henchmen walked into the villa, bound him with chains and carted him away to a waiting William.

It disturbs me to think of the hell Graeme would have gone through. William is the sickest of the sick. He trains his men to do things that most human beings couldn't ever imagine doing. Sadly, by all accounts there was no quick death for Graeme. That wouldn't have been allowed. The verminous bastard partied with him. I received word that during his torture, William was sending out snippets of information to his criminal associates, especially those in Spain and Manchester. The nuggets of information included him using the services of a surgeon from the Bosnian war, courtesy of the

Yugoslavian mafia, who kept Graeme alive for as long as possible to prolong his agony, not to mention William's entertainment. He was no doubt taking immense pride in becoming known as the man who took down Manchester's most dangerous man, an individual that no one else had been able to handle. He apparently even tried to make out that Graeme was the real monster and that the world was better off without him.

The rumours of what William and his gang did to Graeme made it pretty obvious as to who the real monsters were though.

Word has it that William and his men allegedly broke parts of Graeme's body, not to cause his death, but to cause him the maximum amount of pain. The surgeon was rumoured to have injected him with a serum that thickens the blood, so they could chop off bits of Graeme's body without him bleeding to death. There was even a suggestion that they cut off his lips to make pulling out his teeth easier. The most sickening rumour I heard was that they burned and removed his testicles, before shoving them into his mouth.

After two long days of torture Graeme's heart finally gave up.

There was never and probably will never be a murder case regarding his disappearance as what remained of his body was never found.

Stories of Graeme's despicable demise were rife across the criminal underworld. It is impossible to know exactly what is true and what isn't, but I know some falsehoods were told, for instance some believed William had sent me a video of the torture so that I would know what to expect if he finally caught up with me. That didn't happen and I'm grateful that it didn't. I have had enough sleepless nights thinking about what my poor friend went through. I have enough horrible images etched inside my head they still sometimes haunt me when I close my eyes at night.

Days after the killing William was supposedly strolling around the Costa del Sol with his head held high, in the belief he had taken himself to a new level in the criminal underworld. For him, Graeme's murder was about revenge, but also claiming another trophy. He will no doubt have shown photographs of Graeme's head on a plate to somebody somewhere and he will have done so with an perverse sense of pride.

I'm not sure what reward SAS Gerry would have received from William for his part in the murder, but I am convinced that he was involved simply because he wanted to be. He is a total fantasist. Everything about him from his lifestyle right down to his nickname is a sham. He wanted to commit the perfect murder and get away with it. Luring Graeme to Spain, then being involved in his torture and murder was like being a lead character in a movie for Gerry. The man has a bizarre outlook on life and of himself. One thing I don't think he would have been too pleased about however was the bragging from William. Gerry probably feared that that kind of behaviour could ruin everything from his point of view. His perfect murder would no longer be perfect if he was to end up rotting in jail for it. Which begs the questions:

How does William get away with his murders time and time again?

How can a cold-blooded killer openly boast about his killings, seemingly without any fear of being arrested?

I was once told that William had the Spanish police in his pocket, allegedly paying them to not only turn a blind eye but also to protect him. I wondered if that could be true and also whether or not he had any other policing bodies on the payroll.

Chapter 27:

CHASED OUT OF TOWN

William had no doubt wanted to kill me and Graeme side by side. The fact that I managed to avoid such a fate left him reeling. I believe that the brutality of Graeme's murder was supposed to be a message to me. It was supposed to scare me. However it didn't, it just angered me. I have lived and breathed violence my entire life, I have been a street fighter, a drug dealer, a football hooligan, a doorman. I have been shot at more times than I care to remember. Violence went hand in hand with the path I had chosen. William had laid his cards on the table, but I wasn't scared, I just knew I had to be ready to fight fire with fire. And aside from all that, I wanted revenge.

I knew I had to remain visible around town, I could show no weakness. Deep down I was feeling overwhelming sadness at the loss of my good friend, but on the outside I needed to show a steely calm and continue as much as possible as if Graeme's death hadn't affected me. My tears were all beaten out of me as a kid, so I was more than capable of hiding my emotions and coming out fighting - quite literally.

In the few months that followed, William's orchestration of the torturous murder became the talk of Manchester. Graeme's reputation had preceded him for years, he had been a big fish in the North West of England for the best part of a decade, prior to his death and was considered the hardest bloke around (which was at a time when there was a number of serious challengers to that mantle). His murder gave William the notoriety he had been craving. It became apparent that Gerry and Billy however didn't want to be sitting up on that pedestal. Gerry especially wanted to ensure no one would find out about his role in Graeme's demise. After staying out of the country for a few months he was back in England and contacted a friend of mine, asking that a message be passed on to me, requesting a meet.

I agreed and said that I would meet them in any park of their choice. Obviously, the pair of shit bags refused to meet anywhere so discreet and said they wanted it to be in a bar in town. At least one of them was a torturous murderer and the other, if he wasn't directly involved in, was an ex-fighter, yet still they wanted the safety of doormen and security cameras. I agreed to their proposal as I knew they were too cowardly to meet me anywhere else and I was intrigued as to what the pair of scum bags had to say for themselves. I was far from impressed with my so-called friend for ever agreeing to meet with the pair of scumbags in the first place and so I sent back a little message of my own, to make it clear as to how I was feeling, I battered the low life, then ordered him to go straight back to Gerry and Billy before he cleaned himself up.

For the following days I was stressing about how to handle the situation. I considered going down with an army of both mine and Graeme's friends. A pub fight wasn't going to achieve anything though, my thirst for revenge would not be satisfied so easily. I contemplated going kamikaze and shooting them both on sight but knew that wouldn't be the right way to handle it either. That would only have left me in prison, unable to get back at William, and as much as I despised Gerry for what he had done, William was still the pivotal figure behind everything. He was my main target, I opted to simply go to the bar alone and try to keep my emotions in check. Deep down I knew it was a tall task even attempting to remain level headed, when inside I was livid and on top of that I was hurting.

The few hours before the meeting, I spent alone, focusing my mind. I realised I needed a distraction to stave off the uncontrollable rage that may have erupted as soon as I clapped eyes on the snidey cunts. I was almost practicing a role play. I decided to treat it like a game of poker, and I worked on my best poker face as I drove into town.

I parked my car in a side street away from the agreed destination. Walking towards the bar I saw a couple of people who may as well have had 'undercover copper' tattooed on their foreheads. I wasn't perturbed though, I kept walking and focusing on my poker face, all the while telling myself to relax and stick to the plan. I walked through the doors into a packed bar and yet the only face I saw was Gerry's, everybody else became a blur. I sensed he could read the hatred in my eyes. My plan went straight out of the window and I smashed him flush on the jaw. Three doormen jumped in between us while the coward crawled off behind the bar. I was at boiling point, heavily outnumbered and being held back, I could barely move let alone fight, but I was still letting Billy know in no uncertain terms that he would need all his kickboxing skills and more if I ever saw him again, because he was next on my list.

I managed to pull myself free, before being grabbed again. It was the two undercover coppers from outside and they were quickly joined by a handful more.

Down at the station I was informed that the police had been watching my movements for a while and had been concerned that dead bodies were going to start appearing in and around Manchester. By that time they were clearly aware of what had happened in Spain, even though they were doing fuck all about it. Gerry wasn't about to start pressing charges so they held me long enough for town to quieten down before taking me back to my car. I was warned to stay away from Gerry and Billy and told I would be being closely monitored.

It had become common knowledge that I was William's next target, however what I was telling people in no uncertain terms was that he was mine, as were Gerry and Billy. I spent months making sure that everybody knew what those snidey lowlifes had done and that I was prepared to pay good money to have Gerry handed to me on a plate. The pair of them started to lose any respect that they may have had and it didn't take long for the message to become clear to them.

One Sunday evening I had a knock at my door. To my disbelief it was Billy. Incredulously I asked what the murdering prick thought he was doing coming to my house where my children were playing. To which he replied, "Paul please, I've come with a white flag. I need to talk to you, I don't want trouble, can we go to the parkland down the road?"

As soon as he said that I suspected he was playing mind games as I had previously suggested meeting him and Gerry in a park. I wasn't sure quite what he was up to but I agreed to go with him. "I'll just get my coat" I said. That bought me enough time to get my revolver out of the kitchen and conceal it down the back of my pants, it wasn't the best of guns but I couldn't exactly conceal a sawn-off shotgun down there and until I knew what game he was playing I couldn't risk going naked. For all I knew he had a firm waiting for me where we were going.

We walked down the road to the park, neither of us spoke until we arrived there. Eventually he said that he knew I had put a price on Gerry's head. "What makes you think I've not got a price on yours too, you prick, I know you both work for William" I snarled back. Billy began trying to convince me that he was nothing to do with Graeme's murder, but I was having none of his bullshit. To my amazement he even offered to carry out the hit on Gerry if I agreed to let him walk away unscathed. I somehow managed to keep my cool and I informed Billy that I knew the names of everybody

CHASED OUT OF TOWN

that was in the room for Graeme's gruesome end and I also knew everybody involved in getting him over to Spain. I told him in no uncertain terms that my intentions were to carry out revenge attacks on each and every individual involved before my own dying day. At that I turned and walked away, he clearly had nothing of interest for me to listen to, it was either another one of William's attempts to lure me in or it was Billy being a shithouse and trying to distance himself from the whole affair. Regardless, I was having none of it. I left Billy wondering exactly what it was that I knew and whether or not he was actually on my hit list.

Putting a bullet in him was the right idea but it was simply the wrong time and place.

The days passed by but I had no news or sightings of Gerry, so I decided to go looking for him myself. The snake was obviously deep in hiding because I didn't get so much as a sniff of him until some weeks later, while I was at Old Trafford watching United.

Whilst enjoying a lovely half time pie and chips, chatting with friends, Gerry, Billy and a couple of others appeared. Again they were taking no chances, CCTV cameras cover almost every inch of the place and there's an abundance of security to boot. I couldn't believe it when the murdering cunt had the cheek to ask for five minutes of my time.

There was no way I was going to waste any of my breath on that Judas, so he got my red-hot pie straight between his eyes, while my friends attacked his mates.

Credit where credit's due, they did bloody well to get through the gauntlet of kicks and punches that rained down on them as they made their escape up the steps of Old Trafford and out of the ground.

I believe that a couple of days after that incident a car full of men, dressed in black, chased Gerry and Billy in their car, whilst firing shots at them. That seemed to be the point at which the two sniveling cowards realised the situation in Manchester was way too heavy for them to handle, and they got as far away as they could.

Their version of events was that they made a business investment in South Africa which required them to relocate. What they really did was run away like the scared cowards they are.

After the car chase the police came knocking at our door wanting to talk to me. I wasn't in and they began quizzing Jeanette about Graeme's disappearance instead. They suggested he was dead and asked her if I had been involved. They also asked if that was why I was having a feud with Gerry and his pals. Jeanette obviously told them that they had it all back to front, as usual, but she was left with a message for me: I was under 24-hour surveillance and if I went after any of Graeme's old *'friends'* I would be arrested for conspiracy to murder.

I was puzzled.

Why did the police assume Graeme was dead and not just a missing person? Surely they had an informant. If that was the case though, who would be deemed a reliable enough source to inform them of his death?

I wondered if it was possible that they had been informed of the murder by the murderer himself, who at the same time took the opportunity to point the finger at me?

I remembered a conversation that I once had with Tom, where he gave me an insight into William's past. According to him when William was a young man he served in the British army. Tom said that he had a good reputation for being handy to have around in a sticky situation. He was a big, powerful bloke, with a ruthless streak, and he wasn't afraid to be involved in the action. Apparently he was noticed for these attributes by his superiors and in the early eighties during the 'troubles' in Ireland, William earned himself a place in a special unit called The Force Research Unit (The FRU).

The FRU was part of the intelligence corps and was tasked with secretly penetrating terrorist organisations in Northern Ireland. They worked alongside other intelligence agencies such as The Royal

Ulster Special Branch and MI5. The FRU were allegedly involved in the murders of many civilians during the troubles. They were later found to have been colluding with protestant paramilitary groups who were allegedly indirectly involved in a number of assassinations and murders in Ireland.

In what was often labelled 'the dirty war' the FRU were once described as 'the dark corner of military intelligence'.

According to Tom, William claimed to be an expert at kidnap and murder. I found myself wondering if he had learnt his trade during his time in the FRU. I also considered if he was still connected to an intelligence group. That could be one reason to explain why he appears to be untouchable. Was there a possibility that William gained his connections in the criminal underworld whilst legally working undercover and then once no longer a member of the British army, exploited those connections to his own criminal gains?

William may well have been privy to some information that somebody, somewhere couldn't afford to allow to get out. His powers of manipulation are up there with anything I have ever witnessed before.

When the heat was on perhaps he could still call on old friends in high places to pull out his 'get out of jail free' card. I didn't know how much of Tom's talk was mythical, magical or simply made up, but it certainly had a degree of plausibility to it.

William's hotel and other worthy goods were confiscated by the Irish police over drug importation, however they simply deported him to Spain, yet again the British police turned a blind eye to his criminal ways.

The Irish press wrote several articles about William, some of them stating he was a notorious hitman and a drug lord whose victims never got the privilege of a bullet, including one who allegedly had his testicles burned off - which would probably have been Graeme.

Interpol and the Irish Guarda allegedly received information on how Graeme died, so why did they appear to look the other way and refuse to question him about the murder, or for that matter his disappearance. There is little doubt in my mind that William has to be an informer at the highest level. I cannot understand, in this day and age, how else he is able to murder people and get away unscathed time and time again.

Chapter 28:

RISKING EVERYTHING IN EUROPE

The 1998/99 Champions league draw brought me some much-needed joy after what had seemed a very long, tedious year. United were drawn in a group consisting of Bronby, Barcelona and Bayern Munich. After a 3 - 3 draw at home to the mighty Barcelona, our first away match of the group was against the high-flying Germans. As following my beloved reds was one of my lifelong passions, there was nothing and no one that was going to stop me from travelling to Germany that year. I knew I was putting myself at risk by leaving not only Manchester, which was my bolt hold, but the UK. Once out of the country the odds mounted up against me and in favour of William but my attitude was fuck him and his crew, as I wasn't prepared to miss out. Anyway when we travelled we travelled in numbers, so I knew I would be surrounded by both friends and fellow hooligans at all times.

Around 40 of us decided to spend a night in Amsterdam en-route to Germany. Amongst the 40 were some hard core villains, including a hot headed gangster who I was aware had previously worked with William. He wasn't somebody that I would class as a friend, but more of a close associate. I couldn't entirely trust him, but he was travelling with us and we were all determined to have a laugh and stick together whatever happened. Upon arrival in Amsterdam we checked straight into our hotels, before heading out to the bars and joining up with another group of reds that had the same idea as us. A couple of hours into the lads necking as many litres of Heineken as they could, I started to get bored. I was sitting on a pool table minding my own business when a large Dutch chap came up to me. I stood up but the guy was still towering above me. He must have been about 6 foot 5 and quite a mean looking mother fucker. "I'm Ajax's top boy" he blurted out to me in his best English. "Is that right mate?" I replied. "Well tonight ain't your lucky night". I wasted no more time chatting and simply smashed a pool cue over his head. It seemed to have no effect except angering him and he tried to yank it out of my hands. I was being pulled all over but there was no way I was letting go of the cue, not until I was completely set anyway. I pulled against him with all my might and as soon as I leant backwards I released the cue and sprung into him with a ferocious punch which sparked him clean out.

As the AJax lump was falling to the ground two doormen came rushing over. Unfortunately for them they were met with huge glass tankards and beer bottles raining down on their heads. Glass was flying everywhere, it was like a hail storm, only indoors and with chunks of glass instead of hailstones. The three Dutch blokes were in a right mess so we made a sharp exit. Figuring it was going to be too 'on top' for us to hang around the bars in such large numbers, we split into small groups. I found myself with Wing's brother Ben and the hot-headed gangster who was involved with William (Wing is short for Wing commander, which is the nickname we gave to Gary, a head member of the hooligans who used to arrange battles between United's firm and opposing hooligan outfits. To be honest Wing arranged more than just the battles, he arranged the locations, the transport, the escape routes, just about everything necessary for a proper tear up).

We tried to get back to our hotel but the police were appearing everywhere. They were whizzing about on mopeds looking for us. I saw a policeman at the top of a narrow road which we had found ourselves on, so I suggested a quick stop in the coffee shop that we were passing. Thinking we may have evaded them for the time being we ordered a coffee each. As I sat down however I saw a police moped block the shop's doorway. While he was gesturing down the road to other officers I took the opportunity to swap jackets with Ben and asked him to sit at another table, away from me. I knew the police would be looking for a guy in a black leather jacket and without one I thought I had bought myself some time to get away. A policeman entered with one of the doormen, who pointed straight over to Ben, who was sat alone with his back to them. Ben's feet didn't touch the floor before he landed in the back of a police van waiting outside.

We were briefly quizzed and had our hands checked for blood along with two other English customers who happened to be in the coffee shop, before being told we were free to go. Walking off we could hear more mopeds pulling up behind us. We reached the end of the road before I looked back, just as the second doorman appeared at the coffee shop. My timing couldn't have been worse and he caught my eye as I caught his. An eruption of Dutch screams could be heard as he was indicating to the police that I was the one they wanted. We had been given just enough of a head start to make it to the end of the adjacent road and disappear into Amsterdam's maze of alleyways without being spotted.

Arriving back at the hotel unscathed, I told the lads (that had also made it back) about Ben being arrested. I said it was only a matter of time before they traced his hotel. Everyone else seemed to think I was being paranoid and my reaction was over the top. Being a lifelong criminal however, paranoia comes with the territory and I knew my gut instinct was not to be ignored. Even so I was convinced to lie low in the hotel for the night in the hope we could all check out the next day and continue our trip to Munich.

I was sharing a room with a friend called Beb, so me and him decided to chill in our room for a bit and stay well out of the way.

We had been up there for a few hours when the room's telephone started to ring. It was about 1am and me and Beb had both been asleep.

I got up and answered the phone. It was a Dutch bloke asking for Paul Doyle. I assumed that it was the police and I replied saying that I had changed rooms with Mr. Doyle, but I could give them his room number. I offered up some bull shit room number, with no idea who was in there or if it even existed and hung up the phone.

Like a shot, I got dressed and was out of the bedroom window before Beb had the foggiest idea what was going on. I tracked down Keith and Teamo in the red-light district and told them I thought the police were in our hotel. Neither of them were even interested in listening, not until they had been into a brass house anyway. I was left standing out in the street like 'Billy-no-mates' for half an hour until they had finished their business. Once they were both a little lighter on their feet, they listened to what I was saying and agreed to head back with me to gauge what was going on. I was surprised to find that there were no signs of the police around the hotel and the guy on reception looked extremely calm and relaxed, suggesting that he had not been told to look out for anybody (either that or he had been smoking some of Amsterdam's finest green and simply didn't give a fuck). I went back up to my room, where Beb told me that a black Dutch guy had knocked on the door on three occasions asking for me. It was clearly 'on top'. I knew there was a black mob over in Amsterdam that worked directly with William. My bet was that the guy knocking on our door was probably the same guy that rang the room and was more likely to be an enforcer for the mob in Amsterdam than a police officer.

Somebody had betrayed me, either one of the gangsters that were with us, or possibly someone from back home. Either way someone was prepared to throw me to the wolves.

I had let my guard down and in hindsight it had been a stupid mistake to make venturing onto the continent. I knew there was no point stewing over it though, I just had to be ready for their next move. Beb woke up all the lads from our hotel and told them to meet me downstairs. Begrudgingly each one of them dragged themselves out of bed and we gathered in the foyer. It was too late to buy alcohol at that time so I ordered twenty cups of coffee.

Within no time a big black guy strolled in trying to look casual (as casual as you can look walking into a hotel at 3am), we all surrounded him like a pack of slathering wolves. I asked who he was looking for? He said nobody and he just needed to use the phone. I pointed out where the phone was and nervously he looked over towards it, then back at us before saying it wasn't important and he would find another one. With that he left.

He made a wise choice, if he had tried anything he would no doubt have been the first person to have been beaten to death with coffee cups.

I believed that we had made a clear enough statement and everybody went back to bed. Me and Beb switched rooms to be on the safe side. When I woke the following morning there was a message at reception for me. It was from William. The message read: 'I always know where you are Paul. See you soon'.

After returning home from the trip, I received a call from William making more threats on my life and bragging about keeping tabs on me. I didn't pull any punches with my response, I told him that if he had the bottle, he would come out of the shadows to get me himself, but obviously he is a shithouse who lets others take the risks for him, so I wouldn't be expecting him anytime soon. He didn't appreciate my insults and started screaming down the phone at me "I'm coming for you Paul Doyle, if it's the last thing I do".

The call left me with a gut feeling that perhaps he finally would make a move and come after me in Manchester. He would need help from the city's gangsters if he intended to do it though, a lot of whom I had been working with for years. He on the other hand hadn't stepped foot inside the city for at least the previous fifteen years. The odds were in my favour, but I knew not to be complacent.

I decided to make some minor changes to my routine. The pattern of finishing up in Kell's every Saturday was a tough but obvious one that had to go. Unfortunately that particular weekend wasn't the right time for such sacrifices though. It was Valentine's day that Saturday and me and a few of the lads had booked into the four seasons for the whole weekend to treat our other halves. If I pulled the plug on that, William would have been the least of my problems because Jeanette would have killed me herself.

The weekend quickly came around and poor Jeanette who thought she was in for a real romantic night, began doubting just how romantic it was going to be when she realised that I had already necked an E before the first bar. In my defense I was feeling under a lot of pressure at that time, after my close call in Amsterdam and then my renewed belief that William may actually attack in Manchester, I felt I needed to let my hair down, just as much as anybody else.

I began fooling around in the first bar, trying to be the centre of attention and have a good giggle, when I noticed a very attractive lady watching me. She was sat with a guy who was suited and booted and looked every inch a straight member. She couldn't seem to get enough of me and I kept catching her eye. It started to become a little uncomfortable. The attention was certainly flattering, but as I was out with the wife it was a little unsettling. I considered whether it was all in my head or if the Es were playing tricks on me.

Our group moved on to another bar and I presumed that would be the last I saw of her, so I gave her a cheeky little wink on my way out.

Twenty minutes later the same couple arrived again at the bar we were in.

By that point I was pretty high on Es and I convinced myself that she wanted a bit of rough. She chose a table quite close to us, which again was unusual as we don't really look like a group of people that a romantic couple would want to sit next to. I was less bothered about her by that point, In fact the Es had definitely taken control and all that I wanted to discuss was killing William with anybody who would listen.

After a fairly hazy Valentine's night we all headed back to the hotel. I actually couldn't believe it when the same couple were sitting in the lobby. In my messy state I decided that it must just have been a big coincidence and brushed it off. I had more pressing matters anyway, like preparing myself for 2 minutes of romantic love making with the wife.

The following morning I had several missed calls, some from Ned Kelly and some from an international number (William). Before too long I received another call from the latter. He smugly informed me that I was under surveillance. Apparently he had sent his henchman to Kells to do a hit on me but they had discovered that both Kell's and myself were surrounded by undercover coppers. He began laughing at me and naturally the call descended into an argument and then an abusive rant, which my head was in no place for, so I hung up and called Ned back instead.

Ned confirmed what William had told me. Somebody had supposedly phoned Crime-stoppers saying that I was going to be murdered on Valentine's night. I laughed and suggested that someone had been watching too many gangster films and played it down. I figured it was William playing mind games. I realised that it was silly to think that he would come after me in Manchester. Neither he nor his henchmen were going to do that. I knew the devious fucker was going to wait for me to slip up again and cross the channel into Europe. I didn't believe I had anything to worry about, however I felt slightly embarrassed that the attractive girl, who was obviously an undercover copper, had thought I fancied her, and vice versa.

It was one nil to GMP, I was ashamed to say.

Content that William wouldn't venture into Manchester, I decided that if I wanted revenge for Graeme's gruesome murder I had no choice but to go into the lion's den and take care of him on his own turf. So that was exactly what I planned to do.

Once I had made my mind up the excitement was overwhelming. I'd been suffering at home waiting for someone to come for me. The time had come to take matters into my own hands. The odds being stacked so heavily against me wasn't worth thinking about. I was ready to take the chance. I tried my best to keep my mission a secret and only discussed it with a very small number of trustworthy friends.

To get some important details such as William's address I went to see someone I knew could help me and also someone that I knew I could trust, someone whose friend had also been killed by William and someone who understood the rage that I felt towards the savage cunt.

My research was fruitful, not only did I get William's address I also received some other useful information. For instance where he liked to shop, which bars he drank in, restaurants he ate in and also how he liked to walk his dogs on the beach each morning.

After assessing the new leads my plan of action was simple. Do the twat on the beach.

As far as I could see, my biggest headache seemed to be getting in and out of the Costa-del-Sol undetected.

I had a close friend living in Malaga who was willing to let me stay at his place for a week and leave me a few essentials, including his favourite 'tool' and some ammunition. I massively respected and appreciated his courage and loyalty. If anybody found out that he had helped me he would have found himself in grave trouble with either William or the police - depending on the outcome of course. To reduce the risk to my loyal friend, we decided it was in his best interest to have a holiday back in England while I carried out my mission in Spain. I did however need some assistance, so I decided to take my most loyal friend Ashy with me, I was confident that going into the lion's den wouldn't faze him.

Ashy flew to Spain while I drove over using a bent passport. By the time I arrived at the villa Ash had already taken to the easy lifestyle of the Costa Del Sol. He was enjoying the booze and the sunshine in beautiful surroundings. That wasn't why we were there though, so once I arrived the partying stopped and the serious work began. We were not only on foreign soil, much more importantly we were in William's backyard and we had to have our wits about us.

The next morning we were up bright and early, I had to get to the beach before him to catch him unaware. We split up and searched the beach for several hours looking for him and his dogs. After two or three fruitless hours we decided to head off to a cafe for some breakfast, but I was so disappointed I couldn't even eat my sausages. I knew there was still time to get him though so did the same thing the following day, but again to no avail. We stayed out until lunchtime on day two, before Ashy finally convinced me to head back for some food. We went to the same cafe as the previous day. Again I could barely stomach my food. I probably had too much adrenaline coursing through my veins to eat. After a third unsuccessful attempt we walked back to the cafe but I was so annoyed I had begun resenting the Spanish sausages altogether and I refused to even order anything. All I could think of was killing William. It was driving me crazy and I was starting to become obsessed. Knowing it was a do or die mission I decided I had nothing to lose by going to find his house.

I couldn't believe how beautiful his home was. Behind two large gates stood a huge stone villa. A couple of guard dogs roamed around freely, but there was no other sign of life. It was like a fortress with CCTV cameras everywhere. We hung around for a full afternoon, staking it out, before agreeing that it was a kamikaze mission. I decided looking for him in the local bars was probably less dangerous. We stood out like a couple of sore thumbs however, looking mean and moody while the holiday makers were prancing about in swimsuits, with beaming smiles on their faces.

After a long uneventful day we were heading back to our villa when Ashy received a call from back home. It was from a well-known gangster who worked with William. What he said almost put me to my knees. He told us that William and a hard-core firm were searching the streets of Malaga hunting us down. Not only that, but the Spanish police were allegedly out looking for us too. The call seemed to spiral into something out of a movie when he said that the police weren't hoping to protect or even arrest us, but to pass us over to William for blood money. I was speechless. For one of the very first times in my life I was utterly speechless.

I often say that someone above looks down on me, I say it half tongue in cheek, but also half seriously. However when I heard that the precession of bars we had visited searching for William, he had gone into minutes later searching for us, I started thinking it must definitely be true. I had escaped a very close call. I also knew I had either been betrayed back home or we had been spotted in Malaga. Either way William had been alerted to our presence and we were in grave danger now the tables had turned.

Luckily for us we hadn't told a soul where we were staying, but even so that night we took it in turns staying awake and keeping guard.

We had no choice but to abandon our mission the very next day.

Back in Manchester the threatening calls were flooding in. William upped the ante, telling me how he was planning to spend several days working on me, forcing me to eat my own body parts and describing perverse things that he wanted to do to me. The man is seriously fucked in the head.

I was more concerned about figuring out whether or not I had been stabbed in the back though and if so who by, so I didn't allow myself to pay too much attention to the twisted ramblings of a mad man.

Fortunately, I still had many friends and allies that I could genuinely rely on, and it was ultimately the tip off from one of them that saved our bacon in Spain.

Chapter 29:

THE GOOCH GANG

No sooner was I settled back into life at home, feeling comfortable and safe again on home soil, when once again trouble reared its ugly head. My phone rang one morning and on the other end was a very disgruntled senior member of the notorious Gooch gang from Moss Side.

The Gooch gang were largely responsible for Manchester being dubbed as 'Gunchester' in the nineties. Clashes with rival gangs, mainly the Doddington gang (formerly known as the Pepperhill mob) became so frequent that the entire country was reading about the bloodshed in Manchester on a regular basis.

Receiving a call from a less than impressed high ranking member of the Gooch is easily as disconcerting as any phone call from William, in fact as the Gooch do their killing on Manchester territory, the severity of that threat triples in a heartbeat.

Over the years I learned that to survive the streets, it is essential you show the utmost respect to the people who have earned it most i.e. top gangsters and alike. Especially as many of whom would be prepared to put you in a box for disrespecting them. Don't get me wrong, if the respect isn't mutual then arse kissing is not the way forward, but as long as the understanding works both ways, then it allows people to live in relative harmony.

Unfortunately, some of my friends don't really see it like that. They think you have to earn their respect before they will show it. It is understandable to a degree, because they live in that world, the world of a diehard football hooligan. Most football hooligans worth their salt would be prepared to attack whoever confronted them, be it another hooligan, a criminal or a gangster.

It turned out that the night previous to my phone call a good friend of mine, Smiley Bri, had been out drinking in a popular nightclub called Peruvia. A host of footballers, celebrities and gangsters frequented the place back in the day. On the night in question some lad was apparently acting all boisterous and becoming a real nuisance right in front of Smiley Bri. He was seemingly showing off because he was out with a well-known footballer. Annoying Bri is a silly mistake to make though, he doesn't get his nickname because he's always full of the joys of spring, he actually gets it because he never seems as happy or smiley as when he is fighting.

So predictably Bri knocked the fool out cold. The footballer, who was far from happy that his friend had been sparked out then stepped into a world he didn't belong in and stupidly approached a member of the Gooch gang to take revenge on his behalf.

The gangster from the Gooch confronted Bri and started ranting and raving at him. Another mistake, because he also got knocked out, leaving the footballer very red faced and sheepish and Bri in a potential world of shit.

The situation had arisen from 'much ado about nothing' into potentially a very dangerous one. The ruthless Gooch gang have been known to kill people for a lot less than having a gang member knocked out in a public venue. So my morning call from 'G' of the Gooch, was to inform me that he found it totally disrespectful, not to mention embarrassing and that he wanted the name of the 'rough neck' so they could take revenge on him.

I told G that his phone call was the first I knew of the affair and that I was also not pleased to hear about it. I respectfully requested he gave me half an hour to make some enquiries of my own before we spoke anymore about it.

Obviously, I was between a rock and a hard place. I was never going to throw a friend of mine to the wolves, but I also had to be seen to do enough to appease the wrath of the Gooch and hopefully save my mate's skin. After some investigation I discovered Smiley Bri was the man in question. Bri might sound like an idiot, much like a lot of the lads that I enjoy being a hooligan alongside but believe me he is no-one's fool. He's a self-made millionaire with several successful businesses. I have known Bri and his lovely wife for many years and I would go to war before I allowed any gangsters to turn up at his door. Not for the first time in my life I found myself in a tricky situation and not for the first time it was actually through no fault of my own.

I called G back and offered a diplomatic solution to get me and Bri out of the shit.

I explained to him that I considered myself a man of my word and that I have an honourable name amongst my mates. It was therefore not possible for me to do as he had requested and simply hand Bri over to the mercy of the Gooch. To prevent the situation getting out of hand and to prevent gang members from facing unnecessary years behind bars, I said that I was prepared to go to Peruvia the following Saturday night with Bri, so that he could apologise for his inconsiderate actions. Thankfully, G accepted my proposal but he requested that we went alone. Obviously, I agreed but obviously, I lied.

I knew I needed a plan. I was going for a sit-down meeting in a Manchester nightclub with the Gooch, but I may as well have been going to war on a battlefield. There was potentially just as much chance of me ending up dead at either. Peruvia was a stronghold for their gang and I couldn't risk going alone with Bri, nor with just a few close friends. I needed numbers to bring the situation to an end. The first thing I did was to call my usual suspects, then I asked them to call around a few of their own and let the 'meet' at Peruvia become common knowledge amongst our trusted people. Then I sat back, crossed my fingers and waited.

It turned out that I had more than enough backing to take the sting out of the situation, so I arranged to meet the boys on the far side of town before heading over to Peruvia.

Not even I could believe how many faces actually turned up. Big Damian Noonan was there alongside Paul Massey, who in turn had a small army of their own standing beside them. I laughed when I saw the convoy of cars. We made for Peruvia, where it took a number of minutes for us all to get through the door.

G immediately came over to me shaking his head but smiling. "Fucking hell Paul" he said, "I thought it was just going to be the two of you". I started laughing and told him to take a look at his own firm. G looked around and acknowledged my point. Each one of his thirty or so lads were wearing gloves and had hoods up, looking mean, moody and ready for war.

Massey being Massey and Manchester's Mr. Big then stepped in and took over the situation. He was respected by all organisations and G was more than happy to discuss the problem with a man of Paul's caliber. It felt like the good old days again. Days when Massey would have been having a debate and I would be standing by his side ready to pounce. However that night in Peruvia, I would probably have been shot a dozen times before I even had a chance to land my first blow. Massey and G ironed things out and all I had to do was supply the champagne (Big Damian's favourite drink).

The situation had all started with some prick believing himself to be 'Billy Big Balls' because he was hanging out with a professional footballer, but it could have easily escalated into serious bloodshed. It ended up boiling down to street politics though and not for the first time, the wiser, older heads from some of the most serious organised gangs to ever operate in our country were able to diffuse things without any loss of life. People are quick to judge these men and throw scorn on them, however sometimes they really are the keepers of peace and offer a certain level of policing - all be it in their own unique way.

For me it was just another day at the office.

Although the lads had all turned out in force for me, I realised that we couldn't expect to remain in town in such numbers for too long, as the police would be on to us and all hell could break loose. Obviously remaining in Peruvia wasn't a sensible option either, after the champagne had been flowing for an hour or two I knew it wouldn't take much for another tricky situation to arise. There were simply too many gangsters and villains in one club for it to end smoothly.

For those reasons me and a couple of the lads headed off to Kell's to continue our night there. Jeanette was in there with a few of the girls and I figured it was the best place for me to stay off the radar. I took a couple of E's in the taxi and by the time we arrived I was starting to feel a nice buzz. Myself and Dylon found a spot in the corner of the VIP lounge and we began discussing how well the Peruvia 'meet' had gone. Mid conversation Mick brought some Scouse lad over who instantly changed my mood. Now I've not met many shy scousers but this guy was upfront to say the least and after barely a few pleasantries he cut straight to the chase, "I've come over here to give you a chance to earn yourself some money" he said to me. "I need a debt collecting". The abruptness and rudeness of him made my blood boil instantaneously. I'm a drug dealer, a grafter and gambler, I was wearing a £50K watch that sparkled in the dark and this two-bit Scouse prick was insulting me by thinking I was some type of debt collector that should be grateful for him throwing me a bone.

I suggested to Mick that he took his 'friend' away before I put him in an early grave, which luckily he did - as fast as he could.

Dylon could see I was seriously pissed off and told me to forget about it and calm down, so I took another E in an attempt to do just that.

Every now and again after downing a few Es I would turn into a green eyed, jealous monster, and on that particular night it is exactly what happened. Ten minutes or so after the incident with the scouser, I began 'coming up' with a vengeance. As I was starting to get high though I noticed Jeanette and her friend accepting champagne from some smooth sorts at the bar. Again I took exception and I shouted over to her asking why she was accepting drinks from other men. Her response did my mood swing no favours either. "Because they fucking offered" she said. "What do you expect me to do, wait all night for you to get me one?". "Exactly" I shouted back, before telling the fellas to fuck off. Jeanette then told me to fuck off before insisting that the blokes were only being nice. She then accused me of being a jealous prick. I started to defend my actions and was about to explain to her just how right I was when she threw her champagne over me.

Dylon immediately jumped in between us - to prevent me from being attacked, and Jeanette stormed off to the toilets leaving me stood there completely red faced and dripping in Moet.

Brushing booze off me, I sat back down and tried my best to keep to my recent promise, to Ned Kelly, of best behaviour. With everyone staring at me however that promise became less and less important to me. I felt humiliated and angry and somebody needed to pay. My attention quickly turned back to the smart arse scouser who had pissed me off in the first place. I began throwing beer bottles at him. Being high on Es however I was missing him and hitting just about every other cunt in the vicinity. I was pissed off and pilled up though, so I didn't give a fuck and people were giving me a wide berth, rather than attempting to intervene.

That night I went home crawling on my hands and knees, begging for forgiveness and promising the wife that I would never take another Ecstasy tablet. She knew it would be about as successful as my promise to Ned though and made it clear that I was spending the night in the spare room.

The following day I apologised to Ned - on Jeanette's behalf. I advised him it would be in Kells' best interest if she was barred from the place. I got the impression I wasn't in Ned's good books either though. I was fully expecting to be on the police's list of people to talk to, what with our mass gathering of gangsters in Peruvia, followed by my reckless behaviour in Kell's, so I sat back and waited for the call. It never came. No public order offence, no nothing. The daunting realisation was that they were hoping to get me for something much bigger. I was a thorn in their side and they wanted to put me away for years, not just a few months for a petty offence.

The police presence around us had become intense. They were seemingly aware of just about our every movement and wherever we went they appeared, and in force.

One Friday night a group of us travelled to Leeds for a friend's stag do. We got the train, but upon arrival, waiting for us at Leeds station were tens of riot police. A senior Yorkshire copper greeted us getting off the train by telling us that we weren't welcome in his city, due to our reputation for trouble and violence. They sent us packing, back to Manchester, escorted by about twenty officers to ensure we didn't leave the train at any other station.

Everywhere we went we were met with the same 'MOVE ON' attitude. The police forces were clearly working together, which was not that common in those days. Once we were even sent back from Scotland. Usually when you cross the border you are left alone, but they made a special exception to the rules for us.

A number of us had agreed to have a night out in Lincoln, with the Lincoln Reds. We tried to keep it as low profile as we possibly could, but we still ended up with a group of twenty. We decided on a hotel to stay in, split up into groups of fours and managed to get down there undetected. We checked in, got ready for a night out and congregated in the residents bar before hitting the town. It wasn't long however before the police flooded the hotel lobby, with the intention of escorting us out of Lincoln. An officer approached us to discuss the situation. Benny spoke on our behalf and told the copper we hadn't committed a crime and we had already paid the hotel bill; therefore it would be unjust to kick us out. Surprisingly, the policeman actually did listen and eventually agreed that as we had paid for the hotel upfront he would let us stay there overnight, but only in the hotel. We were not to venture out. He warned us that a police car would be positioned outside for the whole night and If we were seen stepping foot beyond the doors we would be arrested. A delighted Benny gave him his word and the police left the building. Immediately we got to work on our plan for sneaking out.

We decided to spend half the evening in the hotel bar (on our best behaviour obviously) to lull the police into a false sense of security and then sneak out of one of the ground floor bedroom windows, before meeting up with the Lincoln lads.

The plan worked perfectly, we were so well behaved and polite in the hotel bar that I think the coppers outside must have wondered what all the fuss had been about. After a couple of hours we started disappearing out of the window, a few at a time and made our way towards the clubs. En-route I noticed all the street CCTV cameras seemed to be watching us. So I figured the bars would be on red alert too. We met some girls outside a bar and offered to pay for them to get in, if they walked in with us, like couples, arm in arm. It worked and our group of four got in. The next couple of groups also got in. Benny and Dot however, who arrived later, were refused entry. The doorman heard their Manc accents and turned them away. Benny started arguing the toss, when out of nowhere a bitch of a female bouncer lassoed Benny around the neck with some device that was intended for capturing stray dogs. The more he struggled, the tighter it got until he was eventually choked out.

We knew we couldn't go into the entrance to help because it was full of security cameras, so we started trying to entice the security team into the darkness of the bar where we could take our revenge.

They must have realised we were baiting them though, so they never came after us. Some of the lads even started taxing the bar, but still they wouldn't come in. One of the clever bastards pressed the fire alarm. With the police and the fire brigade bound to make an immediate response we were snookered. Their quick thinking won them the battle that night but we were not about to forget what took place and we knew it needed addressing.

What we didn't know however was that our chance to take revenge would present itself without any planning whatsoever, and it came in the most unexpected of circumstances.

A decade earlier I had come across a young lad who was making a name for himself in and around Salford. He was often fighting and doing a bloody good job of it too. He was aggressive and hungry, but actually didn't look much like a street fighter, in fact he looked more like a ladies man, but he certainly wasn't afraid to mix it with the best of them. One day we were chatting when I asked, "Why is a good looking young lad like you out fighting all the time, when you could be pulling some tasty young bird and enjoying the quiet life?"

His answer was brilliant "I just love the buzz of winning a fight" he said, with an air of confidence that made me smile. Who am I to argue with that I thought? "I'd like to take you to a boxing gym" I told him "then we can see how good you really are". With a hugely enthusiastic grin on his face he agreed.

I am very proud to say that that young man later made history by becoming both Commonwealth and IBF Inter-Continental light middle-weight champion. He became known as 'The Viking' Steve Foster.

Steve became a great fighter and had the ability to draw a crowd. Wherever he fought an army of loyal supporters would follow him. Mostly they were fellow Salfordians, many wearing Viking hats and beards.

Boxing is a great sport to follow, it is exciting and gets the adrenaline pumping and that combination can make for a good night out. Chuck in a few pints of lager though and it can also make for a very eventful night. Steve was on the bill to fight in a championship fight at the NEC Arena in Birmingham. What transpired that night didn't come as a great shock to me, or to too many of my friends, but it did raise concerns with the boxing commission board.

Steve The Viking's loyal army of supporters travelled in numbers. Most spent the afternoon drinking and shadow boxing each other, in the build up to the main event - Steve's fight. As it turned out however, the actual main event was what occurred in the crowd.

The army of Salford lads went crazy, doing what Salford lads are programmed to do. They started smashing whoever and whatever was in front of them, that being rival supporters or security guards not to mention the Birmingham police force.

The riot made headline news and later many of the rioters received serious prison sentences.

Subsequently to prevent future rioting the police advised it would be best if Steve fought all his fights in Manchester at the MEN Arena. At that time Steve Foster was one of only a few boxers who could get close to filling the place. When he fought the whole city would be buzzing.

So as advised his next fight was arranged for the MEN and for me and all his supporters it was an unmissable event.

I got ringside tickets for myself and some close friends and we met the rest of the lads at Johnson's Bar on Deansgate, which is only a five-minute walk to the arena. The day of the fight was a beautiful summer day and I decided to take my Ferrari down, just to look 'the business'. My plan was to pull up outside Johnson's bar, with the top down, because I knew there would be an audience drinking outside the front. On such a wonderful occasion it was usual for me to leave the house already having dropped an E, and that night was no different.

At the junction for Deansgate, about a mile from Johnson's, my plan started to unravel. There was a road closed sign. The council were re-tarmacing the surface. I was gutted, thinking it was going to spoil my flashy entrance in the Ferrari - I might as well have been in the wife's mini.

Tripping on E's however I decided to ignore the road sign and drive around it. I sped down Deansgate like it was a Formula1 track. As the road surface was just rough gravel it actually made my entrance more spectacular. Driving at top speed on the loose surface caused plumes of smoke to billow behind me. That along with the noise only a Ferrari could make, everybody's heads turned as I approached. I finished my spectacle by skidding to a halt right outside the bar and received a well-deserved cheer from a larger than normal crowd of onlookers.

I jumped out of the Ferrari like 'Charlie-big-potatoes' and still showing off to my audience I threw the keys to my pal Wayne, shouting to him that he could look after it for me (leaving everybody to think that a £120K Ferrari meant fuck all to me). I regretted my decision almost immediately though, as I watched Wayne drive off twice as fast as I had arrived and receive a bigger cheer too.

Most of the lads at Johnson's looked like they were raring to go and ready to box that night themselves. Straight members of the public were hastily walking past the place, not wishing to make eye contact with any of the mob congregated outside. Luckily for me I knew 90 percent of them from either Salford or Old Trafford, so I waltzed in to a multitude of handshakes and high fives, as well as the odd faked right hook to the guts. The atmosphere was electric and I was buzzing from the pill.

When our group decided to start the five-minute walk to the venue, we were followed by a hundred-strong mob who were totally pissed and worse still, most of whom didn't have tickets. I couldn't help but laugh because I knew the security team at the arena had a right headache heading their way.

A lot of the lads had been going around Europe watching United without tickets for years and they knew where the weakest point was to enter the venue - the entrance at Victoria Train Station. Not wanting to miss out on the entertainment and see how well they performed, we went along to watch the fun.

The small number of security guards ran when the Viking's fans charged at them. Obviously, the police were waiting nearby on red alert. That year they had been issued with their latest weapon - CS gas. They started spraying it into the crowd. Unfortunately for the police some of the mob had gas canisters of their own and began to return fire. As the coppers were battling such a large number of Salfordians and experienced football hooligans it wasn't long before they had to retreat. I couldn't help but laugh out loud when I saw the coppers legging it. They ran that fast they must have caught up with the security guards that had fled earlier.

I realised I could have had a problem as the coppers would have loved to have stitched me up for being one of the instigators of the riot, so me, Ashy and Benny kept our tickets in case we needed to prove that we weren't involved in storming the gates. My case wasn't really helped however, because as we headed to our seats we were still being followed by half the mob.

It turned out to be quite a result for the boys. Not only had they chased off the security and the police, but they also got to sit beside us in the best seats in the house. After all, who was going to ask them to move? I think the police must have instructed the security team not to provoke things any further. The last thing they would have wanted was a repeat of the riot in Birmingham, resulting in themselves being headline news.

After watching a boxing masterclass from 'Steve the Viking' a very angry, well known detective came over and confronted Tony O'Neil. Tony is a die-hard United fan and one of the old school main players in the Barmy army. He has been behind the publication of numerous books regaling stories of football hooliganism and is well known around Manchester for that reason.

The officer said, "you had a result tonight, because we didn't want the public to be put at any further risk, but we're coming for you lot". A very smug Tony replied, "Well we're ready to have it now". Not for the first time that night a red-faced copper retreated.

Just as I was thinking our night couldn't get any better, one of the Lincoln lads who was out with us, informed me that the owner of the security firm who choked out Benny, had a coach party of doormen with him, supporting his son who had apparently fought on the undercard. We wanted revenge from the incident in the Lincoln bar, so we stormed around the arena looking for them. When we found them they received a good old fashioned Manchester welcome. Revenge was sweet, more so for Benny. The only person missing was the woman bouncer who had choked him out. If she had been there we would have let them have a fair one to one fight. To be honest my money would have been on her though.

Chapter 30:

DODGING A BULLET

Back in the days when Strangeways was ruled with an iron fist, one of my more undesirable friends was a lad called Robbo. He was one of the new generation that resented the brutality of the system and had the courage to fight back. Even with the screws fists beating down on him, he never stopped raging against the regime. It was the likes of Robbo, Navvy and Paul Massey that made prisons and the prison system far easier, leaving the criminals of today reaping the rewards. The screws would often call Robbo 'The Little Cunt' and to be honest you would struggle to disagree with them. He was remarkably fearless for his size, prepared to fight an enemy well above his own weight and he had a variety of tactics to bring them down to size. For that reason and because of his street nous we would often include him in some of our missions when we weren't serving at her majesty's pleasure.

In the late nineties Robbo's grafting partner was a half-caste scouser called Lyndon. When I first met Lyndon I thought he had a great future ahead of him. He seemed very sharp, smart and willing, not to mention being an amusing character.

The pair came to see me one day offering me some speed at an unbelievably cheap price. I asked how many kilos they had and Robbo replied 80 and assured me it was top quality. With that I raised an eyebrow of suspicion. I knew 80 kilos of quality gear would be worth over quarter of a million and I doubted they had that quantity of merchandise. So to be totally sure I took one kilo and tested it. To my delight and astonishment it turned out to be quality stuff. I knew I could double a kilo up with a kilo of glucose and make a killing on it, so agreed to take it all and I paid half up front telling them the rest would follow when I had sold it on, I therefore asked them to return in a weeks' time

I turned 80 kilos into 160 kilos and sold them to my customers. Within days most had paid up and were asking for more. It was easy money for me, so when Robbo came back for the rest of the cash I asked him if himself or Lyndon could get any more. I had presumed the stuff had come through Lyndon as he was making good contacts in and around Liverpool at that time. I was a bit taken aback however when Robbo informed me that the speed hadn't really been theirs to sell as they had grafted it off a Pakistani lad from Stockport.

Again I felt the eyebrow of suspicion rise. I wanted some answers to some important questions and I wanted them fast. It was essential I knew who it was stolen from because I was the person who had sold it on. In those days it was virtually unheard of for a Pakistani to sell that type of drug and why I wondered would this particular lad had trusted Robbo of all people?

Robbo told me that the guy was called David Barnshawe and he used to sell drugs for a Stockport gangster called Chris Little. Little however was murdered and after working for himself for a while, Barnshawe ended up dealing for another serious firm in Greater Manchester, a firm who had been 'laid on' 300 kilos of top-quality speed from an outfit in Holland.

He said that Barnshawe has no reason not to trust him because they had worked together previously and Robbo had always paid up. When I asked why he had stolen the speed, Robbo simply replied "It was too good an opportunity to pass up".

Even though selling the speed was a great earner for me, I wished it had never been offered to me, I knew I was in the middle of another major rip which could go horribly wrong, and through no fault of my own I was heavily involved due to the fact that I had unwittingly sold the stuff on. I of all people understood what the outcome could be and was less than impressed with the situation I had been landed in.

I told Robbo that as the damage was already done he had two choices; either pay for the speed or never tell another soul of my involvement. Robbo replied entirely as I expected him to, by telling me he couldn't give the money back because most of it had already been spent. We were left with no option.... 'Silence is golden'.

That week I was trying to work out who the local firm could be, with such a good supplier in Holland. I knew half of the outfits in Holland who could supply large quantities of top-quality speed but I couldn't connect the dots and figure out the link. Then one night while I was having a beautiful sleep it came to me like a smack in the forehead, and I knew that if I was right a smack in the forehead was the least of my worries as I was in one hell of a situation.

The only Manchester gangsters that I knew had serious business connections in Stockport worked for William.

The following morning, after a restless night, I contacted a friend who was heavily involved in dealing around Stockport and asked him if he knew David Barnshawe and if so which firm he worked for. The information I got back was exactly what I hadn't wanted to hear. Barnshawe had been working under a well-known pair of Manchester gangsters and a South Manchester gangster. Worse still, news had started to spread that Barnshawe had been ripped off for a large amount of drugs belonging to a drug lord and serial killer who went by the nickname 'BITS AND PIECES' (a name which derived from the state his victims ended up in).

Not only did the criminal underworld know what William was capable of, they also knew that I was the only person stupid enough to rip him off. In no time at all, heads started turning towards me and I received the call which I had been expecting from one of the Manchester gangsters. I arranged to meet the pair of them at a bar in town. As strong as the two of them were, I had no fear of meeting them because me, Mickey and Steve all went back a long way. That little fact didn't stop them from skipping the niceties however and getting straight to the point. They believed I had had their speed, and they wanted to know if it was true. Being well oiled in such meetings I know that it's best to show no signs of weakness, so straight off I told them that I had had their merchandise, but I no longer did, and when I was offered it I had no idea that it was theirs or indeed that it was stolen. I told them it was bought it in good faith.

Obviously, they then asked me who I'd bought it from. "What is this a fuckin police interview?" I asked. I told them I wouldn't answer that question and risk losing my street credibility by grassing someone up. The meeting started to turn a bit heated. Steve said, "We know it was Lyndon and we have already got men out looking for him, but we want the stuff or the value of it back from you". I sniggered and asked; if they knew it was Lyndon then why were they disrespecting me by asking me to grass? I told them that all the stuff had been sold - I had bought it for a competitive price and sold it for a small profit therefore I had no intention of taking a loss, just because someone on their side of the operation hadn't done his job properly "Get them to work fuckin overtime" I suggested in a tone that expressed my annoyance, "you can get your money back that way".

They clearly sensed that neither the money nor the speed was going to be given back, so they tried to unsettle me by telling me the speed actually belonged to William. "Oh my golly gosh" I said sarcastically. "I must be in big trouble. Do forgive me for not shitting my pants". They both smirked but then Mickey asked if I would be quite so cocky if I was talking to Bits and Pieces himself.

I told him to get him on the phone so we could find out.

At first William was being unusually friendly, but once I told him that I couldn't give him the stuff back, the call turned into something from Groundhog Day. His boring threats, which I'd heard a thousand times before started up again. I knew I was jumping into deep water when I started arguing with the prick but I couldn't help myself, and the moment I told him how delighted I had been to find out that the drugs had belonged to him, I knew I had probably gone too far. He started screaming like a mad man. He was going that berserk that he began panting for breath. His ranting became too much to listen to and I passed the phone back to Mickey while he was still going on with himself. Their faces were a picture, they obviously couldn't believe how I had spoken to him. I have better standards than to show a person like him one ounce of respect though. I apologised to the pair of them for the awkward situation and reiterated that it had been an honest fuck up. I offered, simply as a show of respect, to help out by setting up a business arrangement that they could profit from. I agreed to take another consignment of speed and sell it, only taking a small profit for myself (for my troubles) and giving them the rest. Happily, they agreed and so, as before, I doubled up the drugs with some glucose and sold it for a slightly higher price than the previous batch. After doing that a few times they eventually got their money back for the stuff Lyndon and Robbo had grafted.

I had managed to smooth over a difficult situation and took some satisfaction for doing the right thing and for doing it well.

The whole affair was a very serious and regrettable one, but I knew I had handled it correctly.

I even offered Mickey and Steve some sound advice, which was to stop working with William, as most of his colleagues usually ended up doing long prison sentences or disappearing for good, while he sits back and enjoys the good life.

I was pleased when I heard that eventually they did fuck him off.

David Barnshawe unfortunately wound up coming to a pretty gruesome end, however. I since heard he had made a lot of enemies while he was working for the murdered Chris Little and it eventually caught up with him.

Barnshawe was lured to a car park one night, forced to drink petrol, then thrown into the boot of his car, followed closely by a lit match. A tragic way for a young man to die.

Lyndon was also murdered a couple of years later. He was never seen alive again after leaving a pub in Liverpool. His car was found burnt out in a street in Salford the following day, but his body was never recovered. I am unsure of the reason behind his untimely death. I don't believe anybody has been convicted of either murder. I was saddened by the news of Lyndon's death as I thought he had potential to go places. Unfortunately, they simply became two more poor souls that never completed their full journeys through life.

Robbo the 'Little Cunt' later received an unrelated life sentence. As sad as that also is, it was no great shock to me, because he was about the most violent feather-weight villain I've ever met.

It became common knowledge that the price on my head had increased. I was a thorn in William's side and the criminal underworld believed I had ripped him off not only once, but twice. Such a troublesome relationship with one of Europe's most prolific serial killers obviously isn't ideal and at times it did weigh heavy on my shoulders, but things had happened that could never be forgiven or forgotten, so I knew we both had to live with our hatred for one another.

I blanked out the thoughts of being captured by him and his henchmen, because the reality of the hell they would put me through is the stuff of nightmares. I remained upbeat in the belief that I would spoil their party by dying a much more boring death, long before they got me in the hot seat.

I had reached a time in my life where after countless conflicts with villains, thugs, hooligans and gangsters, if I was having a dispute, I liked to give my thinking skills a chance to iron out a situation in order to try to prevent any unnecessary violence. And William aside I generally found myself approaching problems with a more open-minded outlook.

After a good night out in Manchester a group of us decided to go on to an all-night rave. The security at the venue was coincidentally run by Mickey (one of the two gangsters that Robbo stole the speed from). Their head doorman Tommo was well known throughout Manchester for being a ruthless guy who was prepared to step up to any occasion. He was an ex-boxer and wasn't shy about using a weapon. Some months earlier he had shot a bullying Salford gangster in the mouth over a dispute. In my book he generally deserves some well-earned respect from one and all, but there can obviously be exceptions to any rule though, depending on a given set of circumstances.

As our group were waiting to enter the club one of the lads started arguing with Tommo about a previous incident. Knowing the matter had nothing to do with us we all stood back and watched on with interest. After a couple of minutes of arguing our pal pushed passed him and entered the club. To my surprise Tommo then turned to us and snapped "And what are you lot fucking saying?" I was taken aback and thoroughly pissed off by his lack of respect, so I responded by asking what he meant "You fuckin putting it on us now?" I snarled. He didn't reply and just stared at me with a look of resentment. I returned the glare and barged past him and into the rave.

Inside, just through the entrance there was a small bar, I walked straight up to it and ordered 20 bottles of lager, telling the barman that his bouncer would be paying for them.

I knew to expect some repercussions after I was told Tommo had disappeared from his post at the front and probably left the club. The boys were also informed that he had gone and that it likely meant one thing, he had gone home for his 'tools'.

No one in our group would take weapons out with us due to the amount of times we were stopped and searched by the squad, so I knew it was pointless even asking for a weapon. I wasn't bothered though, I was E'd up to the max and full of Dutch courage so I was ready to take on an army with or without a weapon.

Some of the lads with us that night were also friends of his, so when he came back hooded and gloved up they stood in between us while I was shouting abuse at him. Like a stupid twat I ripped open my shirt and told him to take a shot. After the previous year's threats from William of being captured and tortured, I had little fear facing a man with a gun. To his credit, he was far from a fool and on that particular night it turned out that he was prepared to use his thinking skills, while I was the one shouting and ranting. He obviously reassessed the situation and calmly said "Paul let's have a chat before one of us does something stupid". Despite my bravado I was actually delighted to hear those words, however there was still a serious debate to be had.

Having calmed down a little I realised it was time to screw my own head back on. We went into a side room of the club and I got straight to the point, telling him that I thought he was in the wrong due to his earlier approach to us. We had let him have his argument with our mate and nobody butted in. The argument obviously hadn't been our business, but there were enough of us there to have jumped in and finished it off. I told him that as we had respected him by not doing so, he should have respected us too and certainly not started barking at us, not to mention clearing off and fetching a weapon to threaten me with.

He admitted that I made a fair point and agreed that snapping at us had been unjust, he apologised and even paid for the 20 beers that I took, even though he told me I was a cheeky cunt for doing that. We both had a chuckle about it and drew a line under the matter. It was a reflection of the size his character, that he was man enough to apologise, and do it in such a way that he lost no respect. That night I honestly believe I was close to getting a bullet in the chest and he was close to getting a life sentence for murder. The fact that we were able to take a step back from the initial heat of the moment and let our brains engage, meant we came out unscathed and with a mutual respect for one another still intact. From that night on we actually became good friends and more importantly later in life he went on to dedicate a lot of his time to helping troubled children. That, in my eyes, is something that carries a lot more respect than being a henchman for some firm. If we had let violence erupt from our conflict, maybe he would have never ended up in a position to do such a positive thing with his life.

I was beginning to experience more and more incidents in my life where brain over brawn was paying dividends. That meeting with Jimmy Swords, at Kendals cafe, back in the day had taught me about compromise and that it wasn't always a bad thing taking a backwards step.

I wasn't naïve enough to believe peaceful resolutions were the only way forward for me. At 39 years old my rollercoaster of a life had had no shortage of twists and turns, and still lying ahead was a very dangerous twist already in the making, I just wasn't aware of it back then.

Chapter 31:

TROUBLE WITH THE YOUNG ORDSALL FIRM (Y.O.F)

The Ordsall firm which Paul Massey had ruled over for many years started to divide into two factions. A splinter group formed and became known as the YOUNG ORDSALL FIRM (YOF)

The youngsters of the original firm were simply too lawless, they lacked morals, followed no rules and listened to nobody, not even Massey himself. Paul never used to allow drugs to be sold on the streets in his patch. The younger lads wanted to take and sell drugs as and when they pleased and that became a serious bone of contention. They wanted to do things their own way which led to internal fighting.

In a very short space of time the new Young Ordsall Firm became notorious across the north of England. They were ruthless and brave. They were also sly and would commit underhand crimes against other criminals, including kidnapping dealers, robbing them of their drugs and money and then demanding they worked for them from then on.

On one occasion the Y.O.F. sent some of it's members to seek out a lad who had refused to sell their drugs. He wasn't at home when they arrived, but there was a straight, law-abiding friend of his working at his house, putting up wallpaper. To send a message they hacked up the decorator with a machete. Whether it had been intentional or not, the poor bloke was that badly wounded he later died from his injuries.

The YOF attracted such attention for their total lack of respect that they were not seen as people to do business with. They simply couldn't be trusted. They had aspirations of getting to the top. Without people at the top willing to work with them though they were effectively snookered.

That was until one day, when a particular low life, who happened to have taken a serious disliking to me, decided to offer them a way into the big league. He offered them a European connection who would supply them all they needed. There was one small catch however, to prove their worth they were instructed to carry out two contract killings.

The European connection was William and one of the targets was me.

Massey still had links with the YOF so naturally he marked my cards as soon as he heard about the contract. His loyalty to me during our lives together, even when we were often on opposite sides of the battle fields, no doubt prolonged my time on this earth. Receiving news of the contract didn't come as much of a shock to me, what was surprising was the name of the other person who they were supposed to kill. Ged Deaffern, later described by a judge who convicted him as "a Mr Big in the Northwest of England". He was a bloke I had known from back in the day, when he used to live and operate in Salford. He moved to Blackburn to escape from the ruthless streets of Ordsall, but Ordsall had geared up to take the war back to his doorstep.

Ged was a good grafter and had his head screwed on. He was a self-made millionaire from his time working the streets and ran a decent operation in and around Blackburn. He too had ended up working with William and unsurprisingly had fallen out of favour with him.

William had sent him a ton of cannabis, that was to be paid for later, but the police intercepted the load on the motorway just shy of Blackburn. William wasn't prepared to take any blame or accept the loss, so the bullying weasel demanded his money back from Ged.

The rules of the drug game are simple though; if you agree to have drugs laid on then the drugs do not become your responsibility until they are in your hands. Every drug dealer knows and accepts that rule. Therefore Ged naturally refused to take responsibility for the loss.

William being the bad loser that he is, took the quite unbelievable stance that as the police captured the drugs in England, Ged was responsible for the drugs and had to pay.

The YOF were obviously eager to impress their new serial killing, drug lord associate and got to work carrying out their instructions with immediate affect. I was targeted first. While their conniving bosses were still sunning it up in Spain, wining and dining with William, they ordered a supposed hard boy back home to pay me a visit at the reclaim yard. The arrogant prick turned up and said he had been sent by William to collect the money from the outstanding debts. The money for the cannabis with Graeme and the quarter of a million for the speed which Robbo had stolen. Unbelievably he suggested that William, as a gesture of good will, would accept a monthly payment plan.

Calmly I told him he was just a different face with the same boring story which I had heard too many times to remember. I instructed him to ask William when it was going to sink into his thick skull that I would never give him a penny.

As we were talking I started to become more and more irate. As my anger grew I could see his cocky demeanour began to diminish. There was a weakness in his eyes that started to show through. He must have sensed he was close to getting a serious kicking. Over the years I've mastered a technique of how to give a fool a decent enough bitch slap, without inflicting too much damage, so I lashed out with a 50% punch that floored him, he quickly managed to get back to his feet before running out of the yard, leaving me a nice little present - his car, which the lads took great delight in smashing to bits.

I knew I'd taken a risky step, but I also knew, after years of similar conflicts, that I had to stand strong. I was in a dangerous situation and expected a counter attack, having said that, the speed in which it arrived did still surprise me somewhat. I had just enough time to get a handful of loyal heavies down to the yard, to provide some necessary backup, the YOF had been that quick in responding though, that only half of my men had time to arrive. In less than an hour of me bitch slapping their guy, another car full of YOF pulled up in the yard. I presume they had hoped such a rapid response would catch me off guard, so understandably they were less than pleased to find themselves outnumbered by some of my most loyal friends. Their car was completely surrounded and they were effectively trapped inside. I calmly swaggered over and nonchalantly asked what they wanted. One of them snapped that they wanted their friend's car back. With a large smirk I informed him how sorry I was but I couldn't help, as I hadn't seen the car. "We do have a smashed-up wreck that could be sold for scrap though" I taunted. You could almost smell the hatred they had for me. They would not necessarily fear me, as I don't believe they feared anybody, but they knew to be wary.

I then asked when their bosses were due back from their meeting with William before I politely requested a message be passed on when they return. "Tell them I'm ready to do whatever is necessary whenever it's necessary". They were clearly fuming with the lack of respect that I showed, but I wasn't about to bend over for anybody, especially anybody working for William. I could imagine the looks on their faces over in Spain when word got back that their first day hadn't exactly gone to plan and they were already a car down.

I doubt William would have been too surprised by the news however, he would have expected an up-hill struggle with me, as was always the case.

The next day I received information that some of the YOF had been spotted driving by my yard, which indicated to me that William was prepared to write off the money and he simply wanted the hit carrying out. So I figured it may be wise to change tact. As tough as I considered myself I knew that one decent shot and I would be dead, therefore I decided to shout from the rooftops the name of the traitor, who had sold out to William in order to kill a fellow Salfordian. I also made everybody aware that upon his return from cavorting with the enemy I wanted to see him. As soon as the backstabber returned from Spain he was told that I was openly calling him and his men Judas's and so he arranged to meet me for a 'sit down'.

We met in a Salford pub. I took five fierce and loyal friends along, just in case he fancied making another cowardly move. We sat down and he asked me why I was bad mouthing him to everyone and calling him a Judas. He claimed he had merely taken some of the YOF to Spain on a drug deal. I responded by telling him everything I knew. That coupled with the events over the previous week suggested he was telling lies. I told him that no true Salfordian should ever accept a contract on another from somebody in a foreign country, who isn't prepared to do the job themselves. He continued to protest his innocence and claimed he knew nothing about any of the previous week's events. His lies were falling on deaf ears, as I already knew the truth, so I interrupted his bullshit and told him that if I ended up being killed for blood money, then my brothers and an army of my friends would take revenge and his name would be at the top of the hit list.

It was far from a heated exchange. It was actually fairly matter of fact. Simply two criminals discussing a problem that neither of us could really solve.

The lad agreed to 'do me a favour' and ring around to ensure there was no arranged hit on me and if there was he would call it off. Deep down I knew it would only last until the dust had settled or until I dropped my guard but it was progress and I had shown I was prepared to counter any moves they may make.

Word got around that Young Ordsall Firm were furious with their bosses decision to 'cancel' the contract on me. William was probably not too chuffed either and unfortunately their attentions ultimately intensified towards Ged Deafferne. He found himself in even more of a predicament because the YOF still had to prove to William that they were as capable as they had claimed. The first move they made was to tax one of the Blackburn dealers who worked for Ged. They followed that up by attacking whoever was associated with him. A tit for tat war broke out.

His first retaliation was to take revenge on some of the Young Firm by dishing out a couple of heavy beatings. His next move was to put a fifty-thousand-pound price on the head of their firm, Stephen Lydiate.

Over the previous few years, Lydiate had made many enemies with his reckless, ruthless nature and so it wasn't long before the contract was accepted.

While some of his firm were sat relaxing in The Ship Inn, in Salford, watching Man United versus Liverpool, a hitman calmly walked into the pub and put six bullets into Lydiate, before making his escape.

News of the shooting soon spread and initially it looked like a fatal attack. Later it emerged that a bullet proof vest took a lot of the impact, however it was still touch and go whether or not he would make it through the night. Love or hate the guy you have to respect his bravery. What he did next was close to unbelievable and what followed will no doubt go down in Salford folk lore.

Days later, once strong enough to walk again, Lydiate discharged himself from hospital (with one of the six bullets still lodged in him) so that he could take revenge on his rival.

He gathered some of his most loyal men and sent them on a mission to seek out Deafferne. In just one night six members of the Blackburn firm were kidnapped from their homes and taken to safe houses where they were tortured for information as to the whereabouts of their boss. Four of the six were shot in their legs, one member, Jimmy one eye was so badly tortured that he was dripping in blood from head to toe. He was shot in both legs and had a tree branch forced into one of his wounds. That still wasn't enough for the YOF though, they wanted him to suffer the ultimate humiliation and had taken a big gay black guy along with them to rape him. The injuries Jimmy had already suffered though are effectively what saved him from further brutality, as the black guy refused to go through with the rape, due to Jimmy bleeding so severely.

While they planned their next move, Jimmy was held hostage. One of the kidnappers was left to keep watch on him overnight. The guard seemingly took pity on him and agreed to give him some sleeping pills to knock him out. He also made two cups of coffee, one for himself and one for Jimmy, in which he added the pills. Somehow Jimmy One eye managed to switch the cups when his guard wasn't looking and when the pills kicked in, the guard fell asleep presenting the chance needed to make good an escape through a window.

A bloodied and battered Jimmy was found by workmen the following morning, hiding in a skip. They took him to hospital where the police questioned him. Obviously, he wouldn't cooperate but the police, who believed they already had enough information anyway, quickly swooped on the YOF members who they believed to be behind the kidnappings. Most of those arrested were later found guilty of various charges from wounding to kidnap and received long prison sentences. Lydiate received a life sentence for the plot. In total the gang received a combined 41 years behind bars.

William's unscrupulous actions finally did inadvertently lead to Ged's demise. After an unsuccessful attempt to kill him, the utter carnage and trail of destruction that the YOF's had left behind, resulted in Ged becoming very much a man of interest in the eyes of the police. They put an operation on him and a couple of years later he was arrested for several large drug importations. He was subsequently found guilty and sentenced to 22 years.

Salford criminals have a large presence in jails up and down the country, so when a price was once again put on Ged's head, it was inevitable that sooner or later he would run into trouble. A fellow inmate caught up with him behind the high walls of a top security prison and inflicted a number of serious injuries using a homemade 'shank'.

Due to the fact I had shown strength and had a reputation for my own propensity for violence, I had again narrowly managed to avoid a bloody battle, and due to the fact that William is a greedy, arrogant, egotistical savage, an unknown number of men were badly injured, not to mention several others left rotting away with uncomfortably long prison sentences.

From my point of view, the only positive that could be taken from the whole sad affair was that William would have been left furious that once again I had slipped through his net.

I had been consciously working at developing my negotiating skills. A set of skills that could potentially save me from being surrounded by violence for my entire life, and without wanting to blow my own trumpet, I was pleased with my progress. There had been a handful of occasions where I was able to help friends and acquaintances with their problems, just by applying some of my own hard-earned wisdom and rationality to a situation. A number of my pals actually began calling me by a new nickname, in recognition of my change in approach. In stark contrast to 'One Punch', they started calling me 'The Headmaster'.

I already had a fearsome reputation, however news of my newfound ability to diffuse a situation, without the need for violence, spread fast. People from further afield were requesting my negotiating skills instead of my more commonly appreciated 'frightening' skills, but the real beauty of it was; if plan A of negotiating didn't work, I could still happily resort to plan B of violence and bloodshed.

As proud as I secretly was when my friends started to call me the 'Headmaster', I realised I could not let it cloud my judgement. I needed to rely on my instincts in tricky situations. I knew not to let my guard drop or to dish out second chances. My survival instincts, that had stood me in good stead for so long on the streets of Manchester, still needed to be followed if I wanted to stay alive. The world I had created for myself was at times an extremely nasty, scary place, and although my efforts of resorting to violence less frequently worked well sometimes, there was still always a very good chance of a bloodbath waiting around the next corner, and I had to ensure it would not be my blood.

One Saturday night whilst out with a group of friends, I received a call from a close pal - Black Wayne. Wayne is 6'4" and he has the strength and speed to challenge anyone in a one-on-one fight. However on this particular occasion he was trying to deal with a problem that could quickly have escalated into something far more serious. Wayne had his own security business and he was working at a bar in the City Centre. On the night in question the bar had a large group of rowdy Salford lads inside and they had started to cause trouble for the regular customers - in turn creating a problem for Wayne. He called asking for my help because of my reputation, especially in Salford. His hopes were that I could potentially use my diplomatic skills to diffuse the situation before it got out of hand.

Like many people who live outside Salford, Wayne struggles to understand the politics that go on between rival factions within our violent city and just how much volatility and hatred there is between its inner-city gangs. I knew if it was a Salford gang causing the trouble, then it would go one of two ways; they would either be friends or foe, and it would either go swimmingly well or potentially terribly badly.

Wayne being a good friend meant that it didn't matter who he needed my help dealing with, all that mattered was that he needed my help. So myself and five friends immediately set off for the bar. At the entrance to the venue there was a steep set of stairs that lead down to the bar area. Once down the stairs I could see the manager trying to keep control of the situation by attempting to usher the group out as politely as possible. Unfortunately for everybody concerned the group were mainly Ordsall gang members who were never going to take being asked to leave, lying down.

Initially we stood back and hung around at the bottom of the stairs to see if there was any chance of the ticking time bomb miraculously not detonating. My optimism was short lived however, because some of the Ordsall firm spotted us hanging around watching things unfold and reacted quite badly. "Doyle what the fuck are you starring at you cunt?" was shouted by one particular loud mouth. I was obviously disappointed by his disrespectful outburst and my street instincts told me that 'The Headmaster' approach was not going to get me anywhere on that occasion. I had no choice but to rush the rude cunt and knock him out, leaving my more than capable mates to deal with another aggressive upstart that stood his ground. Whilst we were dealing with those two, the rest of the mob ran off up the stairs and started throwing beer bottles down at us. Quickly we grabbed some chairs, flipped them upside down, to use as shields, held them above our heads and charged up the stairs towards the group. When we reached the top the mouthy mob scattered across the square leaving behind just one brave lad, who tried to battle us all by himself. He was a strapping lad, standing well over six foot six, with bravery that I could not fail to admire.

He was shown little mercy though and was battered with fists and chairs until he had no fight left in him. The rest of his cowardly mates totally abandoned him and just watched on as he was quite badly beaten. I tried to coax some of the cowards back by taunting them, "I'm from Salford too but I'd sooner die than leave a friend behind". It was to no avail however and no one came back to help him.

We knew we were overstaying our welcome as A-Division would undoubtedly be on their way, so we scarpered without too much hesitation. Sure enough the police arrived and immediately shut the whole square down due to the big lad being in such a poor state of health. Little did we know then, but the old bill were thinking it could have potentially developed into a murder investigation, so they set their stall out to gather all necessary information and evidence.

One of the main instigators of the trouble and the same lad who shouted the initial abuse at me had the cheek to run straight to Paul Massey to discuss "dealing with me". First he asked for a gun to shoot me with. Massey being a lifelong friend of mine refused his request. So then he tried to get him to organise a fight with me. Massey informed him that it would be like throwing a cat to a Rottweiler and advised the young upstart that he should drop it before he ended up in a similar state to his pal that he had abandoned on the battlefield.

Days later Massey himself filled me in on the conversation, and also told me that the big lad was in a coma in intensive care. He said he was a fairly straight member and a family man and he was very disappointed the lads had left him to take such a beating. I asked Massey to keep an eye on his situation and to inform me if he got out of Intensive Care. True to his word he did exactly that and even arranged a private meeting for us once the lad was feeling well enough for it. I apologised for allowing him to be so badly beaten and offered him a few quid for his troubles. He was Salford through and through, so there were no worries of him talking to the police, I just wanted to compensate him for his time in hospital. He accepted my quite reasonable financial offering and also my additional offer of allowing him to invest some of it back into a transport operation that I was overseeing from Holland to the UK.

The whole affair ended up costing me a few grand, but things could have turned out a lot worse. I almost had a death on my conscience, which would have been heartbreaking under the circumstances, and would obviously have resulted in some serious questions needing to be answered at the police station. Instead of that outcome, I made a new friend and business associate, who actually did very well out of his investment. He also made some changes as to the company he kept.

I knew I was left with no choice other than to resort to violence on that particular night, but it reaffirmed to me that I needed to persist with my 'Headmaster' approach as often as I could, especially with the younger generation of gangsters. Life is precious and sometimes the youngsters need a better understanding that you can't always learn that the hard way.

I didn't need to apologise to the guy for the beating he took, anymore than I needed to compensate him financially, but not only was it a fair thing to do, it also ironed out the situation instead of further aggravating it.

Fate unfortunately wasn't so kind to the lad who had started the trouble, then subsequently requested a gun to shoot me. He was shot and killed himself at a party in Ordsall a short while later. The older I grew the more disturbing I would find it when young lads were getting themselves killed for such stupid, petty acts. Some of them you just cannot appeal to change their ways, and to be brutally honest I doubt I would have listened at that age either.

I began thinking how close that night had come to turning out horribly wrong. It led to me reflecting that it was remarkable I had managed to avoid a spell in prison for quite so long. I was actually feeling out of shape as a consequence. Most people would find the thought of going to prison quite frightening and rightly so because it can be a terrifying place, but I simply look at it as a bit of a health farm, and to be honest my life on the outside was hardly a bed of roses, so I had nothing to fear being locked up.

During the first weeks of a sentence I put myself on a strict diet. Once I feel happy with my weight loss I put myself through some vigorous training sessions. I exercise like a mad man in prison. The sort of regimes that only nutters or SAS troopers would dream of attempting.

I always aim to leave prison with a six pack to be proud of and generally a tip top physique. Upon release I attempt to keep my fitness up by going to the gym regularly, but life gets away from you on the outside and I struggle to keep up with it when there is so much other stuff going on. Besides, during a period in my life when I had spent so much time looking over my shoulder, expecting to be shot or stabbed whenever I left the house, I saw less and less point in looking my best, simply for the morticians benefit.

I was approaching forty, I was five foot nine and weighing in at eighteen stone. There was no denying that I was overweight. There was one bonus to the extra weight though. The more I weighed, the more I could put behind my punches.

As I had spent my entire life mastering the art of punching, my technique was fairly spot on. I throw most of my punches using lateral motions, which means I am able to effectively put my bodyweight into a punch. Having such a powerful punch isn't always such a great asset though. On most occasions I physically have to try to reign it in. More often than not I don't actually want to cause anybody the extra, unnecessary harm - just enough harm for things to be seen my way.

If my challenger was somebody I felt confident of disposing of with ease, then I would tend to lash out with a halfhearted punch. This is a punch with probably about 60 percent effort put behind it.

If he happened to have a particularly terrible attitude or was a rather large individual, he would probably receive an 80 to 90 percent punch, which I knew could be very dangerous for all involved.

With all the best will in the world though, sometimes a full force approach is the only way to resolve a problematic situation.

One weekend I was enjoying a nice peaceful night out in town, with the wife and a few other couples, when one such problematic situation raised its ugly head.

After visiting a couple of pubs and wine bars, we decided to finish the night in The Tapas bar. I was well acquainted with the place and was aware that it had a good array of security cameras. It was renowned for attracting Salfordians, so I guess it is understandable. It was only quite a small place so there wasn't too much in the way of seating areas. Unfortunately on this occasion when we got there our wives were adamant that they wanted to sit down. The reason this was unfortunate was because there were already two factions of Salfordians congregated in the seating areas.

I tried my best to talk the girls out of sitting, to prevent any type of trouble, however I was told to go fuck myself and before doing so, to get the drinks in. I feared the night was going to go south and I stood at the bar just waiting for the first screams.

True enough, before I had even paid for the drinks all hell had broken loose. I turned in time to see my wife and some of the other wives involved in a fist fight with men and women from one of the other Salford groups. The altercation resulted in a daughter of a couple we were out with, being punched to the ground.

The men from our group and obviously the girl's father piled in to take revenge. The other Salford group then also joined in and were attacking our lot. I joined in and we began to force them back. One of their lads in particular put up some strong resistance, before we raised things a gear and bombarded him with beer bottles and glasses. You would struggle to have counted the number of bottles that rained down on the guy's head. By the end of the conflict several of their crew were unconscious, the majority of the others were either bruised, bleeding or just cowering away. There is always one exception though.

As I was attempting to make a swift exit with the wife, I noticed this big lump standing in the doorway, blocking our path. He was a huge fella and he gave me a gladiator stare which meant one thing - he was going to attack. I had no choice but to shove Janette right out of the way and launch at him, throwing my first punch before he could throw his. Having seen him in action earlier I knew he was a tough strong bloke, so I hit him with pretty much full force. He was out cold before hitting the floor. I shouted back for one of our group to get the security videos from the doorman and by the time we got back to our car, we assumed the incident was long behind us and we had nothing more to worry about.

Later that week a friendly copper informed me that A Division had a warrant out for my arrest. I had been caught on CCTV punching the guy in the Tapas Bar. Apparently there was a separate CCTV system for the entrance way and the immediate street outside and we had failed to remove that recording. Nothing else from the whole night had been salvaged apart from me sparking the big lad in the doorway. The copper also told me that the film was crystal clear and he personally had seen it because some of the coppers were showing it around in the police canteen. "It was one hell of a punch" the copper declared (which I must admit I was quite chuffed about), "but you may find yourself in trouble this time Paul".

Assuming full well that I was going to be arrested I packed a sports bag full of stuff that I could take with me for my stay at HMP Strangeways. T-Shirts, jogging pants, trainers, radio, electric hair cutters etc. I actually had a little chuckle to myself while I was packing my array of belongins (as prison is a far cry from the old days when you had no more than a toothbrush and paste, a bar of soap and a bucket to piss and shit in, not that I'm complaining of course).

I was all packed and awaiting an arrest, but the boot at the door never came. I presumed they had had second thoughts about arresting me for something as trivial as an assault, So I decided not to look a gift horse in the mouth and arranged a big night out in town.

That Friday me and the lads went out and I was determined to accept no less than a belting night. Most of the evening was fairly run of the mill, I was enjoying myself getting high on ecstasy, but was eager for more. I was a bundle of pent-up energy and insisted that we went clubbing earlier than we normally would have. The well-known phrase be careful what you wish for became prominent the moment I burst through the doors of the club. I was ready to make a lasting impression on the dance floor and I believe that is exactly what I did. No sooner than my eyes had adjusted to the dark, the excitement which I had longed for erupted into life. The doors slammed shut behind me and mayhem ensued. A full squad of armed police were pointing guns at me whilst screaming like kids "GET DOWN ON THE FLOOR".

Now when I'm high on pills the Salford street kid tends to come out of me. That meant two fingers were raised on each hand and the squad were told to go fuck themselves. I had no intention of lying down on the floor, wearing my best clobber, and surrendering to those cunts.

Two officers rushed at me and grabbed my arms, forcing them behind my back, while the others advanced while pointing guns at my head. I was cuffed and dragged outside before being chucked in a van and taken to the City centre police station for a long night in the cells.

Being high on Es, every minute in that cell felt like an hour. I became so bored that I found myself wishing it was like the old days when officers would burst in and kick fuck out of you every half hour, just to pass the time.

After an uncomfortable night without any sleep two detectives finally took me to be interviewed. Normally I would give a 'no comment' statement, but on this rare occasion I thought it was in my best interests to play ball.

I had been arrested for a Section 18 (which is the most serious assault charge, indicating intent to cause harm) so I figured the bastards were clearly wanting to put me away for a long stretch.

I started to state my case, I argued there was no weapon involved, no kick to the head, no prolonged attack. "All I did was hit him once" I kept repeating myself too, hoping to drum it into their thick skulls. They knew I wouldn't take the charge lying down but I knew they wouldn't drop it easily either.

The arresting officer then made an unbelievable statement, he claimed that they were going to prove I had used a weapon. I was bewildered by that, knowing they had crystal clear CCTV footage and no weapon would be seen on it. I told him again there was no weapon.

"Why don't you give us your full version of events then Mr. Doyle?" the patronising cunt said.

So I did.......

"Me and the wife had been out for a quiet night with some friends which ended up in a venue called the Tapas Bar. Halfway through a pleasant evening I went for a dance on my own, however the music stopped and the lights came on because there was a disturbance in the other room. I entered the other room to see if my wife was okay, when I noticed my friend's daughter had been knocked out and my wife was complaining that she had also been assaulted. I suggested to her that we should leave the place in case we were attacked again. As we were making a speedy exit, the wife warned me to be careful, as the lad who had been assaulting people, was standing in the doorway seemingly waiting for us. I looked towards him and noticed him staring at me in a very aggressive, somewhat frightening manner. Therefore out of fear of being hit, I threw a wild swing at him and to my shock he went down. At that point I said to the wife; Quick love let's leave before he gets up and beats me up".

The two detectives looked at me in exasperation. One of the coppers suggested that I told a good story and even asked if I had expected to be arrested and pre-planned that particular one in advance.

"Good God no, not at all, getting arrested came as quite a shock", I answered.

The police then showed me the footage of the punch. They told me that they had blurred out the victims face and were not using his name for fear of reprisal.

One of the coppers then suggested to me that if an individual realised they had the ability to throw a punch, like the one I had thrown, it may be deemed plausible, in a court of law, that their fists be classed as weapons.

Right then I knew what game they were playing. They were willing to move heaven and earth in order to get the section 18 to stick.

"Do you have a nickname?" one of them asked.

"Yes the Headmaster" I replied, "due to my desire to avoid violent conflicts for myself and others". They wanted to trip me up and get me to admit to being a violent man, one who was well aware of his significant ability, but I had no intention of being coaxed. I said, "The punch I threw was out of fear for myself and my wife".

"Is it not true that you are widely known as One Punch Doyle" I laughed and confirmed "I had previously been nicknamed One Punch because one of my brothers had knocked me out with a single punch when we were young boys". I swiftly diverted the line of questioning and said that I was glad they had the incident on video because it would show there was no obvious intent on my part to cause any significant harm, and before my lucky punch landed I believed they would be able to see the fear in my eyes.

The cat and mouse game went on for three long hours and despite my best efforts to rubbish all of their accusations I found myself being charged with a section 18 and the prospect of 10 years in prison. Nevertheless I was granted bail.

As the desk sergeant was signing my release papers, I suggested that it seemed unusual for them to be granting me bail when I could be facing a 10 stretch. I cockily said there must be a bigger operation on me. To which he stunned me by replying "Mr. Doyle you are one of the most sought-after men in Manchester after the years of carnage you've brought to the streets of our City, but we've got you this time, so enjoy your last few weeks of freedom".

Unrelenting I replied, "Don't be so sure, but when this is over could you do me a copy of that video, so I can show the grand kids". Not for the first time in my life a copper told me to fuck off out of his station.

In the cab on my way home I was thinking to myself that a stint in prison wouldn't be too bad. Afterall I was carrying a couple of stones too many, not to mention having Europe's nuttiest serial killer hunting me, as well as the GMP classing me as one of their priority targets.

A stint at her majesty's pleasure could be a bit of light relief I told myself, trying to remain upbeat.

Chapter 32:

'PIG' SICK

Realising that I could be going away for a long time, Jeanette thought it would be nice to throw me a surprise 40th Birthday party. Don't get me wrong it was a lovely idea, but I was a bit bewildered when she asked me for twenty grand to pay for it. I said to her "Jeanette forgive me love, but how is it a surprise party when you've just told me we're having it and asked me to pay for it?" To which she replied, "The surprise is where you're having the party". "Oh, right" I said, still totally bemused. An hour or two after handing Jeanette the cash I received a call from Ned confirming the booking of a function room at Old Trafford. I've never claimed to be the smartest person around, but sometimes I wonder if every other cunt is on a different planet.

I paid for my own 'surprise' party upfront and it's 'secret' location was divulged to me within a couple of hours of me handing over the cash. Aside from those two minor details I also had to put together a large majority of the guest list, as the function room which Jeanette had booked held almost 1000 people and I wasn't prepared to look like Billy no mates, at my half empty Birthday bash.

I spent hours phoning around as many people as I could think of to invite. I even asked my children's school teachers, much to their surprise. In fact I was that desperate not to end up with an empty venue that I considered advertising it on the local radio.

A large chunk of the invites obviously went out to Manchester criminals and gangsters, not to mention an army of United hooligans.

My wife was also busying herself inviting her friends and relatives.

A few days before the big day I received a phone call from Ned, informing me that the police contacted him regarding the party. They had tried to shut down the event for fear of trouble. I was described to him as being the leader of an organised criminal gang and a notorious football hooligan.

Ned told the police he couldn't cancel the night as it was already paid for, so the spiteful coppers insisted that it had to finish by midnight, or else they would look into removing Old Trafford's drinks license.

Following Ned's warning I decided to contact the owner of the Tapas Bar. He agreed to allow us to finish the night off there - for a small sum of £5k.

Even though I had good friendships and or working relationships with 90% of my guests, I wasn't so naive to think that everyone would get on like a house on fire. The place being set on fire was probably more likely.

I knew there would be some statement making to be done, but even I was surprised to hear the Higher Broughton firm, who were notorious for being successful business men, had used the opportunity to showcase their wealth, by ordering five limousines so they could arrive in style. When I got wind of it, I ordered two for me and the family.

When the big night finally came around I was upset to see several riot vans parked by the entrance. My guests had to walk through a gauntlet of police and were openly filmed by the press as they arrived and entered Old Trafford. In reality it worked out quite well for the Higher Broughton boys, as their extravagant arrival was made all the more impressive by all the attention. They swaggered out of their limos to the applause of some of my other guests and the *pig sick* faces of the watching policemen.

Looking around the function room, admiring my guests I couldn't help but smile. I felt like a real part of the great grafting city that was Manchester. My satisfaction was short lived though, because whilst gazing around in admiration, I spotted my good friend Daz Hancock with an expression of fury on his face. I watched him barge past a couple of people and out of the fire exit. I wasn't aware of what had gone on, but I knew instantly that Daz would have left to get himself a weapon, which meant I had about 30 minutes to smooth over the situation before he returned.

Daz is the type of bloke that wouldn't give a shit about the police surrounding the place, he would plough in and get himself a thirty stretch, then worry about it later.

I had to plead with a strong firm of lads to apologise to Daz, as a favour to me. We were only ten minutes into the celebrations and I knew that if they didn't back down it would all have been over no sooner than it had really begun. Very reluctantly they agreed to keep the peace. It still took me another twenty minutes to calm Daz down though, once he had arrived back, baying for blood.

The next three hours followed suit. I was like a headless chicken running around trying my best to stop wars breaking out between my friends and associates. In all my years as a doorman I never worked as hard as I did that night. In fact if the truth be told, I owed a big thank you to the old bill for enforcing the midnight closure. I felt like I couldn't relax until we were safely away from Old Trafford. Having said that, there was still the problematic task of getting my guests across town to the Tapas Bar. The limo drivers were insisting they could only take 8 passengers at a time. That was until one of them was dragged from the driver's seat and dumped on the pavement, then the remaining drivers became more accommodating, allowing 11 or 12 passengers to squeeze into each car.

As the Old Trafford part of the night drew to a close I felt a huge surge of relief. Against all the odds nobody had been killed or arrested and I had finally kept a promise to Ned that there would be no trouble. I hadn't half had to work for it though. I was determined to enjoy the rest of the night with my collection of hooligans, armed robbers, gangsters, drug dealers and one or two from the really dark side of the underworld fraternity.

Inside the Tapas bar tempers were getting short. The police presence was the main reason for that, not to mention a few bullshit arrests that they made outside. They could see that tensions were rising but were too thick to see that it was all their own doing.

Before too long a senior officer walked into the place with a handful of coppers and tried to close the bar. My guests started verbally abusing and mocking them. One foolish young upstart didn't find our sense of humor to his liking and tried to arrest one of the lads in front of everybody. The rest of the guests quickly rushed in and the police sensibly retreated.

After standing around for a while, outside, scratching their heads, the senior copper reentered and requested to speak to a nominated person on behalf of the guests. Benny was out like a shot, he just loves to try and get one over on whoever he can, and to be fair he was the only person capable of having that debate at that time of the night, the rest of us were far too disgruntled, pissed up or high. Benny got the police to agree that if we all left quietly then the few individuals that had already been arrested would be released without charge the following morning, or at least when they had sobered up, whichever came first.

I wasn't happy with that offering though as I had booked a coach to pick me and my fellow hooligans up at 4am from outside the Tapas bar, to take us straight to Wembley (where United were due to play Arsenal later that day). I told Benny he needed to do a better job. So off he went to try again.

The copper finally agreed that the party could continue until the coach arrived at 4am, but then everybody had to leave and in an orderly fashion if we wanted the arrestees to be released.

Benny did well really, although personally I was slightly disappointed that the night didn't look like ending with a full-on battle against the police. That would have been a perfect finale.

By the time the coach arrived, of the 40 lads who were booked on the Wembley trip, only 18 were capable of making it. The others were either off their heads on drugs or totally bladdered. The coach was therefore used as a taxi to drop some of my guests home before we started our trip down south. All in all the night had been a success, which is more than could be said about United's 3 nil drumming to Arsenal in the charity shield. Two limousines were apparently found abandoned later that day on the Wembley approach road.

The following weekend I decided to catch up with the owner of the Tapas Bar, to find out what the police had been saying about the party. United played the first *real* game of the season on the Saturday, so after arriving back in town I suggested to the lads that we dropped by before starting our night out. We got to the bar and were greeted by a young steroid junkie doorman, whom none of us recognised. I explained to him that I had come to see the owner to discuss a previous event, but he rudely told me he didn't care who I had come to see, we weren't getting in because our group was too large. Momentarily I bit my lip and gave him another chance. I said to him for a second time I wanted to speak with the owner and we weren't interested in spending the night in the bar. "The owner isn't in" he replied before suggesting "you should try the pub down the road they're not as strict". With that he arrogantly turned away from me.

At 40 years old I was too long in the tooth to let a pushy little 'sted-head' prick speak to me like some sort of a twat, so I asked him "Are you trying to be brave or are you just a stupid fucking cunt?"

He turned back towards me and started getting in my face, so I had no choice but to give the stupid fucker a slap. It actually was a slap too, so I was amazed to see him hit the floor like a sack of shit. I leant over him and said, "Fuck me mate, imagine what you would be like if I hit you properly". I told him to count himself very lucky that I don't treat people as poorly as he did, then I suggested he fucked off home and learned some manners before I changed my mind.

My mates were half wetting themselves at the pathetic state of the young wannabe tough guy as we stepped over him and walked in. I was making my way straight up to the office when I noticed the CCTV playing behind the bar. I stopped and looked, interested to see what the doorman would do next, but he was nowhere to be seen. Just coming into shot however was another doorman, that I did know and to my astoundment he was chatting with a copper.

I called the lads and told them we had to leave sharpish. As we rushed out of the place I slowed down to throw a glare at the doorman. "See you soon Paul", he cheerily said as I walked by.

At that point a rush of blood came over me. The cheeky bastard I thought, he's there informing on me to a copper and has the brass balls to wave me off like he's a mate.

Unlike the steroid popping doorman that had run off home, I knew this guy was capable of putting up a decent fight, but copper or no copper I had started to see red, so I had to address the matter.

"You cheeky, snidey twat" I snarled, "saying bye to me like you're my mate. My mates wouldn't call the police on me every time I come to their club. I presume it was you that handed over the footage of me banging that bullying twat the other week too, and now what? Another clip of me slapping your pussy bouncer?"

"What the fuck are you on about Doyley" he replied, "I think you should cool down".

Full of anger I barked back "I'm on about people like you phoning the fucking police every time I turn up here". With that I stormed off in a huff before things got out of hand. I was a hundred yards down the road by the time Ashy caught up to me shouting "Doyley you fucking dickhead, come back, the copper's a kissogram".

Extremely red faced I went back with my tail between my legs and asked the doorman if he would accept my most sincere apologies. Luckily, he saw the funny side of it all and he played it down brilliantly. He did in a more serious tone however suggest that I took a bit of time out, as he had never seen me looking so stressed.

Hearing that I looked stressed hardly came as a surprise to me, there seemed to be a police presence every which way I turned and on top of that I had the whole William saga, I was an international drug trafficker, and I had the prospect of a ten year stretch hanging over my head for GBH. Things had gotten very hot in my kitchen - I agreed that he was probably right and asked if he would do me a favour by passing a message on to the bar owner that I wanted a quick chat with him as soon as possible, then once again I apologised for my mistake before sheepishly leaving, somewhat quieter than I had arrived 15 minutes earlier.

The very next morning I received a call from the owner. He informed me that the police had told him and apparently all the other licensed premises in Manchester to call them as soon as I was spotted entering. He insisted however that they had not done so. He also confirmed that he had personally ensured that there was no evidence of me slapping his doorman the previous night. I told him I was pleased to hear it because I had been considering demanding the five-grand back from my 40th, however in light of his offerings I said I would let the matter slide. We finished the conversation on somewhat of a lighter note. He told me that the kissogram had actually been set on fire later that night, for using the guise of a police woman. As harsh as it sounds I couldn't help but laugh. What the fuck did they expect, parading around like that in a predominantly Salford bar.

The words of advice from the doorman at the Tapas bar stayed with me for a little while. With the speed and direction my life seemed to be moving, it had started to feel like I was living multiple lives.

There were a few key things that I could cling to, simply to ensure I didn't lose my true identity. My wife and kids have always meant the world to me and I would always try to do right by them. I knew that focus would help keep me grounded. My close friends were there to help me on that front as well. I was often the butt of their jokes and if there was ever a set of mates to keep somebody's feet on the ground, then believe me, I had them. And at the heart of a good friendship I believe lies a sense of humour – after all without the ability to have a laugh, what have you really got? I was determined to hold my head up and keep on smiling.

My sense of humour is something that I am quite proud of actually, although I have to admit it may seem a little bit twisted at times, especially for folk who don't know me. On more than one or two occasions my jokes have landed me in rather hot water and often with the old bill.

One such occasion my desire to have a chuckle ended up costing me quite a few quid and even led to my younger brother Mark getting a 2 year stretch in Strangeways.

It all started with Mark giving me a lift to the yard one day in his van.

We pulled up at a tee junction when he asked me if the road was clear on my side for him to pull out. My eyes must have lit up, "YES" I said, "but be quick about it". Mark put his foot down and pulled out straight into the side of a passing police car. It was a joke that I regretted almost immediately as I felt a surging pain in my neck and side, and my hysterical laughter only made the pain worse.

It felt like somebody was force feeding me laughing gas when two angry coppers rushed over to us and began giving Mark a bollocking. They couldn't really do much because it was just a traffic accident but seeing me holding my side in fits of laughter went down like a lead balloon.

Mark also appeared to not find my joke very funny.

Even though I was the one that ended up getting hurt, he still gave me a verbal volleying. In fact he called me some names that I wouldn't like to repeat.

I did profusely apologise for smashing up his van, but I also explained to him that I thought it was an obvious thing to do as I couldn't have passed up the opportunity to mangle a police car with no fear of being arrested.

My words appeared to be falling on deaf ears, Mark just wouldn't accept my apology. He continued to sulk for days, right up until he wanted a favour from me. After about a week or so he appeared at my yard asking me to lay on 40 kilos of speed. Not only did he want it laying on, but he also wanted it at a very cheap price, claiming he would use the profits to buy himself a new van.

When it comes to selling drugs I always try to be very professional, so I asked Mark who the drugs were for. He told me some cockneys had asked him if he could sort it. Puzzled I asked him "What cockneys and why are they coming up to Manchester to buy speed?".

Mark being a loving little brother said, "Shut up you suspicious old cunt, you fucking owe me so just give me the stuff and stop being a shithouse".

As he was clearly not in the mood for my interrogations and as I did feel a little guilty about his van, I decided (against my better judgement) to trust that he knew what he was doing and I arranged for my driver to drop 40 kilos with him the next day. I told my driver to subtly quiz Mark about his deal and find out what he could.

Upon his return he told me that the deal was taking place at the Novotel hotel in Worsley. Immediately my heart sank. The Novotel had automatic gates which open as you enter but require you to request permission to exit via an intercom system.

That makes it the perfect place for the police to attempt a sting.

I tried to call Mark but all I got was his 'phone off' tone, which made me think he had possibly already been nicked. I sent somebody to check out the hotel and unfortunately my instincts were right, the place was swarming with old bill.

Mark had stupidly walked straight into their trap. The coppers had wanted to implicate me, however I had covered all my bases and Mark was never going to grass me up, so he ended up receiving 2 years, which wasn't the worst result in the world, but it was pretty costly under the circumstances.

If I hadn't tricked Mark into driving straight into the police car he would never have found himself behind bars. I should also have done my job properly and not allowed him to guilt trip me into laying on the speed without having more information about who it was for. The arrest proved to me that the police were very hot on my heels, and showed the lengths they would go to, to catch me out. As a professional criminal Mark's arrest should really have worked as a tell-tale sign for me to take a little break. I had a small empire to run though and if I stopped the supply, my customers would start going elsewhere. I was well aware it was a big risk that I was taking, but I deemed it a necessary one, after all I am a gambling man. I have quite an apt saying, that I like to remind myself of from time to time - If you waste too much time crying about the losses of yesterday, it will affect your earnings tomorrow. It's kind of a Dust yourself off and carry-on approach (but for a gambler) so that was the approach I chose to take.

With the police net seemingly closing in on me, I needed to make the most of life while I was a free man. One way I liked to achieve that, was by treating myself to a lovely lunch, as often as I could, in a particularly fine establishment. In fact me and the boys were spending so much money there back then, that when the police planted a bug at our preferred table, the staff gave us a 'heads up' as to what was going on. Obviously, we took advantage of this and sent the old bill on the odd wild goose chase. In hindsight I suppose it was a bit of a stupid thing to do, but they were gunning for me anyway and it provide us with a few chuckles, so what the hell.

At the same time Tony Blair was really getting tough on crime. He was trying every trick in the book to clamp down on organised criminals and even a few tricks that weren't in the book.

During his reign of power police squads like Manchester's very own A Division were not only allowed but encouraged to use heavy handed tactics in tackling organised crime gangs. Another major change was the previously frowned upon method of 'entrapment' - tricking criminals into committing crimes.

Previously this would often have resulted in cases being thrown out of court, but it became more acceptable, with only certain bits of evidence being deemed inadmissible.

Unless it was undeniably clear that a policeman had purposely lured someone into committing a crime, which they otherwise would not have committed, then the evidence stood. The snide trick became more prevalent and cases (which would previously have been deemed as entrapment) found their way into the prosecution system.

One day while I was enjoying one of my lavish lunches I received a telephone call from my brother in law, Mongy Mike - the reason he goes by such an odd nickname is because he is monged out of his head on cannabis twenty four hours a day - which was nothing to do with me by the way. Mike called asking if I would meet him in the car park so he could introduce me to a guy called Baz. This bloke had apparently been buying and selling stolen goods in and around Salford. Mongy informed me that Baz had some parcels of gold to sell at 8% below scrap value. I couldn't resist the chance to make a quick quid, so I agreed to meet them.

The moment I set eyes on Baz I felt something wasn't right. I gave Mongy a frown as if to say What the fuck? The cunt looked every inch an undercover copper, but before I could laugh at the pair of them and fuck them off Baz's phone rang. Loud enough for all to hear Baz said to the person on the other end of the line "I'm with a friend of yours now, I'll put him on". The devious cunt then passed me his phone. To my surprise the person on the other end was none other than my old mate Paul Massey. Me and Massey said a quick Hello and exchanged pleasantries before I handed the phone back. I immediately assumed that I had misjudged Baz, there was no way he could be an undercover officer and be involved with Massey. Massey was far too smart for that; he could sniff out an undercover from a mile away. For that very reason I broke one of my own golden rules - never let your guard down when meeting somebody for the first time.

Baz knew he had weaseled his way in with me and began to exploit it. He wasted no time in pulling out a parcel of gold chains and necklaces, with a street value of £25k The sneaky twat then told me that he had heard of my reputation and knew I was trustworthy, so he was willing to lay the gold on. I should have smelt a rat again at that point. My reputation was so terrible that my own friends wouldn't even trust me with a nine bar of weed, never mind the fact that half of Manchester's criminal underworld, at that time, believed I had not once but twice ripped off Europe's craziest serial killer.

Nevertheless I was dazzled by the gold and the deal and proceeded to make an arrangement with Baz to take the gold on bail at a very good price of just £18,000.

I spun it around in no time making myself a tidy profit and when Baz returned to collect his money, naturally I asked if he could get me more. He told me that it came from a firm down south and he didn't think it would be an issue but would have to speak with them first. Little did I know, but I was being groomed like a school kid.

When we next met he had another equally impressive case full of gold, however he said his acquaintances down in Sussex would appreciate being paid in powder, as there was a bit of a drought at that time. Cocaine was just starting to boom up and down the country and Manchester was a hot spot to buy it (being so close to Liverpool). Like an unprofessional prick I told him that I didn't sell cocaine but I could supply his friends with cannabis as payment. Yet again he went away to ask the question. He returned saying his friends would accept my cannabis on this occasion, however he continued to pester me for coke. I told him on numerous occasions that I didn't sell the stuff. I had a very lucrative business selling weed and I didn't need the hassle of dealing in class A drugs. His requests continued to come and he began doing my head in. In the end he wound me up so much I decided to give him some shit weed, which I was struggling to get rid of. Those southerners are years behind Mancs and scousers so I knew it would still be fine for that lot.

Baz was back a few days later telling me his guys down south were more than happy with the Cannabis but they were quite disappointed that I was refusing to set them up with some powder. Surprisingly Baz said that it didn't even matter about the quality - which I was initially a little stunned by, but again I just presumed those backward southerners were still trying to catch up with the times. To do the pestering twat a favour, I gave him Ant's number. Me and my mates refer to Ant as 'the porn star' however he was more commonly known as 'the snowman' amongst his work colleagues, as he occasionally dabbled in cocaine and always had a stash of his own.

Baz met up with Ant and bought a couple of ounces off him. Some days after that I received a call from Ant asking me just how well I knew Baz, because he was pestering to buy a kilo of the stuff. When I took the time to stop and consider exactly how well I did know him, I started to feel that I may well have slipped up. I got in touch with Massey to find out who Baz really was.

Massey's response to me was "You're having a laugh aren't you Doyley, I've only met him once, he told me he'd been working with you for years". I informed Massey that the first time I ever met Baz was when he received the phone call from him. Massey said that the only reason he had called that day was because Baz had sent him a text saying that he was with me and I had wanted to say hello.

Massey had a sick sense of humour, like mine, and so when I told him that I had served Baz up with cannabis and he now wanted a kilo of cocaine, he burst out laughing and said he thought it was time I took a holiday.

It was very hard for me to accept that I was being set up by one of Tony Blair's boys in blue and I wasn;'t prepared to take it lying down.

Chapter 33:

SWOOP ON THE UNTOUCHABLES
– Operation Victory

I arranged a meeting with Massey and Damien Noonan, I needed some 'professional' advice from people similar to myself, who liked to live on the wrong side of the law, and more importantly knew how to manipulate it. Big Damien's initial suggestion however was simply to wrap a bat right around the devious cunts head and chuck him in the ship canal. As much pleasure as I would have taken from doing that, I felt for once, that I really needed a more subtle approach.

Massey put me in touch with a solicitor friend of his, for some legal advice and we hatched a plan. Damien introduced me to two of the most colourful characters I have ever met, who were willing to put themselves in the firing line in order to flip the cards and do a sting on Baz.

Raymond Wright and Anthony Flitz are both well known throughout the English prison system. Those two would graft hard to make a living on whichever side of the prison walls they happened to be on, and they were key to our operation.

To any normal human being, Raymond and Anthony would without doubt appear to be quite disturbed individuals. They detest the police and rage against the system. Those two criminals actually fantasize about committing the perfect crime. They are wonderfully bizarre individuals, to call them eccentric would be a huge understatement and injustice. When Damien told them we needed their help to stitch up an undercover copper Flizy almost wet himself with excitement.

Before we could pull off our little scam I had to get my house in order. I knew the police would be coming through my door as soon as we had accomplished our goal, which meant I had a rare opportunity to tie up all my loose ends and ensure my family were secure while I was away at her Majesty's pleasure.

I sold my reclaim business and swerved a massive VAT bill. With that money I paid off the mortgage on the family home, so the wife and kids could continue to live without the stress of mortgage repayments hanging over their heads.

I made the foolish mistake of introducing a friend to my Dutch contacts and allowed him to be in charge of my transport operations. That was to prove a costly error, however (money and betrayal live in close quarters. If there is sufficient money up for grabs there will always be some lowlife willing to stab you in the back for it).

Once I had taken care of all that I had to, and I was ready for my dawn raid from the old bill, we put the wheels of our plan into motion.

Ant the porn star told Baz he would put him in touch with his suppliers who would be more than capable of supplying a kilo of white powder. Baz was obviously delighted and agreed to meet Ant's suppliers (Ray and Flizy) at their earliest possible convenience.

Ray and Flitzy met Baz and told him that they had the best powder in Manchester, "Brilliant and white" they kept saying, while tapping the end of their nose. They told him that It was a little more pricey than normal, but they were prepared to exchange it for thirty thousand pounds worth of gold. Baz, as we knew he would, jumped at the opportunity and agreed to meet them later that week.

The exchange was smooth, the goods passed from car to car within a matter of seconds and the transaction was complete. We were over the moon. We had been handed £30k of gold jewellery and it had cost us about a tenner. The kilo of white powder that was given to Baz had been wrapped up like you would expect to receive a kilo of cocaine, fresh from the docks, however it certainly wouldn't have had the desired effects if you were to stick it up your nose.

The powder was actually Daz washing powder - to keep your whites whiter than white.

Inside the parcel, along with the Daz was a note that read:

"You got exactly what you asked for".

Everyone was buzzing with how smoothly it had gone. It was exhilarating knowing we had got one over on the bastards. The Noonan and Massey rode off into the sunset with their heads held high but it was slightly more bittersweet for me because I knew I would be getting sent down any day. I also suspected I would find myself at the top of some bullshit indictment. What I didn't know though, was just how long I would be going away for.

For the previous few years, the police had known that there was a price on my head, and they, like me, knew the reality of that threat. They also knew that I had not taken a backward step, had not tried to make peace, nor had I tried to hide away. For them, the whole situation was to all intents and purposes a pressure pot just waiting to blow. For that reason I had had either undercover or uniformed police popping up here, there and everywhere both night and day.

News had spread about me being stitched up by Baz, but undeterred by the police presence, my enemies still wanted one last pop at me before I was safely tucked up in Strangeways.

I was fairly relaxed about the police coming for me. As for my evil enemies however, I had to remain constantly on guard.

I was not about to lie down and be taken alive to face my final hours screaming for mercy at the hands of a torturous monster like William.

During the hours of daylight I had the added protection from loyal friends. Once I returned home in the evening, it was just me and my loving family that would be left to fight the fight, if the enemy raised its ugly head.

When I was a young lad in the reform schools I used to sleep with my clothes on and with some type of homemade weapon, at the ready for anyone who thought I'd be an easy target while I slept. I believe I have only existed for so long because I have always tried to stay one step ahead of the game.

Since an early age I had imagined leaving this world after an honourable battle to the end, like a Roman gladiator in the Colosseum. And as stupid as it might sound, I have always felt safe when I am fighting, as if someone or something was protecting me. It gave me an air of invincibility which stood me in good stead on many occasions. No doubt the day will come when that aura of safety abandons me, but until then my inner strength has to remain strong and my determination to outwit my foes needs to be on point.

When I was back at the house and darkness had fallen I would prepare myself for the unknown. I'd wedge a bar across the hallway at knee height, so if anybody came rushing in, the pricks would trip over it and find themselves at the mercy of my two, 12 stone rottweilers, Ronny and Reggie. Unfortunately, I'm not as brave as my dogs so if I followed them into the fight I would be wearing a bulletproof vest and swinging a double-bladed sword. I could no longer risk keeping a gun on the premises as I was expecting the police raid and having an unlicensed shooter would increase my sentence significantly. Even without a gun though, I was confident that myself, Ronnie and Reggie would be a match for most.

During the hours of darkness Jeanette came into her own (and I don't mean between the sheets) like any good Salford girl she would be my night watchman. Every second counts in those sort of ambush situations and I needed all the help I could get. She spent hours keeping guard, looking out onto the street for any signs of trouble.

One quiet Wednesday night, not long after it had gone dark, Jeanette noticed a blacked-out car crawling along at the bottom of our cul-de-sac. We knew we were being watched. Almost immediately after the first car a second car drove by. I know the game inside out and it only ever takes two or three heavies to go through someone's door and professionals would only check the area out once or twice before an attack, that meant something was about to go down.

I sent my family upstairs and put the dogs in the hallway, as my first line of defense, whilst I grabbed my weapon and positioned myself ready for battle.

Two or three minutes passed but nothing happened. I presumed something or someone must have unsettled them, a neighbor or a dog walker perhaps. I continued to wait, poised to pounce. I called up to Jeanete in hushed tones "What the fuck are they waiting for, can you see anything?" She suggested it could have been the police, but the police wouldn't have a car full of heavies doing drive-bys, that would have been as subtle as a sledgehammer in a greenhouse.

I figured they must have been waiting for me to go to bed, so to draw them in I turned off the tv and all the lights. I repositioned myself once again and allowed my eyes to adjust to the darkness. Doing that actually relaxed me as I realised it would work to my advantage. Adrenaline began pulsating around my body and I felt a giddy surge of energy in the knowledge that it may well have been my judgement day.

I peered through the side of the curtains just as the two cars pulled into the cul-de-sac again. This time they were together and obviously ready to move in. They parked a few doors down and all the car doors opened on both vehicles. I was heavily outnumbered, which strangely increased my excitement. Ronnie and Reggie got up and headed straight to the front door. Their senses told them we were about to have visitors. They began to bark like crazed wild animals, I hissed at them both to stop, but they didn't. The next second my street was alive with flashing lights and my hallway lit up like Christmas. I didn't know what the fuck was going on, until the all too familiar sound of police sirens pierced my ears. In the blink of an eye our quiet street resembled a police car park.

The police obviously had me under 24-hour surveillance and must have got onto my attackers just as quickly as my night watchman - Jeanette. I couldn't help but grin as I settled back down and put the tv on to drown out all the commotion outside. My neighbours must have presumed it was me being arrested, but unfortunately for them that wasn't the case.

Once the adrenaline had left my body, I felt sick to the stomach. My emotions were mixed, partly I felt let down that nothing had come of it all, and partly angry at the realisation that it could all happen again, that very night, or the next, or the next. We had been ready and prepared for their ambush, but what if Jeanette wasn't as sharp next time around, what if I wasn't home and my wife and kids were there alone? I almost resented the police, for essentially saving my bacon. Ronnie and Reggie had clearly been hoping for some action too, they stood staring at the front door for hours that night in anticipation. They were still sleeping there when I woke the next morning.

Once common sense had prevailed, I felt blessed. My family hadn't been exposed to any frightful violence, not to mention the fact I had once again dodged a bullet.

I gave the neighbours a little wave and proceeded to take my kids to school that morning, as if nothing had even happened. After that, I headed to the gym to burn off some pent-up frustration. In order to avoid the busy Altrincham, post school drop rush hour, I went via the country lanes. I was on a quiet road no more than a few minutes from the town centre when a car came screeching up behind me. I could make out masked faces through the rear-view mirror, and there were four of them. To say I was gob-smacked would be an understatement. The dust had barely settled from the previous night and I was under attack once again. Without a weapon onboard I knew the odds of survival were stacked against me, so I couldn't risk stopping to take them on. That chain of thought was further affirmed when my back windscreen exploded from gunfire. I had no option other than to get either back on the busy roads of Altrincham or better still the M56 motorway.

I've never claimed to be the world's best driver and I realised that I was going to have to think fast and drive faster if I wanted to escape. I made a sharp right turn which for a second left me feeling like the car was going to flip, no doubt rendering me trapped inside and at their mercy. Luckily at least two of the wheels remained firmly on the road though and my stomach stopped doing cartwheels. I began to weave in and out of both lanes, preventing them from positioning themselves alongside me or worse still from getting in front.

I was driving like a mad man just to keep them at bay. More shots were fired, and I heard the ping of metal hitting metal as bullets ricocheted off the frame of my car.

The motorway was about a mile or so away, and I was only a few hundred yards from a busy A road. My next hurdle however, was getting from the quiet B road onto the bustling A road, as it was a pretty major junction, not to mention regulated by traffic lights.

Fortunately for me everything within spitting distance of us was pulling out of the way as fast as they could and the run up to the junction was relatively free. I was relying on a huge stroke of luck with the lights though, or I knew I would be flying into the side of some poor unsuspecting sod making their way to work.

The lights changed to red while I was about 50 yards away, but totally flooring it I drove straight through. It was a tough call to make, but I wasn't prepared to be shot to bits like a sitting duck. I sailed through safely enough, just as the traffic was starting to move. I presumed I had just been handed the piece of luck that was desperately needed, but as I looked in my rear-view mirror, I saw the crazy bastards chasing me do exactly the same thing. Inches from disaster they left total chaos in their wake.

It was half a mile and one straight road to the motorway. Their near miss had cost them a few seconds and bought me just enough time to get onto the M56 before they could make up the ground. Once on the motorway I was safe, my only concern was getting the car windows fixed.

Life had become a rollercoaster of emotions, there were more ups and downs than on 'the big one' at Blackpool pleasure beach.

I drove straight to Ashy's house to update him on the developments of the previous twelve hours. As I arrived he was in the middle of making a sausage sandwich. "Want one?" he asked as he peered out at my car's missing rear window.

"No" I said, staring back at him quite dumbfounded. "Aren't you going to ask why my car looks like it's something out of the Bonnie and Clyde movie?"

"This should be good" he said.

Shaking my head in disbelief, I walked passed him and into the house, before filling him in on the events of the previous night, as well as my kamikaze car chase. He continued making his sausage sandwich, so totally undeterred that I actually stopped mid flow and asked "Are you even listening to me Ashy? I've been telling you how I've spent my morning dodging bullets and you seem more concerned about that sausage butty". Ashy's response was brilliant to be fair to him; "You've been escaping death your whole life Doyley, so what's new?"

He knows me as well as anybody has ever known me and to hear the stories came as no great shock to him. "You've always had a fuckin knack of getting out of the kitchen when the shit gets too hot. Want me to follow you to the garage, so you can get your window replaced?"

I looked at him and chuckled. "Yes mate, that would be good," I said.

By the grace of God, I was proving to be too elusive for my foe, but I was increasingly puzzled as to why the old bill had still not carted me off. I took to sleeping on the sofa with my tracksuit on, so I could rush to save my front door from being booted off its hinges by some police issued size twelves and a battering ram (Those bastards love nothing more than smashing a door to bits, just to inconvenience you as much as humanly possible). I had found myself in that all too familiar predicament more times than I cared to remember, and I know that it is just as unpleasant for your family as it is for you, when the bullying twats' man-handle you in front of your nearest and dearest.

Early one morning I woke to some noise outside and when I looked out, I saw that my wait was finally over. A regiment of Rambo cops were charging down my driveway. I just about managed to get to the door first, but before I could say 'welcome do come in', I was bent over so far that my nose was nearly tucked up inside my own arsehole. They cuffed my hands so tightly that I could feel them turning blue.

I half expected and could accept what they were doing to me, I had experienced it a thousand times before, what happened next though really made my blood boil. One of the dirty shit house rats roughed up Jeanette, resulting in her suffering a broken jaw - simply because she refused to put her cigarette out.

They carried me out of the house whilst I was screaming at the bullying cunt, and threw me head first into a van.

Down at the station it was all the same old shit. Each interview was as equally boring as the last and just as boring as the next. It was tedious. I did have a chuckle to myself when they mentioned Ray and Flitzy though.

It turned out mine wasn't the only my door to have gone through that morning, they had raided a whole host of us at the same time. It didn't really surprise me as that was fairly standard procedure, to minimize the chances of anybody fleeing. What did surprise me though was the number of houses that were hit. Police stations around Salford and Manchester were full that day and there was even a helicopter circling the city the following morning when myself and the first few defendants were due up in court. The realisation dawned on me as to just how major an operation they had had on us.

The Manchester Evening news had a field day the week we were all up in court, with daily updates from the proceedings, including headlines like "*Swoop on the untouchables*" and "Manchester's biggest ever attack on criminals"

They wrote that police carried out dawn raids on more than forty houses. The swoop came after officers infiltrated the criminal community in the Salford area over a period of 8 months, where they bought drugs and stolen property from Villains in the area.

'Operation Victory' was the largest of its kind and was set up to target criminals who were considered untouchable and tarnished the city's reputation. 500 officers arrested 53 people and seized numerous criminal items including a sawn-off shotgun and two hand pistols along with drugs cash and stolen goods.

Chief Supt Chris Wells, Head of Salford Police, said "it was a very successful operation aimed at the most prolific and high-volume criminals".

As I stood in the dock, armed police surrounded me, aiming to portray me as a dangerous gangster, the prosecution stated that I was the leader of a criminal enterprise and claimed I was the "tip of the iceberg". I found that quite funny, as the exact same words had been used 20 years earlier when Operation 20 man had hauled me, Massey and the rest of the boys up in front of the courts, for our misdemeanors both home and abroad.

This time I was facing charges of conspiracy to supply cocaine and cannabis to an undercover police officer, and I was remanded into Strangeways.

Strangeways is a totally different place to what it had been before the riots of April 1990. The screws interact with inmates for a start, whereas before they were just miserable cunts that wouldn't even give you the time of day. In fact, the whole prison system is unrecognisable now compared to how it used to be.

After going through reception, a large group of us were put onto K wing, which was still the induction wing and still a shit hole. Induction wings usually are the shittiest wings in a prison. I think the bastards just like to shock new inmates when they first get sent down. Unlike nowadays, TVs were still a luxury back then and you couldn't be issued one until you'd done at least six weeks of best behaviour. That brought tears to my eyes, because United were in the Champions League against Juventus that night and it was being shown on ITV.

Initially I was padded up with a good friend of mine who told me to stop moaning about the football. He was far more concerned about the overall state of the wing and the lack of tv was the least of his concerns. I was in the middle of a heartwarming chat, trying to cheer him up and telling him that K wing was always in such a state, but things would soon look brighter, when out of the blue one of Strangeways' most iconic screws came to our cell and said, "Nice to have you back again Doyley, grab your stuff, I've got you a cleaning job on B wing".

I almost dropped to one knee to thank the Lord, but my pal started moaning again and ruined the moment for me. I had told him that things would soon look brighter, it just so happened that they brightened up for me a little quicker than they had for him. He was far from impressed and I could still hear him cursing me as I left the landing.

Being given a single cell on B wing, with a tv already in it, was like a dream come true and I was able to watch the match in peace.

The next day I thanked the screw and told him I owed him one. As a further kind gesture, he managed to get a lot of my friends onto B wing too, including moaning Minnie who I had left the night before. On association that night I phoned Ned Kelly and arranged to get the friendly screw a couple of Champions League tickets for the following home match as way of a thank you. Even that innocent little incident somehow made the newspapers though. The story stated that "Salford's Mr Big had been offering Manchester United tickets to prison officers in return for favours". There was actually an inquiry launched on the back of that article too.

The funny thing about it was that the blame fell at Paul Massey's feet, because of his reputation as Manchester's Mr Big. He was also in Strangeways at the time (but in Cat A) and sent me across an amusing letter, quizzing me as to why it was, he had got the blame for what I had been up to.

In court at a pre-trial hearing, I pleaded Guilty to supplying cannabis but only admitted supplying a phone number to an undercover copper, so he could purchase cocaine. My mitigation was that the crime was only committed because of the constant badgering and harassment from the undercover officer. It was clear that there was no financial gain for me to be had from the cocaine deal, and my solicitor informed me that the maximum sentence I could get on a guilty plea was seven years.

As per normal the police went for the jugular on the day of sentencing. Coppers surrounded the courthouse with riot vans, making a total spectacle of things. Furthermore, only one member from each of the defendant's families was allowed in the courtroom. My fellow co-defendants all turned up dressed in smart suits.

Knowing the judge was going to throw the book at me, I wore a Man United T-shirt with Champions written across it.

There were 7 of us in the dock and I was the first up, as I was at the top of the indictment. Just before the Judge began labelling me as a lowlife criminal, or words to that effect, a beeping noise started coming from the dock which caused him to pause before furiously demanding to know if one of us had some type of electrical device upon us.

My half-brother Marcus, who I love dearly, has a heart defect and he needs to wear a watch that beeps if his heart rate becomes too fast. All us defendants burst out laughing when Marcus informed the judge that he was close to having a heart attack.

The old chap in the wig was incredulous at our sick senses of humour and turned purple with rage. He actually looked like the one most likely to have a heart attack by the time he had finished screaming.

After the comical break in proceedings the purple-headed prick resumed, stating "Mr. Doyle when the likes of you come before the courts it is in the public interest for me to give you the maximum sentence permitted, my hands however are tied to that extent, as I can only give you seven years".

You cheeky bastard, I thought to myself, as I shook my head in disgust.

The others in the dock each received five years, which was also on the steep side.

Seven years is obviously a long time, and the police had certainly got one over on me. If the truth be known though, the criminal justice system probably saved my life with that stitch up.

The sentence wasn't going to be the end for me, it wasn't even the beginning of the end. I knew I could do a seven stretch, I had done more than that before. Prison is all in the mind and I had long since mastered how to bide my time. Upon my release however I would step out into a world that had changed considerably, a world where thinking skills had become more important than having a knockout punch. A world which somehow seemed smaller, where guns and drugs were flooding our country from far and wide, with relative ease, and every Tom Dick and Harry seemed to want in on it.

Ahead of me still lay some of the biggest challenges of my life, including facing twelve major indictments for drug importations worth an alleged street value of £300 million.

ACKNOWLEDGEMENTS:

It gives me great pleasure to thank those who deserve the utmost credit for making this book a reality; my son Leo and Andy Brown for assisting Joe Brown in working his magic, and those behind the scenes that further supported the arduous work that went into pulling this off.

I would like to truly thank my loyal friends and fellow soldiers, better known as The Men In Black. Die hard Manchester United fans and hooligans, many of whom are well known characters nationwide. Their bravery and solidarity helped me through some nightmare predicaments where becoming just another number on a cold slab often looked unavoidable.

To all the friends who have stood by me through thick and thin, from the young boys I spent too many years growing up with in the reform schools, to the men that have my back to this very day. I feel blessed for the times I have shared with each and every one of you.

To the lost souls who never completed their full journeys through life, I raise my glass. The fact that I am still here today and able to tell my story is quite remarkable, as about 90% of my closest friends are no longer with us, but the memories I have shared with them helped make me the person that I am today.

My biggest acknowledgement is reserved for my beloved family who have always been my rock.

Printed in Great Britain
by Amazon

29605270R00219